Courtly
Performances

Raphael Sanzio. *Baldesar Castiglione.*
Louvre Museum, Paris. Photo Alinari-Art Reference Bureau.

Courtly Performances

Masking and
Festivity in Castiglione's
Book of the Courtier

Wayne A. Rebhorn

University of Texas
at Austin

Wayne State
University Press

Detroit 1978

Permission to quote copyrighted material is gratefully acknowledged to Anchor
Books, Doubleday & Company, Inc., for portions of *The Book of the Courtier* by
Baldesar Castiglione, translated by Charles S. Singleton, edited by Edgar de N.
Mayhew, copyright © 1959 by Charles S. Singleton and Edgar de N. Mayhew; and
to The Johns Hopkins University Press for the portions of Chapter 6 which were
originally published in *Modern Language Notes* 87 (1972): 37–59.

Library of Congress Cataloging in Publication Data

Rebhorn, Wayne A   1943–
  Courtly performances.

  Bibliography: p. 225 - 223.
  Includes index.
  1. Castiglione, Baldassare, conte, 1478–1529.   Il
libro del cortegiano. 2.   Courts and courtiers.
3.   Courtesy. I.   Title.
BJ1604.C6R43   170'.202   77-17066
ISBN 0-8143-1587-9

For Marlette

ꙮ Contents

Illustrations

~ Acknowledgments

The debts I have incurred during the writing of this book are many and substantial. Fellowships from the American Council of Learned Societies and the Research Institute of the University of Texas gave me the leisure to bring this study to completion and to have the manuscript prepared for publication. My debts to previous critics of Castiglione and to countless scholars of Renaissance art and history, social psychology, game theory, and anthropology are expressed as fully as possible in my notes and bibliographies. A special debt of gratitude is owed to my mentors René Wellek and Lowry Nelson, Jr., for their constant support and assistance; to R. J. Kaufmann for his wise and patient guidance and helpful criticism on more than one occasion over the last few years; and to Thomas M. Greene, who first introduced me to Castiglione and taught me to love Renaissance literature and who has been a most helpful critic and the best of mentors since I first came under his tutelage many years ago. I am also extremely grateful to those friends and colleagues whom I burdened with the reading of various chapters of my manuscript and who have responded so kindly with their corrections and suggestions: Thomas M. Greene, R. J. Kaufmann, Daniel Javitch, Dain Trafton, and Roger Abrahams.

The greatest debt of gratitude is owed to my wife. With eternal patience and careful scrutiny, she has read my manuscript again and again as it went through various stages of writing and rewriting, and at each stage she has given me the substantial benefits of her critical judgment, her own keen analyses, and her constant aid and encouragement. She has lived through the writing of this book with me, and I dedicate it to her out of love and gratitude, since in many ways it belongs to her as much as it does to me.

Introduction:
Idealism, Masks, and Festivity

When Sir Thomas Hoby published his translation of *The Book of the Courtier* in 1561, he appended to it two brief lists of rules he had extracted from Castiglione's dialogue: "A Breef Rehersall of the Chiefe Conditions and Qualities in a Courtier" and "Of the Chief Conditions and Qualityes in a Waytyng Gentylwoman."[1] Most likely, Sir Thomas intended these lists as aids to his fellow countrymen, for they, like him, worried about the "barbarity" (Hoby, p. 9) of English manners, which they inevitably perceived whenever they compared themselves and their court with the refined civilization of France and the much more refined courts of Italy. To remedy this defect, they eagerly studied books such as *The Courtier,* Giovanni della Casa's *Il Galateo,* and Stefano Guazzo's *Civil Conversazione,* because such works offered handy, comprehensive sets of formulas they could apply to the task of polishing their native manners.[2] That Castiglione's helpful work also sparkled with the wit of its conversations, the elegance of its social intercourse, and the subtle interplay of its personalities and ideas, so much the better. What mattered to most Elizabethan

All references to *Il Libro del Cortegiano* are to the edition of Bruno Maier (Torino: Unione Tipografico-Editrice Torinese, 1964), second edition. They consist of: a roman numeral for the book (or *Letter* for the dedicatory letter to Don Michel de Silva); an arabic numeral for the chapter; and a second arabic numeral for the page of the above edition. Whenever possible, such references will be included in the text.

All references to *La seconda redazione del "Cortegiano,"* edited by Ghino Ghinassi (Firenze: Sansoni, 1968), will use the same abbreviated form employed for *Il Libro del Cortegiano,* but will be prefaced by *Sec. red.* They, too, will be incorporated into the text whenever possible.

All translations of the *Seconda redazione* are my own. Those of *Il Libro del Cortegiano* are taken from *The Book of the Courtier,* translated by Charles S. Singleton (Garden City, N. Y.: Doubleday, 1959), and are followed by the relevant page number.

gentlemen, however, as well as to most gentlemen throughout Europe from Portugal to Poland, were the rules for conduct they could extract from Castiglione's work or could rely on someone like Sir Thomas Hoby to have extracted for them.[3]

Without doubt, *Il Cortegiano* may appropriately be considered a "courtesy book," that is, an etiquette manual, a Renaissance Emily Post. In order to educate a rustic nobility, help the nonnoble to ape the manners of their betters, and generally increase the level of civilization among their countrymen, the inhabitants of Provence, France, and especially Italy had been scribbling down rules of courtesy in prose and verse at least since the thirteenth century.[4] For example, in about 1290 Fra Bonvicino da Riva, a friar at Legnano who eventually became a professor of grammar at Milan, produced a little tome he called the *Zinquanta Cortesie da Tavola*, a poem in quatrains prescribing how one behaved while dining.[5] According to the good *frate*, during a meal one did not make disparaging remarks about the food, put one's hands in one's hair or on any foul part of one's body, speak with a full mouth, pet cats or dogs, or clean off one's fingers by licking them. Considering the table manners its rules set out to correct, obviously an indispensable book for thirteenth and fourteenth century Italians! Most other courtesy books, from sections of Brunetto Latini's *Tesoretto* (c. 1265) to Erasmus's *De Civilitate morum puerilium* and della Casa's *Galateo*, do not differ substantially from Fra Bonvicino's: they offer relatively compact lists of rules which are extremely practical, tersely formulated, and usually negative in character and which are organized quite unsystematically, so that rules for conversation will often be randomly interspersed among others dealing with personal appearance and table manners. As the following excerpt reveals, the "Breef Rehersall" that Hoby appended to his translation of *Il Cortegiano* summarized its contents into a perfect example of the form the courtesy book had maintained almost unchanged since the time of its origin.

> To be handesome and clenly in his apparaile.
> To make his garmentes after the facion of the most, and those to be black, or of some darkish and sad colour not garish.
> To gete him an especiall and hartye friend to companye withall.
> Not to be ill tunged, especiallie against his betters.
> Not to use any fonde saucinesse or presumption.
> To be no envious or malitious person.

12

To be an honest, a faire condicioned man, and of an
upright conscience.

(Hoby, p. 369)

While Castiglione clearly intended to improve the manners of
contemporary Europe by writing his *Cortegiano,* interpreting the
work essentially, if not exclusively, as a courtesy book lessens it by
reducing its many complex concerns to a single one and ignoring
Castiglione's interest in defining an ideal type, depicting an ideal
society in operation, and creating a memorial befitting the men
and women of Urbino he loved so much. In the first place, there
are vast diferences in form between most courtesy books and *Il
Cortegiano.*[6] Not only does Castiglione present his teaching
through conversations and speeches rather than lists of rules, but
he shows himself far more interested in the analysis of behavioral
situations and the moral problems they pose than in producing a
set of specific prescriptions for social success and ethical behavior.
His book must have genuinely disappointed Renaissance gour-
mets who sought in its pages a clue to the sophisticated dining
practices of Italian princes, and a courtly arriviste would have had
to search through genuine courtesy books, such as Erasmus's *De
Civilitate,* to solve the mystery of how one goes about blowing
one's nose in public. As the exception that proves the rule, when
Castiglione does urge the courtier to dress in black or at least in
dark colors like the Spaniards, he shows himself most interested
in defining the social contexts where such dress is and is not
appropriate, describing the image it enables the courtier to project, and analyzing the psychological effect it has on others. *Il
Cortegiano* leaves the traditional etiquette manual far behind as it
works with the basic principles underlying social interaction. In
keeping with such analysis, it attempts not to formulate a set of
rigid rules and maxims hopelessly wedded to the specific aspects
of a particular culture, but to make the reader conscious of the
general nature of social operations as well as their moral dimen-
sion, so that he may then evolve his own, flexible approach to the
particular social realities of his own culture.

If treating Castiglione's *Courtier* as a courtesy book does not do
justice to the complexity of its social analysis, it does not even begin
to deal with the major concern of the work, that of presenting a
human and social ideal for its reader's imitation. Although Castiglione's book has long been praised—and condemned—for its idealism, the exact nature of that idealism still needs adequate
definition. In what way exactly, for instance, is Castiglione's cour-

13

tier ideal, and of what does his ideality consist? In fact, how does Castiglione make all the courtiers and ladies of Urbino, intended as refractions of the courtier they create, into ideal characters, and how can they be both ideal and yet "realistic," believable people? Equally important for understanding Castiglione's book are questions concerning the world he depicts in it. Just how does he make it reflect the nature and operations of human societies in general while presenting it as an ideal model for all to imitate? And of what exactly does this society's ideality consist? The six chapters of this book will attempt to provide answers to these basic questions concerning the idealism at the heart of *Il Cortegiano*.

In formulating those answers, two key concepts—masking and festivity—are needed, and it is essential that both be defined clearly from the start. At the center of Castiglione's social idealism in *The Courtier* is the concept of masking.[7] Like many others in the Renaissance, he conceives social activity as essentially a matter of playing a series of roles, each entailing certain predetermined attitudes and modes of activity, status relationships, and types of dress and deportment—in other words, each having its appropriate, *figurative mask*. In keeping with his interest in the universal rules of social behavior, Castiglione does not descend to particulars in describing the masks his courtier should wear. Whether one should grow a beard or remain clean-shaven, wear feathers in one's hat or go bare-headed—such questions he leaves to individual discretion. Instead, Castiglione wants the aspiring courtier to become aware of what masking involves, of the different roles required by different social situations; and he especially wants his courtier to develop an ideal flexibility, a protean quality which will enable him to shift from role to role with the lightning speed of a quick-change artist. Castiglione mocks those un-self-conscious men at the opposite extreme from his ideal, who mechanically perform the parts assigned them, counting their steps as they dance and offending the ladies by playing the soldier off the battlefield as well as on it (see I, 26, 125 and I, 17, 110–11). He suggests that such men are more than buffoons, that they are profoundly unfree, enslaved to the tyrant roles they do not understand and cannot manipulate. By contrast, through his understanding of role playing and his mastery of the myriad forms assumed by human activities, Castiglione's ideally flexible courtier not only achieves social success, but the truest sort of freedom as well.

While Castiglione's subtle, complex, refined art of masking obviously offered especially valuable instruction for those who actually served at court, Carlos V of Spain would never have placed *Il Cortegiano* on his bookshelf alongside Machiavelli's *Principe* and the Bible, and Roger Ascham would not have recommended it to all his young gentlemen pupils, if its teaching applied only to courtiers. Courtship can well be conceived in more universal terms; as the following extract from Diderot's *Neveu de Rameau* brilliantly argues, everyone can be considered a courtier in some situations.[8]

Lui

... Il n'y a dans tout un royaume qu'un homme qui marche, c'est le souverain; tout le reste prend des positions.

Moi

Le souverain? Encore y a-t-il quelque chose à dire. Et croyez-vous qu'il ne se trouve pas, de temps en temps, à côté de lui, un petit pied, un petit chignon, un petit nez qui lui fasse faire un peu de la pantomime? Quiconque a besoin d'un autre est indigent et prend une position. Le roi prend une position devant sa maîtresse et devant Dieu; il fait son pas de pantomime. Le ministre fait le pas de courtisan, de flatteur, de valet ou de gueux devant son roi. La foule des ambitieux danse vos positions, en cent manières plus viles les unes que les autres, devant le ministre. L'abbé de condition, en rabat et en manteau long, au moins une fois la semaine, devant le dépositaire de la feuille des bénéfices. Ma foi, ce que vous appelez la pantomime des gueux est le grand branle de la terre.

He

... In an entire kingdom there's only one man who walks, and that's the sovereign; all the rest take positions.

Myself

The sovereign? There's still something more to say about that. Don't you believe that from time to time he finds beside him a tiny foot, a tiny lock of hair, a tiny nose that makes him play a little pantomime? Whoever has need of another is indigent and takes a position. The king takes a position before his mistress and before God; he

> dances his bit of pantomime. The minister plays his role
> as courtier, flatterer, valet, or beggar before his king. The
> ambitious crowd dances your positions in a hundred ways
> each more vile than the next before the minister. The
> fashionable priest in his long coat and clerical bands does
> it at least once a week before the official who fills out the
> list of benefices. My word, what you call the pantomime of
> beggars is the great dance that shakes the earth.

Since societies inevitably have their hierarchies and no man can be
completely self-sufficient, everyone will find himself at least occasionally "taking a position," compelled to court others to gain his
ends. While Diderot's characters regard this inevitable courtship
and mutual dependence as something unsavory, even vile, Castiglione and his culture, several centuries before Diderot, entertained a much more elevated view. Consequently, in his *Cortegiano*
Castiglione accepts the inevitability of courtship and tries to teach
his readers how to wear the proper masks with dignity, how to
gain social status and rewards without sacrificing themselves, how
to "take a position" without being or appearing vile.

If Castiglione does not accept Diderot's cynical view of masking
as personal debasement, neither does he share Machiavelli's opinion of the mask as an instrument of deception. While he is
bothered by the possibility that masking may create a false impression of its wearer's real personality and abilities, he trusts that no
man can play a false role successfully for very long without some
aspect of the gap between man and mask becoming apparent.
Consequently, he continually urges the courtier not to lie about
his abilities (II, 39, 251–52) and to shape his mask so that it
reflects qualities he really possesses (II, 27–28, 232–34). Conceived in terms of masking, the individual's personality falls
within the realm of art, becomes subject to his creative will.
Through continual control and conscious direction, he can shape
himself to play perfectly those social roles that constitute the essential forms of a humane and elegant civilization. For Castiglione, masking is thus neither a sacrifice of self nor a vicious betrayal of others; it is the indispensable means by which man may
hope, with his art, to transform himself into an ideal.

If masking allows Castiglione's courtiers to become their ideal
selves, festivity enables their society to transform itself similarly.[9]
Festivity involves—and especially involved for the Middle Ages
and Renaissance—a temporary suspension of the rules governing
ordinary social intercourse: status relationships are altered, aban-

16

doned, or even reversed; social and religious institutions temporarily lose their authority; the political order is travestied; economic laws are suspended; and men and women come together in an atmosphere of play and with real feelings of communal closeness. To be sure, all festive celebrations are not alike. There is a world of difference between the exuberant, raucous, antiauthoritarian, popular celebrations of carnival and the feast of fools, and the decorous, more controlled and socially proper, elite activities of courtly celebrations, such as those depicted in Bembo's *Gli Asolani,* Castiglione's *Cortegiano,* and, in a slightly different fashion, the *cornice* of Boccaccio's *Decameron.* In the social situations depicted in these works the impulse to festivity is no less strong than in popular celebrations, but that impulse is shaped by a very different set of implicit social rules. These rules blunt its antiauthoritarian impact and actualize its communal energies in the form of personal relations marked by heightened decorousness and self-conscious affability. In other words, although both types of festivity witness the transformation of society into community, in popular celebrations the emphasis falls on freeing men and women from normal social restraints, which are parodied and travestied. In the kind of festivity depicted in *Il Cortegiano,* normal social restraints are simply set aside rather than mocked, and the emphasis falls on transforming social intercourse to reflect the greatest humanity and sociability consistent with fairly elevated standards of decorum.

Masking and festivity are completely compatible concepts. In many festive celebrations, such as carnival and Hallowe'en, literal masking actually did—and does—occur. The mask provides a way of suppressing the everyday social self and freeing oneself for definite kinds of self-transformation. The mask allows for the release of otherwise repressed emotions and permits the individual to affiliate himself with the new community formed for the duration of the festival. Although in most festivities, the participants do not literally wear masks, they often do wear special clothing, and in every case they adopt special forms of physical and verbal behavior quite distinct from those dictated by their everyday social roles. It is just this sort of figurative masking—the adoption of special forms of social behavior—that characterizes the fictive world of Castiglione's *Courtier.* From this perspective, then, masking and festivity appear not merely as related concepts; they are inextricably bound together.

The first three chapters of this study will accordingly deal, albeit in different ways, with masking in *The Book of the Courtier.* The first analyzes Castiglione's conception of the ideal courtier as a masker, an actor who consciously shapes his image to satisfy the audience that watches him perform on the great stage of his courtly world. A book on the art of masking, *Il Cortegiano* draws on ancient philosophy and contemporary humanist thought as it formulates a particularly aesthetic conception of the human personality, comparing the social self shaped by the individual to a painting shaped by the hand of its creator. The second chapter then deals with the people of Urbino, those half-real, half-ideal courtiers and ladies, and with the means Castiglione uses to characterize them as simultaneously real, historical figures and exemplary variants of the ideal courtier. In particular, it takes seriously Castiglione's image of the self as a work of art and finds in the principles and practices of High Renaissance portraiture the key to characterization in his book. This chapter thus also helps demonstrate the genuine unity of Castiglione's work, for the very means he prescribes for the ideal courtier's self-actualization he also uses effectively to create the ideal characters of his courtiers and ladies. Finally, the third chapter focuses on the supreme masker, the most memorable courtier in *Il Cortegiano*, Castiglione himself—or rather, it focuses on the mask he creates for himself in the prologues to the four books of his work. Although Castiglione's narrative persona drops off after each of those prologues, its brief presence in the work has a tremendous effect on the reader's response, for it frames the entire work, establishing at the start of each of its books a distinct perspective, a set of values, and an emotional tone that direct the reader's reactions to everything that follows. It also offers in Castiglione's own image the most direct and immediate example of what characterizes the mask of the ideal courtier.

The second half of this study concerns itself with the nature of the festive world Castiglione depicts in *Il Cortegiano*. Chapter 4 examines the assumptions he holds about human nature and the generalizations he derives from his observation of social interaction—assumptions and generalizations not so very different from those of such contemporaries as Thomas More and Niccolò Machiavelli. It also analyzes how his courtiers and ladies create an ideal social world, not by rejecting the actualities of human drives and social relationships, but by transforming social life into a form of festive play. Castiglione presents an ideal world that refuses to pessimistically accept things as they are and avoids a totally unrealistic flying off into utopian fantasies.

In order to analyze the social rules that govern Castiglione's

18

ideal world and are largely responsible for its ideality, Chapter 5 examines the particular genre he has chosen to exploit. To be sure, like so many other Renaissance works, *Il Cortegiano* may be considered an example of *genera mixta,* the conflation of a host of genres invoked by different aspects of the work.[10] Castiglione's book thus not only has genuine affinities with the medieval and Renaissance courtesy book, but also with the philosophical treatise on manners and morals (discussed in Chapter 1), the Renaissance portrait (Chapter 2), the pastoral (Chapter 3), and utopian and play literature (Chapter 4). Chapter 5 makes a claim for the priority of a different genre, however, on the basis that Castiglione casts his work in the form of a dialogue and that he himself stresses the importance of that form by drawing the reader's attention to it in his prologue to Book I.[11] In other words, as Castiglione, at the start of his work, underscores his fiction of supposedly real, historical conversations, he establishes the dialogue as its dominant generic form and thus relegates to the background its possible relationships to other genres.

To be more precise about the genre of *Il Cortegiano,* Castiglione actually presents his work as a symposium, a particular subspecies of the dialogue with its own distinctive, formal characteristics which relate it directly to the major concerns of this study. By their nature, symposia depict ideal social situations; they are festive celebrations in which groups of individuals engage in various forms of serious play *(serio ludere).* Governed by a distinct set of social rules, symposia separate their worlds from everyday reality and require that the individuals who participate in them shed their normal identities and transform themselves into more perfectly sociable beings. At symposia like Castiglione's, the social situation dictates that everyone figuratively wear the mask of his ideal social self.

If the first five chapters implicitly demonstrate the tight unity of concept, character, and form that mark *Il Libro del Cortegiano,* the sixth and final one focuses specifically on the challenge to that unity raised by the oppositon between the ideals of Castiglione's first three books and those of his last. Building on the conclusions of the previous chapter concerning the nature of the work's social world, this sixth chapter finally argues that such contradictions in subject matter cannot dispell the unity of Castiglione's symposium, for within that particular sort of festive world such contradictions are not really out of place. Rather, they are relegated to the status of being merely the opinions of different characters whose arguments and disagreements are the essential lifeblood of the symposium. In other words, Castiglione maintains the unity of his book, not by homogenizing its ideational content, but by signalling the reader to interpret it according to its consistently imagined, artistic form.

In their different ways, each of the following chapters deals with the artistry of a book that occupies an important position at the vital center of Renaissance culture. On one hand, *Il Cortegiano* harks back to the great achievements of the quattrocento in Italy: its rediscovery of ancient texts and recovery of ancient art forms, its exalted new conception of art and the artist, its idealization of civilization, and its optimism about man and belief in his limitless possibilities. Castiglione refines these enthusiasms in the elegant conversations of his dialogue and, through his art, gives them a congenial form that would make them all the more accessible to the educated elite of contemporary Europe. At the same time, *Il Cortegiano* anticipates and contributes to the ever-growing refinement and sophistication of manners throughout Italy and the rest of the continent. As it broods darkly on the "barbarian" invasions, which the disunified Italian city-states could not stem and which would soon bring the entire peninsula under foreign domination, it also anticipates the gradually increasing aestheticism of life in the courts of Italy and throughout Europe, where more and more absolute rulers would encourage aesthetic, rather than political, self-definition for their subjects and where the display of artistic elegance would consequently become a dominant passion.[12] In the subtly controlled art of Castiglione's *Courtier,* as in the art of its significantly greater coevals—Raphael's Stanza della Segnatura and Michelangelo's Sistine Chapel ceiling—the humanism of the fifteenth century comes to glorious fruition and strikes a momentary balance with the love of beauty, elegance, and refinement that would soon become the hallmark of later Mannerist courts. For just two short decades at the beginning of the sixteenth century, these masterpieces of High Renaissance culture magically harmonize moral ideals with elegant manners, optimistic ideals of political and social action with aesthetic self-cultivation, and virile, directed energy with grace and refinement.

Even at the time of his culture's greatest triumphs, however, Castiglione sensed the fragility of its harmonies, the instability and impermanence of its forms; and he fittingly shaped his book, not as a paean to an eternal civilization, but as a plaintive elegy for its premature demise. Although he began his *Cortegiano* in 1507 or 1508, during the glorious, optimistic period when Raphael was just starting work on his frescoes in the Stanza della Segnatura and Michelangelo was contemplating the Sistine Chapel ceiling, Castiglione continued to revise it through the next two painful decades. This period witnessd constant wars with foreign states, the degeneration of Urbino under Francesco Maria della Rovere and its ultimate loss to a grasping Leo X, and Castiglione's own personal tragedies, the premature deaths of his wife and many of his closest friends. Finally, far away from Italy at the court of Carlos V, isolated in what he called a *solitudine piena d'affanni* (*Letter,* 1, 71: "desert full of woes"[2]), he finished his long labors by composing the sad, nostalgic letter to Don Michel de Silva, which he added as a preface to his book. He set this preface down during the spring of 1527, the fateful, gloomy spring that saw the Sack of Rome cruelly extinguish and scatter the last dying embers of High Renaissance civilization. Consequently, as it nostalgically mourns the vanished dream of an ideal city populated by beautiful, heroic men and women, *Il Libro del Cortegiano* seems to sing the swan song of its culture, whose ideals, ambitions, hopes, and ultimate frustrations its author knew so well. Understanding the art of Castiglione's minor masterpiece will thus yield more than intimate knowledge of a book; it will offer insight into an entire age.

1/ Spectacles in a Courtly Theater

⟣⟠ Early in Book I, Ludovico da Canossa describes the various manly exercises he thinks appropriate to an ideal courtier whose principal profession is arms. Hunting is valuable, he says, because it bears a definite similarity to war; swimming, running, and throwing stones may prove useful occasionally to a soldier; even tennis and vaulting on horseback offer good physical conditioning. Yet, in every case, Ludovico finds a second justification for these exercises beyond their utility in training a warrior: every one of them involves the courtier in performing before an audience of peers and superiors and thus offers him the chance to win his essential reward, their admiration for his accomplishments. Note that Ludovico reserves special praise for vaulting on horseback:

> . . . abbenché sia faticoso e difficile, fa l'omo leggerissimo e destro più che alcun'altra cosa; ed oltre alla utilità, se quella leggerezza è compagnata di bona grazia, *fa,* al parer mio, *più bel spettaculo che alcun degli altri.*
>
> (I, 22, 119; my italics)

> . . . though it is tiring and difficult, [it] serves more than anything else to make a man agile and dextrous; and besides its usefulness, if such agility is accompanied by grace, in my opinion *it makes a finer show than any other.*
>
> (39)

This passage makes explicit the theatre metaphors underlying Ludovico's entire discussion; he sees the ideal courtier essentially as a performer who produces beautiful spectacles continually for an appreciative audience. In this view, the court becomes a great theatre; an individual's actions, really acting; and the ideal courtier, the star of stars.

These theatre metaphors hardly remain Ludovico's private prop-
erty, however, for they recur repeatedly throughout Books I and
II, as Ludovico, Federico Fregoso, and others define the way an
ideal courtier should behave.[1] For instance, in discussing the *arte*
of telling jokes and witty stories, Bibbiena labels it an *imitazione*
consisting of gestures, sounds, and modes of speech, and he
warns the courtier particularly against descending to the level of
buffoneria (II, 50, 267). In both cases, Bibbiena implicitly thinks of
telling jokes and witty stories as a comic performance and of the
courtier as a comic actor or entertainer. Similarly, whenever Federico discusses the all-important question of how the ideal courtier puts his good qualities into practice, he inevitably characterizes
him as a man on show, a manipulator of appearances, a performer before an audience. At one point, Federico declares:

> E se poi se ritroverà armeggiare nei spettaculi publici,
> giostrando, torneando, o giocando a canne, o facendo
> qualsivoglia altro esercizio della persona, ricordandosi il
> loco ove si trova ed in presenzia di cui, procurerà esser
> nell'arme non meno attillato e leggiadro che sicuro, e
> pascer gli occhi dei spettatori di tutte le cose che gli parrà
> che possano aggiungergli grazia. . . .
>
> (II, 8, 201)

> Whereas, if he happens to engage in arms in some public
> show—such as jousts, tourneys, stick-throwing, or any
> other bodily exercise—mindful of the place where he is
> and in whose presence, he will strive to be as elegant and
> handsome in the exercise of arms as he is adroit, and to
> feed his spectators' eyes with all those things that he
> thinks may give him added grace. . . .
>
> (99)

Fully aware of the nature of spectacles, Federico notes that audi-
ences have notoriously short attention spans and advises the courtier to appear on stage as early in the show as possible. Significantly, Federico illustrates this general rule directly from the art of
acting: he praises a *nobile istrione antico* who always strove to be the
first to recite his part in a play (II, 8, 202). What is more important, according to Federico, the courtier does not cease being an
actor when he leaves the great stage of public spectacles; whether
he stands before a full house in the theatre of the court or gives a
private performance in his prince's chambers, the ideal always
wears the actor's mask (persona).

24

Ma se 'l cortegiano, consueto di trattar cose importanti, si ritrova poi secretamente in camera, dee vestirsi un'altra persona, e differir le cose severe ad altro loco e tempo ed attendere a ragionamenti piacevoli e grati al signor suo, per non impedirgli quel riposo d'animo.

(I, 19, 219)

But if a Courtier who is accustomed to handling affairs of importance should happen to be in private with his lord, he must become another person [lit., put on another mask], and lay aside grave matters for another time and place, and engage in conversation that will be amusing and pleasant to his lord, so as not to prevent him from gaining such relaxation.

(112)

For all of Castiglione's characters in his first two books, the ideal courtier produces an endless series of brilliant performances, pausing only long enough to exchange one mask for another.

Although occasionally the courtier will literally put on a mask as he participates in courtly entertainments or public spectacles, Castiglione's theory essentially is concerned with a *figurative* masking. That sort of masking means arranging one's personal appearance properly, wearing the right clothes, and behaving in such a way that one plays perfectly the roles society offers.[2] To use the words of Count Ludovico, Castiglione's spokesman in Book I, the courtier's mask is just like his ideal lady's make-up: it is not smeared on in thick layers that seem to cover her face with a wooden mask and turn her into a statue; rather, it is applied sparingly, so that it moves freely with the changing expressions of her face and appears a natural part of it. Thus, make-up minimizes defects and enhances beautiful features, transforming an ordinary face into an attractive work of art (I, 40, 154).[3] As Castiglione's spokesmen present their ideal courtier in terms of acting and role playing, it is just this sort of nonliteral masking they have in mind, masking in which the individual does not hide behind an elegantly featured work of art, but becomes that work of art himself.

The theatre metaphors structuring Castiglione's view of the world and of his ideal courtier correspond to a basic reality of Renaissance society. While a long-established commonplace declares that the king was never alone, in fact, scarcely anyone was ever alone in the palaces, townhouses, and humble cottages of Renaissance Europe. The work of the French demographic historian, Philippe Ariès, has shown that constant social interaction was

25

the norm for Renaissance men and that they found it difficult to imagine life without the continual presence of society.[4] The modern distinction between public and private was less sharply defined in sixteenth-century society, when one's "family" included servants and retainers as well as relatives, and when there was no room in one's house into which one could withdraw in order to enjoy complete privacy. Even in the privy, privacy was sometimes hard to find; Renaissance pedagogues, servants, and advisers routinely accompanied their masters and mistresses into what might otherwise seem the ultimately private domain. In response to this almost totally public, totally social world, many Renaissance writers from Erasmus and Castiglione to Shakespeare conceived it as theatre. They assumed that men were always on display, and that whether they played roles or not, others would judge them and respond to them in terms of those roles. Thus, while Castiglione doubtless endorsed Gasparo Pallavicino's opinion that honorable men should not judge others by their dress, he nevertheless agreed with Federico Fregoso that everyone did in fact judge men that way, reacting continually to their dress, their speech, their manner of walking, even their hair style (see II, 28, 233–34). For Castiglione as well as many other Renaissance writers, man was always on stage performing before an audience which would judge him, whether he stumbled through his part, played it to the hilt, or went down proclaiming that he played no part at all. Therefore, to prevent garbled lines and missed cues, Castiglione offers his *Libro del Cortegiano* as a guide to courtly acting; since all the world's a stage, he will teach his would-be courtiers to become witty, brilliant entertainers, not ridiculously inept buffoons.

In Castiglione's vision of life, his ideal courtly actor defines his identity primarily through art and much less through political association with a state or a ruler. This particularly aesthetic conception of character is hardly Castiglione's invention. It existed as early as the Hellenistic period of Greek antiquity and strongly affected Roman conceptions of education—in the works of Cicero, Quintilian, and Plutarch—that in turn shaped Castiglione's own ideal conceptions. According to H. I. Marrou's monumental *History of Education in Antiquity,* Hellenistic culture was essentially aesthetic as a result of the particular social and political changes wrought on Greek civilization by Alexander and his successors.[5] A world based on the ordered city-state gave way to one without any stable political center, where the state seemed merely the plaything of the whimsical goddess Fortuna. The traditional means of self-definition through identification with the *polis* lost its viability, and Hellenistic men turned instead to education, culture, and art for ways to explain who they were. No longer simply a matter of techniques to prepare children for adult life, education and the culture it produced actually became the goal of life. One positive result of this change was that, as the Greeks conquered and incorporated into their world numerous non-Greek peoples, they ceased defining themselves exclusively in terms of racial characteristics and relied instead on the culture and education that Greek and non-Greek could share alike. On the other hand, if culture became a universal concept potentially linking all men together, the Greeks also limited it more and more to the arts and particularly to literature. They imagined that only the artist, the man of letters, could possess supreme happiness in this life and immortality in the next; art became a religion, and heaven beckoned as an eternal, literary soirée.

Hellenistic aestheticism did not descend directly to the Renaissance, but underwent fundamental changes in the moral alembic of Roman culture. The general seriousness and moralism of the Romans and their basic, political identification of themselves with Rome profoundly affected the Hellenistic program they inherited. Specifically, while they learned to conceive of education and culture as ends in themselves, they still continued to envisage the ends of education and life simultaneously in the practical terms of service to the state. As a result, in the fifteenth and sixteenth centuries, when Renaissance humanists created an educational philosophy based primarily on a reinterpreted Quintilian, Cicero's recently unearthed *De Oratore,* and Plutarch's freshly translated *On the Education of Children,* they embraced both the moral-political and the aesthetic sides of the Roman ideal.[6] Infused with a Christian moralism, the ideal orator of Cicero and Quintilian re-emerged in the guise of Vergerius's, Pontano's, and Erasmus's ideal princes, Thomas Elyot's governor, della Casa's gentleman, and, of course, Castiglione's courtier. According to the theories of humanists like Vergerius, Leonardo Bruni, Elyot, and Sadoleto, the student received education for the practical, usually political, role he would play in adult life, and at the same time he was taught to pursue the rather different goal of his own self-perfection.[7] To some extent, all these Renaissance thinkers turned to education as the sole means to render men completely and truly human. "Men are not born, but made," declared Erasmus in a statement that reflected perfectly the beliefs of his fellow humanists.[8] At birth, the child's mind was a *tabula complanata* waiting to be written on by the skillful hands of parents, servants, educators,

27

and companions.[9] They felt that, with no care, the child would rapidly degenerate to the level of the beasts, but that with a good education he would rise to the heights of true humanity. Thus, emphasizing literature, history, and rhetoric, and departing from antique conceptions of the liberal arts by including music and the visual arts, the humanists set about to fashion their ideal, a free man (*liberus*) fully prepared by the *artes liberales* for the supreme accomplishment of self-realization.

Castiglione shared with the humanists their optimistic assessment of man and their belief in his educability, and the form assumed for his ideal courtier in Book I of *Il Cortegiano* reflects the twin goals of moral-political training and personal self-realization they inherited from antiquity. He thus defines the ideal courtier partially as the military and political servant of his prince and partially through the largely aesthetic culture which enables him to realize himself as a human being and which he manifests in literary learning, musical and artistic appreciation, and witty, urbane conversation. Yet Castiglione shifts the balance in this program, both diminishing the Roman emphasis on political service and emphasizing the goal of personal self-development, and he parts company with his fellow humanists by stressing the particularly aesthetic means to reach this second goal. When concerned with their goal of self-realization, fifteenth- and sixteenth-century humanists, like their Roman ancestors, devoted most of their attention to the moral and intellectual development of the individual.[10] Their fundamental category of thought was ethical and political philosophy, not aesthetics; they wanted a good man far more than a beautiful one. While Castiglione firmly insists on the moral excellence of his ideal courtier, that the ideal be a man of substance valuing the good above all else (see II, 22–23, 223–26), he also consistently stresses the value of the arts, presents the courtier as an artist fabricating images of himself to offer his audience, and, through analogies with music and painting, metaphorically conceives his human personality, the end product of training and effort, in aesthetic terms as a work of art. Probably without conscious intent, Castiglione obeys the humanists' own cry to return *ad fontes;* in fact, he leaps over both his contemporaries and their Roman ancestors to reach back and revive an aesthetic vision of life that had lain dormant since the time of Hellenistic antiquity.[11]

Castiglione also differs from predecessors and contemporaries in another extremely important way. Both the Romans and the humanists of the Italian Renaissance essentially concerned themselves with the formation of the child, with those early portions of life that were devoted to formal instruction and moral training, and were always, to some extent, meant to take place in a world somewhat divorced from everyday social realities. Some Renaissance thinkers, like Erasmus and Roger Ascham, even went so far as to discourage any education outside the artificial, controlled, moral, and bookish realm they wished to create for the child.[12] Castiglione, on the other hand, was a man of the world, and *Il Libro del Cortegiano* concerns itself not with the ivory tower education of a moral paragon, but with the larger question of how a humanistically trained, morally conscious individual is to operate in the real world of society. Castiglione's answer is to conceive that world as a great theatre in which the courtier becomes ideal by acting out a series of different roles that are adapted to suit the exigencies of time and place, morally proper, and always projecting the best conceivable image of his personality. Clearly, Castiglione must have felt that a malleable infant, once hardened into the morally rigid shape his humanist masters imagined for him in the carefully controlled and limited environments of their schools, would be totally unable to meet the demands of a complex, constantly changing world. Thus, in *The Courtier,* Castiglione implicitly rejects any attempt to train the individual in an abstract morality divorced from society; he does not ignore moral issues and advise pure opportunism as later writers on the art of courtesy would do, but he does insist that his ideal be shaped through constant interaction with society, that he confront morally vital questions in real situations.[13] He wants his ideal courtier to become an eternally flexible, protean actor of many masks, an intrinsically moral man who continually refashions his beautiful image to fit the myriad scenes he finds in the great theatre of his world.

Castiglione's first two books concern themselves with the talents, techniques, and styles of acting necessary for the would-be courtier if he is to succeed in playing the varied roles social intercourse demands. To become a consummate actor primarily involves the development of a total, moral self-consciousness, a complex condition that includes several distinct kinds of awareness. In the first place, the courtier must possess a knowledge of his general talents, resources, strengths, and limitations. When Castiglione's spokesman, Federico Fregoso, warns the courtier to avoid exercises and situations that might expose particular insufficiencies (e.g., II, 10, 204–5), the advice rests on the assumption that the courtier knows himself well enough to understand his weaknesses both absolutely and in relation to the strengths and weaknesses of those around him. In general, Federico declares that the courtier should merit the rewards he receives, but that he should know exactly what his own merits are and not try to behave in a way unsuited to his personality. Federico concludes: "Però bisogna che ognun conosca se stesso e le forze sue ed a quello s'accommodi, e consideri quali cose ha da imitare e quali no" (II, 20, 222: "Thus, everyone must know himself and his own powers, and govern himself accordingly, and consider what things he ought to imitate and what things he ought not" [114]). Secondly, the courtier's self-consciousness involves a broad understanding of society and its rules, what it defines as desirable behavior and rejects as indecorous and unbecoming. A third component of this ideal self-consciousness relates directly to the courtier's understanding of social norms and processes, for he must develop an awareness of his immediate environment, his immediate social context, that will aid him in adapting to it. At one point, Castiglione's spokesmen emphasize the importance of respecting the social context by joking about *le circonstanzie* (II, 8, 200), the circumstances in which any action takes place and to which the courtier, while remaining true to himself and his moral principles, nevertheless must adapt his words and deeds if he desires them to succeed. Such a courtier will never commit the faux pas of terrifying the ladies like some braggart soldier with talk of blood and battle in the midst of a purely social gathering (II, 9, 202–3). Finally, the most essential ingredient in the courtier's self-consciousness is his constant awareness of the image he presents to others. More important than the reflection he sees in his mirror is the reflection of himself he sees in others' eyes. As he enters a room, he looks cautiously at eyes that smile or frown on him, and as he performs his part, he carefully alters gestures and words at the merest flutter of a lash. Without such complex self-consciousness, this Renaissance star could never manipulate his image successfully and before long would find himself playing to an empty house.

As he creates the beautiful images others see, Castiglione's courtier is unmistakably an artist who consciously and deliberately employs two distinct kinds of art in achieving his ends. On the one hand, Castiglione speaks repeatedly of *arte,* a particular, manipulative skill, by which the courtier fashions his attractive personality. In a most revealing image, Castiglione compares the courtier's fashioning of himself to an artist's disposing of the elements in his painting: the ideal is instructed to present his virtuous qualities so that they offset one another,

come i boni pittori, i quali con l'ombra fanno apparere e
mostrano i lumi de' rilevi, e così col lume profundano
l'ombre dei piani e compagnano i colori diversi insieme di
modo, che per quella diversità l'uno e l'altro meglio si
dimostra, e 'l posar delle figure contrario l'una all'altra le
aiuta a far quell'officio che è intenzion del pittore.

(II, 7, 199)

as good painters who, by their use of shadow, manage to
throw the light of objects into relief, and, likewise, by their
use of light, to deepen the shadows of planes and bring
different colors together so that all are made more apparent through the contrast of one with another; and the
placing of figures in opposition one to another helps them
achieve their aim.

(98)

In the above passage, art is a manipulative skill which the artist
consciously uses to arrange, contrast, and harmonize his figures.
By analogy, the art of the ideal courtier must likewise be a tool
with which he actively, consciously arranges and highlights the
distinctive features of his mask.

Particularly in the second book, when the courtiers discuss humor and tell jokes, Castiglione establishes this identification of the
courtier's *arte* as a matter of manipulation and conscious effort, a
skill that can be learned and must be consciously applied. While
Castiglione agrees with Federico Fregoso that nature provides the
raw materials of wit and talent and energy, he likewise insists with
Bibbiena that art, associated repeatedly with study and judgment,
polishes and corrects one's conceits, separating the good from the
bad (II, 43, 257: "ma il giudicio poi e l'arte i [dei concetti] lima e
corregge, e fa elezione dei boni e rifiuta i mali"). The substance of
a joke may be the gift of nature, as it flashes into the head of the
teller with an immediacy that precludes conscious effort, but the
joketeller remains a performer who must have a quite theatrical
repertory of gestures, expressions, and techniques if his joke is to
produce laughter (see II, 50, 267). Nature may be indispensable,
but without the guiding hand of art, its products will be shapeless,
directionless, and inevitably indecorous. In Castiglione's thinking,
nature proposes, but art disposes.

The courtier's art arranges the materials nature gives him so
that they satisfy three requirements: they must continue to appear
natural; they must satisfy the rules of social decorum; and they

31

must reveal a fundamental beauty. Thus, a man with a handsome face but a large bald spot on his head is advised to wear something to cover it up (II, 40, 253), a strategy Castiglione himself adopted, especially when he sat for a portrait. Wearing a hat as he did seemed natural enough when everyone else also wore hats, and if chosen carefully, a hat could not fail to satisfy the requirements of social decorum. What is more important, it would allow the viewer to focus on the dignity and beauty of the wearer's face, rather than on his bald spot, and where hat and face perfectly complemented one another, the viewer could enjoy the additional beauty of an harmonious ensemble. As Castiglione's terms suggest, the courtier's *arte* is essentially an art of arrangement; it permits individual components to be viewed at their best and offers in addition a harmonious whole with its own, special beauty. Operating with such a conception of art, the courtier could hardly be mistaken for a method actor. Less Brando than Barrymore, he self-consciously creates a series of magnificent poses when playing his roles. A beautiful personality, like the painting and music to which Castiglione specifically compares it, is something *composed*. Federico Fregoso's image captures its essence: a brilliant jewel placed in a beautiful setting.

Nevertheless, in transforming life into a series of matchless poses, the courtier must never appear to be a poseur. His acting is rendered all the more difficult because while using his awareness of self and others to create attractive images, he dare not give any sign of the conscious effort involved in his act. When Castiglione's spokesmen criticize affectation, as they do repeatedly, they do so not because it seems effeminate or indecorous, but because it reveals conscious effort to play a role. In Castiglione's world, men fear deception, and the appearance of conscious effort provokes censure, anger, and contempt, since it shows that one is trying to appear something clearly beyond one's abilities, something one is not. Because smooth social interaction depends on the maintenance of men's trust that appearances duplicate realities, the bungled performance of the would-be courtier "leva in tutto il credito e fa l'omo poco estimato" (I, 26, 124: "this robs a man of all credit and causes him to be held in slight esteem"[43]). Instructively, Ludovico da Canossa praises those ancient orators who preserved men's faith in them by dissimulating their learning in their speeches and thus appearing simple and artless. Had such artifice called attention to itself, "arìa dato dubbio negli animi del populo di non dover esser da quella [l'arte] ingannati" (I, 26, 125: "[it] would have inspired in the minds of the people the fear that they could be duped by it"[44]). Only by hiding the conscious effort involved in art and hence in the ideal courtier's performance can social intercourse proceed smoothly and enmity be avoided.

To accomplish this end of hiding art and its effort, Castiglione calls for a second kind of art, which he labels *sprezzatura* and for which Ludovico da Canossa offers two slightly different definitions. In the first, the count explains that the courtier will perform gracefully only if he uses in every performance "una certa sprezzatura, che nasconda l'arte e dimostri ciò che si fa e dice venir fatto senza fatica e quasi senza pensarvi" (I, 26, 124: "a certain *sprezzatura* [nonchalance], so as to conceal all art and make whatever is done or said appear to be without effort and almost without any thought about it"[43]). The context of this sentence suggests that the ultimately untranslatable *sprezzatura* indicates an easy facility in accomplishing difficult actions which hides the conscious effort that went into them.[14] A little later, Ludovico offers an illustration of what he means by the facility involved in *sprezzatura* by likening it to the virtuoso performance of the artist.

> Spesso ancor nella pittura una linea sola non stentata, un sol colpo di penello tirato facilmente, di modo che paia che la mano, senza esser guidata da studio o arte alcuna, vada per se stessa al suo termine secondo la intenzion del pittore, scopre chiaramente la eccellenzia dell'artifice. . . .
>
> (I, 28, 129)

> Often too in painting, a single line which is not labored, a single brush stroke made with ease and in such a manner that the hand seems of itself to complete the line desired by the painter, without being directed by care or skill of any kind, clearly reveals . . . excellency of craftsmanship. . . .
>
> (47)

No wonder *sprezzatura* would become a central term in Mannerist aesthetics and particularly in the theory of Lodovico Dolce, where it would indicate an ease and spontaneity of execution thought to be the surest signs of artistic genius![15]

In Book II, Federico Fregoso uses *sprezzatura* in a slightly different way, which suggests the need for further refinement of the definition given above. Federico lauds the notion of playing while masked, because the individual can thus devote his attention to what is important and use *una certa sprezzatura* towards that which

33

is not (II, 11, 206). Simply translating the word in this passage as nonchalance ignores the important element it retains from the verb that is its root. The verb *sprezzare* means to scorn or despise, and nonchalance is far too cool, too neutral and unaggressive, to suggest that meaning. Yet surely when Federico demands that one use a certain *sprezzatura* toward what is not important, he implies an attitude of slightly superior disdain rather than one of complete indifference. Similarly, when Castiglione describes a face made up to reveal its natural beauty and concealing the art that went into its creation, he employs a phrase, *sprezzata purità* (I, 40, 155), meaning at the same time both an unaffected, unostentatious purity and a purity that is scorned, looked down on by the one who possesses it and manipulates it so masterfully. One final example confirms the connection between *sprezzatura* and *sprezzare*. When Count Ludovico reworks his definition of what creates truly graceful dancing, he declares that such grace comes from

> quella sprezzata desinvoltura (ché nei movimenti del
> corpo molti così la chiamano), con un parlar o ridere o
> adattarsi, mostrando non estimar e pensar più ad ogni
> altra cosa che a quello, per far credere a chi vede quasi di
> non saper né poter errare. . . .
>
> (I, 26, 125)

> that cool *disinvoltura* [ease] (for when it is a matter of
> bodily movements many call it that) in many of the men
> and women here present, who seem in words, in laughter,
> in posture not to care; or seem to be thinking more of
> everything than of that, so as to cause all who are watch-
> ing them to believe that they are almost incapable of mak-
> ing a mistake. . . .
>
> (44)

Here the count uses *desinvoltura*, a synonym for *sprezzatura* that refers specifically to the ease and nonchalance of physical move-ments,[16] and he most instructively modifies this synonym with the participle *sprezzata*, thus emphasizing the latter's quite different connotations. He does not describe mere indifference, the free-dom from complexities and entanglements that *desinvoltura* sug-gests, but a scornful indifference. Moreover, he underscores the element of slight disdain involved by means of a suggestively dou-bled verb, *non estimar e pensar,* indicating that the dancer talks or laughs to show not merely that he does not have to think about his dancing, but that he is superior to it and does not esteem it as well.

Lest the identification of *sprezzatura* with scornful indifference create misconceptions, a further qualification is necessary. When he speaks of a *sprezzata purità* or a *sprezzata desinvoltura,* Castiglione surely means that one's easy behavior should imply scorn for the potential difficulty or restriction involved, not for the beauty of a face or the grace of dancing. To manifest *sprezzatura* is to imply scorn for normal, human limitations, physical necessities, and the restrictions of most forms of behavior. As the previous quotation indicated, to use *sprezzatura* is to make it seem that one cannot err, to create the impression that one is the complete master of every role one plays, every action one undertakes. Count Ludovico underscores this particular function of *sprezzatura* when he offers his second definition of the term:

> Questa virtù adunque contraria alla affettazione, la qual noi per ora chiamiamo sprezzatura, oltra che ella sia il vero fonte donde deriva la grazia, porta ancor seco un altro ornamento, il quale accompagnando qualsivoglia azione umana, per minima che ella sia, non solamente sùbito scopre il saper di chi la fa, ma spesso lo fa estimar molto maggior di quello che è in effetto; perché negli animi delli circunstanti imprime opinione, che chi così facilmente fa bene sappia molto più di quello che fa, e se in quello che fa ponesse studio e fatica, potesse farlo molto meglio.
>
> (I, 28, 128)

> Thus, this excellence (which is opposed to affectation, and which, at the moment, we are calling *nonchalance*), besides being the real source from which grace springs, brings with it another adornment which, when it accompanies any human action however small, not only reveals at once how much the person knows who does it, but often causes it to be judged much greater than it actually is, since it impresses upon the minds of the onlookers the opinion that he who performs well with so much facility must possess even greater skill than this, and that, if he were to devote care and effort to what he does, he could do it far better.
>
> (46)

Not only does the scorning indifference of *sprezzatura* reveal the courtier's masterful knowledge; more importantly, it magnifies his image, suggesting that however accomplished he may appear to be, he is potentially even greater.

This conception of *sprezzatura* as a means to manifest the courtier's superiority cannot be separated from the emphasis Castiglione's spokesmen place on his nobility. Ludovico da Canossa explicitly demands that the ideal be of noble birth, and Federico Fregosa repeatedly warns him against mingling in the games and amusements of peasants, "perché sta troppo male e troppo è brutta cosa e fuor della dignità vedere un gentilomo vinto da un villano" (II, 10, 204: "because it is too unseemly and too ugly a thing, and quite without dignity, to see a gentleman defeated by a peasant"[101]). Even though Gasparo Pallavicino attacks both speakers on the issue of nobility, he simply prefers a courtier whose nobility is natural, a matter of talent and training, and not due merely to an inherited title (see I, 15, 106–7 and II, 10, 204–5). Essentially, Gasparo and all the other courtiers consider their ideal a member of the superior social class to which they themselves belong. Although inferior in the social hierarchy, which all respect, to the even more elevated class of princes and kings (see II, 18, 218), this elite group holds itself far above the "vulgar herd," distinguishing itself by means of its classical education, highly refined manners, and cultivated tastes. Even in its humor, it constantly preserves a sense of social superiority ("servando sempre la dignità del gentilomo") and always avoids comic behavior that might suggest the antics of uneducated peasants (see II, 50, 267). Finally, it should be noted that if Castiglione's courtier is always an actor playing before a group of spectators, he is much less concerned with impressing the common people with his performance than his peers and superiors. Not only does he not compete with peasants, but, sneers Federico, he should never strive to attain excellence at certain games like chess, since that would only serve the base purpose "a far maravigliare il vulgo" (II, 31, 239: "to cause the vulgar to marvel"[128]).

A hostile critic might ask Castiglione why his courtier must use *sprezzatura* to create the image of himself as a superior being when he is supposedly a superior being in fact. In reply, Castiglione would simply point to the social world he knew so intimately and would say, as Federico does, that in this world men normally react to appearances and esteem or despise one another long before they can penetrate beneath men's masks and understand, however imperfectly and incompletely, realities. At several crucial points in *Il Cortegiano*, Castiglione underscores his conviction that no man can really distinguish appearances from realities absolutely, understand others and their motives with complete clarity, or totally free his perceptions from the bias of personal perspective. The question of how to distinguish reality from appearances arises twice in *Il Cortegiano,* and each time it receives a carefully qualified answer which suggests that Castiglione recognized no completely successful method for dealing with it. At one point, when asked how one separates true love from that which is merely feigned, the Magnifico replies: "Io non lo so perché gli omini oggidì sono tanto astuti, che fanno infinite dimonstrazion false e talor piangono quando hanno ben gran voglia di ridere" (III, 54, 415: "This I do not know, because nowadays men are so cunning that they make no end of false demonstrations and sometimes weep when they can hardly keep from laughing"[260]). Moreover, although the Magnifico then goes on to offer his *donna di palazzo* advice about how to deal with this problem, his advice presents no method for separating the true from the feigned, but essentially amounts to a defensive strategy for her. Unable to see through men's deceiving masks, she protects herself by remaining distant and skeptical in response to those who flatter her, refusing to talk of love, and laughing at others' protestations of affection. The Magnifico concludes: "in tal modo si farà tener per discreta, e sarà più sicura dagli inganni" (III, 54, 416: "in this way she will cause others to deem her discreet and she will be better insured against deceit"[260]). Similarly, in another passage, after Federico Fregoso has declared that the ideal courtier should only obey the truly good and honorable commands of his prince, he completely evades Gasparo Pallavicino's difficult question of how one discerns the truly good from what merely seems so: "Perdonatemi, . . . io non voglio entrar qua, ché troppo ci saria che dire, ma il tutto si rimetta alla discrezion vostra" (II, 23, 226: "Excuse me, . . . I do not wish to go into that, for there would be too much to say; but let the whole question be left to your discretion"[117–18]). Finally, Castiglione also includes an incident in *Il Cortegiano* to dramatize the incompleteness characterizing human perception. At the start of Book II he reports that, when asked to recount the discussions of the previous evening, all the courtiers gave the prefect Francesco Maria della Rovere slightly different versions of what had been said (II, 5, 195–96). Even in such a neutral matter as simple recollection of the past, there is no escape from the limitation and subjectivism of personal perspective, no hope for absolute clarity and completeness of vision.

Undaunted, Castiglione believes that his ideal courtier can successfully solve this apparent problem of communication and human intercourse. The ideal will solve it by creating images of himself which effectively proclaim abilities and talents he may not be able to demonstrate convincingly at first sight or sufficiently often. Essentially, his image making will be an art of suggestion, in which the courtier's audience will be induced by the images it confronts to imagine a greater reality existing behind them. Note how Federico urges the courtier to accomplish exercises outside his profession with such faciltiy that people judge him even more excellent at what is his profession (II, 39, 251–52). Although Castiglione assumes his courtier will possess the abilities his image suggests, for the sake of social acclaim the ideal need only produce images that successfully activate the imaginations of his viewers. They will then flesh out and enhance the image they see and contribute substantially to the power it has to move their admiration and applause. Thus, although the courtier's image making may begin as compensation for the inadequacy of human perception, it clearly becomes a distinct advantage as it allows him to make himself into a much more enticing and compelling figure than he might otherwise be.

It should thus be apparent that when Castiglione speaks of *sprezzatura* as the means by which art hides art, he does not describe a form of behavior that involves total artlessness, and he never implies that his courtier should appear before others as anything less than a brilliant performer. To be sure, Castiglione attacks sloppy, extreme, and exaggerated behavior, but not because it is artful. Rather, he attacks it because, in its insufficient or overly great artfulness, it calls too much attention to the fact that a performance is occurring, instead of letting the performance speak for itself. Such behavior shows an incomplete mastery of art or an offensively cunning and inept attempt to dispense with it. It offends those in its audience because it seems to rob them of their freedom and dignity; it demands overtly that they pay attention and look up to someone who wants them to think he is greater than his performance reveals him to be. His attempt to command attention and admiration can only result in hostility and contempt or in tolerant, but slightly condescending laughter such as that which Castiglione has his courtiers direct at the petulant, self-important Unico Aretino. By contrast, the ideal courtier will succeed with his spectators because, in singing or dancing or conversing with perfect mastery of the art involved, his performance reveals implicitly that he is, in fact, the consummate artist he appears to be. Moreover, because his art remains unobtrusive, it does not threaten those in his audience by demanding their appreciation, but makes it seem that he actually performs for their sake and that he looks up to them as his judges. Thus, as he performs difficult feats effortlessly, he frees his observers to marvel at his mastery and use their own imaginations to enhance the image he displays to them.

At one point in Book II, Castiglione's characters consider the desirability of the courtier's appearing really masked in public, and their reflections on this literal, rather than figurative, masking define a model for the kind of courtly performance Castiglione must have desired.

> . . . in camera privatamente, come or noi ci troviamo, penso che licito gli sia . . . ballar moresche e brandi; ma in publico non così, fuor che travestito, e benché fosse di modo che ciascun lo conoscesse, non dà noia; anzi per mostrarsi in tai cose nei spettaculi publici, con arme e senza arme, non è miglior via di quella; perché lo esser travestito porta seco una certa libertà e licenzia, la quale tra l'altre cose fa che l'omo po pigliare forma di quello in che si sente valere, ed usar . . . una certa sprezzatura circa quello che non importa, il che accresce molto la grazia: come saria vestirsi un giovane da vecchio, ben però con abito disciolto, per potersi mostrare nella gagliardia; un cavaliero in forma di pastor selvatico o altro tale abito, ma con perfetto cavallo, e leggiadramente acconcio secondo quella intenzione; perché sùbito l'animo de' circonstanti corre ad imaginar quello che agli occhi al primo aspetto s'appresenta; e vedendo poi riuscir molto maggior cosa che non prometteva quell'abito, si diletta e piglia piacere.
>
> (II, 11, 206)

> . . . privately, in a chamber, as we are now, I think he could be allowed to . . . try morris dances and *branles* as well; but not in public, unless he is masquerading, for then it is not unseemly even if he should be recognized by all. Indeed, there is no better way of showing oneself in such things, at public spectacles, either armed or unarmed; because masquerading carries with it a certain freedom and license, which among other things enables one to choose the role in which he feels most able, . . . and to show a certain nonchalance [*sprezzatura*] in what does not matter: all of which adds much charm; as for a youth to dress like an old man, yet in a loose attire so as to be

able to show his vigor; or for a cavalier to dress as a rustic
shepherd, or in some other such costume, but astride a
perfect horse and gracefuly attired in character: because
the bystanders immediately take in what meets the eye at
first glance; whereupon, realizing that here there is much
more than was promised by the costume, they are delighted and amused.

(102–3)

This key passage nowhere suggests that the masker should make
an obvious and conscious effort to convince everyone he really is
the old man or shepherd his disguise proclaims him to be. Rather,
his masking itself reveals him to be an artful actor, someone who
obviously plays a part. Such a man does not threaten his audience
because his artifice is totally apparent, and, appropriately, Castiglione manifests little concern that his courtier's identity should be
recognized underneath his disguise. In fact, he even suggests that
the youth leave his costume undone and that the shepherd ride a
good horse, partially so that both can thus more conveniently
perform their acts, but also because that way they will keep their
spectators from mistaking them for real old men and rustic
shepherds. Like Renaissance painting and sculpture, this courtly
masker is "una artificiosa imitazion di natura" (I, 50, 175: "an
artificial imitation of nature"[my translation]), and in Renaissance
culture, to speak of something as *artificioso* was to accord it the
highest praise. Furthermore, if the courtier does not deceive his
audience because he employs obvious artifice, he also does not
deceive them because he surpasses, rather than falls short of their
expectations in his performance. Ultimately, his mask gives him
the necessary freedom, the artistic freedom, to serve his spectators
by creating a beautiful image that will be pleasing in itself and in
contrast with the lesser image everyone at first expected.

The perfect ease and mastery which the courtier creates by
using *sprezzatura* constitute two of the central features present in
all the different courtly masks he wears on the great stage of the
world. They help define the fundamental courtly style he displays
in every role he masters with his art—no matter whether he wears
the mask of soldier, political advisor, lover, or comic entertainer.
These qualities are not the only features of that style, however,
for Castiglione supplies a fairly elaborate set of concepts and
terms to define it in a quite complex manner. These other stylistic
features include: *gravità* and the closely related concept of *dignità*;
purity, simplicity, and naturalness; and the absolutely central term

40

grazia. Analysis of these terms and particularly of *grazia* should again show how profoundly Castiglione is related to the Hellenistic tradition and should help explain why the ideal character of his book appealed so powerfully to large segments of Renaissance Europe.

However important other terms may be for characterizing the courtier's ideal image, the key term in Castiglione's behavioral aesthetic is *grazia.* It has a particularly ambiguous position in his book; from one perspective it stands alongside all the other terms and simply defines one component of the ideal image. From another perspective, it is the generative term of the series, necessitating the addition of all the others in order to define the elusive qualities it signifies. In the first case, grace is presented as a "condimento d'ogni cosa, senza il quale tutte l'altre proprietà e bone condicioni sian di poco valore" (I, 24, 121: "seasoning without which all the other properties and good qualities would be of little worth"[41]). Grace is what the courtier wishes to manifest by using *sprezzatura* and is an essential feature of his civilized behavior. Identical with urbanity, elegance, and refinement, it is synonymous with the highest achievement of culture. Moreover, it also has a fundamentally aesthetic meaning.[17] From Leon Battista Alberti in the early fifteenth century to Vasari in the middle of the sixteenth, *grazia* was used to describe the important achievement of art: a harmonious elegance and refinement which Vasari considered the real product of genius and which he opposed to a beauty achieved through strict following of rules. The paintings of Castiglione's close friend Raphael especially called forth praise for their *grazia.*[18] In the light of this background, attaching an aesthetic meaning to the word *grazia* in Castiglione's book should hardly seem extravagant. When Castiglione's courtiers dub their ideal the knight of grace, they not only grant him the refinement normally associated with civilization, but the kind of artistic elegance perceived in the postures and gestures of Raphael's characters. Thus, once again, the courtier's image is unmistakably a work of art.

At the same time, *grazia* also generates a host of other terms to describe the style of the courtier's ideal image. In addition to *sprezzatura,* one of the most important is *gravità.* As with all the terms used to define the courtier's style, Castiglione stresses that *gravità* is a quality the ideal manifests regardless of the role he happens to be playing. Castiglione presents it as a quality appropriate for every age in a person's life and especially for young men who might otherwise translate their nervous energy into incessant activity, earning themselves the reputation of flightiness and childish instability. Federico declares he likes to see "un giovane, e massimamente nell'arme, che abbia un poco del grave e del taciturno; che stia sopra di sé; . . . perché par che abbian non so che di più che gli altri giovani" (II, 16, 213–14: "a young man, especially when he is engaging in arms, be somewhat grave and taciturn and be self-possessed, . . . because such youths appear to have a certain something which the others lack"[108]). *Gravità* should also characterize both male and female behavior, even though Castiglione takes pains to differentiate the forms it assumes in each of the two sexes. Especially nervous about potential attacks on the courtly ideal for being too effeminate—attacks reflected in the misogynistic criticisms of Ottaviano Fregoso and Gasparo Pallavicino in Books III and IV—Castiglione emphasizes the virility of his courtier at every turn. Even his grace is modified as "virile" (I, 19, 114). To the ideal lady, created as the complement for the courtier, go all the traditionally feminine virtues: delicacy, tenderness, restraint, and a pleasing affability (III, 4–5, 341–44). Corresponding to these opposing male and female images, Castiglione presents two kinds of *gravità*, the difference between them determined by the character and function of the two sexes. For the man, *gravità* serves both to protect him from attack and to add a certain weightiness to his image, which will aid him in his aggressive courting of society. The gravity and reserve of the lady is less an offensive than a defensive weapon, a means to stifle rumors and innuendoes which others all too willingly spread about her behind her back (III, 5, 344–45: "quella gravità temperata di sapere e bontà è quasi uno scudo contra la insolenzia e bestialità dei prosuntuosi"). For both, however, the quality remains an essential part of their ideal images at every stage of life and no matter what particular role they choose to play.

What *gravità* means in terms of behavior comes to light in several comments by Federico Fregoso, who insists particularly on its importance for the ideal. Arguing that dress is often interpreted as a revelation of character, Federico quickly prescribes his preferences: he likes clothes that "tendano un poco più al grave e riposato, che al vano; però parmi che maggior grazia abbia nei vestimenti il color nero, che alcun altro; e se pur non è nero, che almen tenda al scuro" (II, 27, 231: "tend a little more toward the grave and sober rather than the foppish. Hence, I think that black is more pleasing in clothing than any other color; and if not black, then at least some color on the dark side"[121–22]). In another passage, Federico reinforces this preference by arguing that if

Italians tried to imitate the lively manners and costumes of the French, they would merely render grotesque what did not suit their character. Instead, he urges his fellow countrymen to complement their natural tendency to liveliness by imitating the *gravità riposata* particular to Spaniards (II, 37, 248). The image that Federico desires his courtier to project is one of seriousness and sobriety, a weightiness of personality that invites the respect of others by encouraging their all-important trust and confidence. Like his *sprezzatura*, the courtier's *gravità* is also a particularly suggestive quality, a matter of understatement which insinuates that depths of wisdom and reserves of energy lie behind what everyone sees, whereas the overstatement of wearing constantly flamboyant costumes would make the courtier seem ridiculous for trying too hard to stand out beyond everyone else. Finally, as the outward manifestation of self-control and confidence, *gravità* documents that essential *dignità del gentilhomo* (II, 50, 267; see also II, 11, 205–6) which the courtier is always to preserve as the nucleus of his self-esteem.[19]

If *sprezzatura* and *gravità* define stylistic traits of ideal, courtly behavior, so do several other, profoundly suggestive concepts: simplicity, purity, and naturalness. Although opposed to affectation, artificiality, and fussiness of every sort, simplicity and purity are not merely negative qualities, to be defined as the absence of certain undesirable, extravagant forms of behavior. In the contexts where they occur, the terms possess a number of suggestive associations. For instance, at one point, Castiglione speaks of a "pura ed amabile simplicità, che tanto è grata agli animi umani" (I, 27, 127: "pure and charming simplicity which is so appealing to all"[45]), and at another, he describes a face, its natural beauty not destroyed by excessive make-up, as having a *sprezzata purità* (I, 40, 155). As he notes the powerful, attractive force simplicity and purity exert on those who observe them, he clearly invites positive, moral associations like goodness, honesty, and innocence to be derived from the terms. Thus, the courtier who possesses *simplicità* and *purità* seems a morally superior being more than a mere performer.

Castiglione never uses an abstract noun equivalent to the notion of naturalness, but he does use the words *natura* and *naturalmente* to describe forms of behavior opposed to affectation and related to the notions of purity and simplicity. For instance, Count Ludovico praises certain ancient orators who dissimulated their learning in their speeches in order to make them appear composed "simplicissimamente, e più tosto secondo che loro porgea la natura e la verità, che 'l studio e l'arte" (I, 26, 125: "in the simplest manner and according to the dictates of nature and truth rather than of effort and art"[43–44]). Again, a little later, he praises the courtier's facility in handling weapons, since it makes him seem as though "il corpo e tutte le membra stiano in quella disposizione naturalmente" (I, 28, 128–29: "his body and all his members fall into that posture naturally"[46]). In both passages, Ludovico is primarily interested in the courtier's avoiding affectation and the disastrous appearance of artifice and calculation, but as he links nature to truth and simplicity as well as to a desired harmony between body and mind, he suggests that *natura* also has more than negative meanings for him. In the contexts where he uses it, the term does not suggest the messy, sometimes chaotic, natural world men live in, but rather seems to point to an ideal nature, the kind Castiglione's culture depicted in idealized landscapes, pastoral pleasances, and ultimately, in images of the Garden of Eden. In short, when Castiglione praises his courtier for the naturalness of his image, he suggests that this sophisticated artist, this ideal representative of civilization, paradoxically reflects something of the prelapsarian qualities his ancient forbears had in paradise.

A brief review of the constituent elements defining the image of Castiglione's "graceful" courtier will serve to bring out more fully its edenic character. First, the courtier is a man who appears fully at ease in this world; his *sprezzatura* makes him seem the total master of self, society's rules, and even physical laws, and it creates the distinct impression that he is unable to err. His *gravità* testifies to his possession of human dignity; his simplicity and purity suggest moral wholeness and innocence; and, finally, his naturalness evokes a harmony with the natural order from which most men have fallen away. Unmistakably, this "gracious" courtier recalls the innocent Adam, who, before the Fall, likewise did not err, enjoyed harmony among his various faculties and with the natural world, and stood erect in his God-given dignity. To be sure, Castiglione's courtier lives in Urbino, not the Garden of Eden, embodies all the characteristics peculiar to his culture, and appears as a consummate artist and performer, not a "natural" man. Nevertheless, during his inspired performance, the ghostly presence of Adam hovers over him, animating the image he projects with the affective energy that only recollection of man's first father could generate. However much Castiglione may have cultivated the cherished ideal of Renaissance Italian courtly society, and however much classical authors like Cicero, Quintilian, and

Plutarch fertilized his conception, only the warm sun of Eden could make it grow and send forth its bloom. As a result, the courtier's image acquired a power to affect the members of its culture, men who were still deeply responsive to Christian archetypes and who might otherwise never have granted Castiglione's ideal the central place it assumed in their lives.

In no sense, however, should one conclude that Castiglione makes his courtier into a religious ideal or uses the central term *grazia* as an essentially religious or theological concept. Although in Bembo's Neoplatonic oration, he will use *grazia* in a theological sense and envisage a religious goal for the courtier, Castiglione remains a thoroughly secular thinker in his first two books.[20] Nevertheless, Castiglione's use of *grazia* to define a secular quality in a secular context is structured by its traditional meanings and associations in the domain of theology. In other words, the term generates or calls forth a set of terms and relationships on the secular level which have precise analogues on the theological level. According to Kenneth Burke, *The Book of the Courtier* establishes a connected hierarchy of such systems of terms, leading smoothly from the lower, secular level to the ultimate one, which, in Castiglione's culture, was necessarily theological.[21] In Burke's analysis, the reverence that the courtier pays his social superior, his lord, is an analogue to the reverence he pays his ultimate superior, his Lord God, and Burke argues further that Castiglione structures his work to lead from the first sort of reverence presented in Books I, II, and III to the ultimate reverence of Bembo's speech in Book IV. Similarly, Burke would argue that the earthly grace the courtier creates in his acting is analogous to its ultimate form, that divine grace which Adam once enjoyed and which others can still achieve as Bembo does, through Neoplatonic rapture. Thus, while *grazia* remains a secular conception in the early pages of Castiglione's book, its theological meanings and associations influence its use on that secular level and help explain its implicit power and suggestiveness. Moreover, it should be noted that the theological implications in Castiglione's use of *grazia* are strikingly Catholic in a world teetering on the brink of the Reformation. While Count Ludovico agrees with Cesare Gonzaga that grace cannot be learned, he does insist that most men have the potential to acquire it by their own power (I, 25, 122–23). On a theological level, Castiglione would reject the extreme Protestant position, according to which man could not earn grace at all, in favor of the more traditional Catholic position that encouraged men to work and thus contribute something themselves to their achievement of grace.[22]

While *grazia* defines a quality of the courtier's image, Castiglione also uses it to indicate the reward of glory and honor, the applause his ideal receives from his audience, and particularly from his lord, as a result of his gracious performance. Strikingly, at no point in *Il Cortegiano* does Castiglione suggest a belief in virtue as its own reward. Quite the contrary, his characters insist that *l'onore*, that is, public praise and recognition, "è il vero premio delle virtuose fatiche" (I, 18, 111: "is the true reward of all virtuous toil"[34]), and they condemn the performance of good deeds when no one else observes them and when there is, consequently, no possibility of reward (II, 8, 200–201). Thus, for the courtier to be truly *aggraziato,* he must not only be "gracious" in appearance, gestures, and conversation, but he must also be "graced" with the recognition and esteem of others. Castiglione's use of a single term to define both conditions suggests his optimistic belief in the close relationship between them; in fact, it could be argued that one of his fundamental purposes in writing *Il Cortegiano* was his desire to reveal the connection between gracious behavior and the grace of social rewards. However, just as good Renaissance Catholics never asssumed that they could command their Lord's grace through the performance of gracious works, so Castiglione recognizes that though the courtier's performance must be gracious if he is to please his lord and gain his good graces, even the most perfect manners, dress, and language cannot insure he will receive his just reward (see II, 32, 240–41).

Although he enjoyed European fame as a perfect courtier, Castiglione knew only too well the ultimate irrationality of grace in this world. For reasons he seems never to have understood and which have remained obscure to later historians, when he returned from Milan to the court of Mantua in 1499, Castiglione simply did not find favor with his lord Francesco Gonzaga. That dissatisfaction turned into open hostility after Castiglione entered the service of Duke Guidobaldo in 1504; and for the next decade, it prevented him from setting foot on Mantuan territory and visiting the members of his family who were there. Only in 1515–16 did Castiglione regain Francesco Gonzaga's favor and eventually become his ambassador at the papal court.[23] Thus, it is most appropriate that in *Il Cortegiano,* although its author argues gracious behavior usually receives its reward of grace, he also reveals his awareness that the connection between the two kinds of *grazia* is neither necessary nor inevitable. Nothing less than a gift from his earthly lord, as from his heavenly one, grace lies ultimately beyond even the most perfect courtier's control and testifies to the

46

final unpredictability of the two lords he serves. Although *Il Cortegiano* celebrates the fact that grace usually lies within the reach of art, it adds the sober qualification that art's reach sometimes exceeds its grasp.

When the courtier's audience claps enthusiastically in response to his performance and rewards him with the grace of its praise, Castiglione defines its characteristic reaction with a most important term: *maraviglia*. For instance, Ludovico da Canossa urges the courtier to use *sprezzatura* to hide the effort involved in difficult or unusual feats: "perché delle cose rare e ben fatte ognun sa la difficultà, onde in esse la facilità genera grandissima maraviglia" (I, 26, 124: "because everyone knows the difficulty involved in matters that are rare and well done, whence facility in them generates great marvel"[my translation]). Later, in Book II, Federico Fregoso sums up his own advice to the ideal courtier, again focusing on *maraviglia* as the response he should seek in his audience.

> E per concluder dico, che bon saria che 'l cortegian sapesse perfettamente ciò che detto avemo convenirsigli, di sorte che tutto 'l possibile a lui fosse facile ed *ognuno di lui si maravigliasse, esso di niuno.* . . .
>
> (II, 38, 249; my italics)

> And, to conclude, I declare that it would be well for the Courtier to know perfectly all we have said befits him, so that everything possible may be easy for him, and that *everyone may marvel at him and he at no one.* . . .
>
> (135)

These key passages leave no doubt that marvel or wonder is the basic response the courtier seeks to arouse in everyone about him and that it is essential for his social success.

During the sixteenth century, *maraviglia* (which also appeared as the verb *maravigliarsi*) embraced a wide variety of meanings, including marvel, wonder, surprise, the unexpected, the extraordinary, the monstrous, and the supernatural, and it indicated an intensity of response ranging from mild surprise to total astonishment.[24] Marvel was the typical response elicited by displays of virtuosity, technical feats, and witty word games like the double entendres that Bibbiena declares "più presto movano maraviglia che riso" (II, 58, 278: "cause marvel rather than laughter"[157]). On a deeper level, marvel could also involve vibrant impressions of beauty, revelations of unimagined aspects of reality, or startling

47

flashes of insight into the strange truth of things.[25] In either case, it meant not only a delight in being surprised, but an enthusiastic admiration for the cleverness, intellectual inventiveness, and profundity of the performer. Hence, it was a reaction that Renaissance artists especially sought to produce by creating unusual, fantastic, bizarre, and surprising works.[26] In his *Cortegiano*, Castiglione uses *maraviglia* in just this sense on several occasions, praising the marvelous music produced by voice and viol playing in concert (II, 13, 209) and lauding Sannazaro's poems *con le maraviglie* (II, 35, 245). Since he presents his ideal courtier as nothing less than the artist of his own personality, a virtuoso actor who has perfected his art to the point where he can toss off the most demanding roles with the most assured ease, it is singularly appropriate that his audience should respond to him with *maraviglia*, just as they would marvel at the incredible beauties and ingenious creations of Raphael and Michelangelo.

Castiglione uses the word *maraviglia* repeatedly throughout his *Cortegiano*, and not always as a term of praise. Often, it has an almost neutral meaning of "surprise," a mild reaction to something unusual or unexpected (see, for example, II, 19, 220, and III, 24, 370). At other times, however, it expresses a most negative response. For instance, at the start of Book II, Castiglione employs it to indicate his irritated incredulity that old men would indiscriminately worship the past and condemn the present (II, 1, 187: "Non senza maraviglia ho più volte considerato onde nasca un errore ... etc."). In another place, Cesare Gonzaga similarly expresses his amazement (*maraviglia*) that women escape the ingenious snares laid for them by their would-be seducers (III, 50, 408). In both passages, *maraviglia* does not indicate admiration for what is involved, but it ironically calls attention to something unexpected which is not at the same time desirable, entertaining, or revealing of higher truths, and it expresses the speaker's feelings of contempt, irritation, or indignation in response to what he sees. An even more important, negative use of *maraviglia* occurs early in the discussions of Book I, when Ludovico expresses his wish that the ideal courtier be neither too short nor too tall, "perché e l'una e l'altra di queste condicioni porta seco una certa dispettosa maraviglia e sono gli omini di tal sorte mirati quasi di quel modo che si mirano le cose monstruose" (I, 20, 115: "because either of these conditions causes a certain contemptuous wonder, and men of either sort are gazed at in much the same way that we gaze at monstrous things"[36]). This passage indicates the significant distance that separates Castiglione's conception of the marvelous from that which would dominate Mannerist courts later in the century. In rejecting the grotesque and the monstrous, he rejects what Mannerist artists and critics and their patrons found absolutely fascinating, as they titillated their refined palates with ever more unusual, strange, and rare phenomena.[27] In Castiglione's conception, the marvelous is still primarily the beautiful and the seemingly natural. Moreover, it is valued not merely because it surprises or shocks, but because it presents itself as a product of human intelligence and offers some sort of valuable revelation. Castiglione and his courtiers would bristle with annoyance at being shown the freaks and prodigies of nature, might tolerate Raphael's decorative grotesque designs, but would love his elegant paintings best of all.

Another way to understand yet more fully the response involved in Castiglione's concept of *maraviglia* is to remember that from antiquity through the Renaissance, it was the expected and desired reaction to paradox. Both Cicero and Quintilian translated the Greek term *paradokson* (paradox) appropriately with words derived from the Latin verb *admiror,* meaning to wonder or marvel at, and later in the sixteenth century, the English rhetorician Puttenham, when considering paradox as a figure of speech, instructively called it "the wonderer."[28] For all of them, paradox was a species of *serio ludere,* a playing with words, concepts, or value systems that could be a gay, frivolous amusement, an engrossing pastime, or a profound experience intimating truths and realities far beyond normal experience. Thus, although paradox always depends on an audience's delight in surprise, the reaction of wonder it produces may include a number of different emotional intensities and involvements, from raised eyebrows to open-mouthed astonishment. Upon closer scrutiny, the marveling response to paradox actually turns out to be two-fold: the paradox first arrests the mind of the perceiver in an amazement that is akin to bafflement; then it stimulates the puzzled mind to an exploration or questioning of what it has experienced, thus intensifying its involvement in the experience and in some cases, at least, leading to the perception of deeper truths.[29] The wonder produced by paradox is itself ultimately paradoxical: the simultaneous experience of mystification and revelation.

As the preceding analysis would suggest, the *maraviglia* aroused by the ideal courtier's performance might productively be considered a response to paradox, especially since it invites definition in paradoxical terms, whether it is considered a matter of disciplined spontaneity, the easy resolution of the difficult, or the artful imitation of nature. Moreover, Castiglione's courtier himself can be read as a creature of paradox: while he is a man like all men who has neither transcendent authority nor superhuman abilities, strives hard to appear average, and values *mediocrità* as his chief virtue, at the same time, he performs with an ease and mastery that suggest absolute superiority to the physical and social restrictions that bind ordinary mortals. To such a paradoxical performer, as to his paradoxical performance, the response of marvel thus seems most fitting indeed.

At times, this response seems little more than a simple pleasure in wit and inventiveness; the courtier's audience admires without intense involvement his ability as a performer to play with words and entertain them with stunts and clever stories, just as they admire Bibbiena for his comic performance during the second evening. At other times, the response seems far deeper, and it derives its intensity precisely from the fact that the courtier represents for his creators the realization of their profoundest needs and desires. The image he creates unites the culture's ideal of witty sophistication and urbanity, the artful refinement of civilization at its height, to its happy dream of prelapsarian innocence, simplicity, and nature. The courtier is both the first citizen in the City of Man and an image of Adam reborn in Paradise. In fact, all the major attributes that define his style have a basically double character, expressing both the conscious ideals and the unconscious dreams of Castiglione's culture: his *dignità del gentilhomo* corresponds to his worldly position and the values of civilization while it recalls Adam's more fundamental, God-given dignity; his grace reveals an easy mastery of social forms and at the same time invokes the state of grace man enjoyed in Eden; his simplicity and naturalness indicate the civilized man's perfect taste, which is free from affectation, but they simultaneously suggest Adam's innocence and harmony with nature. The observers' wondering response to the courtier thus testifies to the pleasure they experience as he fulfills their dreams. Moreover, in doing so, he satisfies two even more profound needs: their need to find order in the world and to feel that man is truly free. In effect, the courtier provides his audience with a sense of congruence between what they deeply hope to see and what they actually do see; he creates the vision of the ideal achieved in the midst of an imperfect, historical world. The courtly performer momentarily obliterates the gap between "is" and "ought," between reality and desire; he gives a taste of Eden to men who still eat the fruit of a fallen earth. Moreover, in addition to this intimation of order, he gives them a glimpse of freedom. For Castiglione, as for the most others during the Renaissance, freedom did not come from rebelling against the law, but from mastering and fulfilling it perfectly and thus rising above it to what constitutes man's only real independence (see IV, 21, 473). This is precisely the freedom the courtier manifests as he creates his image of total mastery over limitations of every sort and plays every role he undertakes to absolute perfection. He is thus a perfect expression of order and a perfect expression of freedom—one final paradox to arouse the ecstatic wonder of his audience.

Significantly, the term *maraviglia* appears at one point in Castiglione's book where, although it does not refer to the courtier at all, it nevertheless reinforces what has been said of the profundity of the reaction involved. At the end of Book IV, after the lords and ladies of Urbino have descended from the speculative heights of love to which Bembo led them, they pull back the curtains and discover that a beautiful, rosy dawn has come and that the star of heavenly love shines benevolently over a paradisal landscape. They react to this wonderful discovery *con molta maraviglia* (IV, 73, 543). They are amazed that their conversations lasted through the night, for the pleasure they experienced in listening to Bembo was so great that they did not perceive the flight of the hours. They are equally amazed to see the star of love irradiating the countryside about them, as though the vision they all shared with Bembo has momentarily spread out to affect the entire world. Castiglione provides sufficient detail here to leave no doubt that their *maraviglia* is a profound response to a mysterious and paradoxical experience. While his courtiers and ladies remain caught in the process of history and the limited space of their room, they suddenly experience the surprising sensation that time has been obliterated and that their little room has momentarily merged with the great world about it. Historical time and finite space seem for a brief instant eternal and infinite, as the inhabitants of Urbino achieve an incongruous, unexpected, fleeting intimation of ultimate order and ultimate freedom in the midst of this life. No more truly marvelous ending could have been found for a book concerned with a profound and paradoxical ideal, a divinely human artist to whose transcendent performance wonder is the only fit applause.

2/ A Portrait of Urbino

While *Il Libro del Cortegiano* pursues the explicit end of describing an ideal courtier, it simultaneously aims at another: erecting an enduring memorial for Duke Guidobaldo, the court of Urbino, and the people who inhabited it. To reach this second goal, Castiglione deliberately chooses to portray his former masters and friends as they were historically, to present them replete with all their defining *proprietà e condicioni* (*Letter*, 1, 71). Playing the role of court historian, Castiglione thus, at the start of Books I and IV, catalogues the courtiers' occupations and achievements, the distinguished posts they held, and in several cases, the battles they waged heroically against adverse fortune and death. He also describes Urbino's beautiful palace, which was built by Duke Federico, and recounts the glories of both his former master, Duke Guidobaldo, and his present one, Duke Francesco Maria della Rovere. Moreover, by mentioning the more widely known historical figures of Julius II, Henry VIII, François I, Ferdinand, and Isabella, as well as historical battles and events, Castiglione imbeds his vision of Urbino firmly in the context of contemporary Renaissance history. Carrying even further this inclusion of historical material, he also carefully fixes the date of the discussions at Urbino by expressly relating them in his text to two actual historical events: his diplomatic journey to England in the fall and winter of 1506–1507 in order to receive the Order of the Garter for Duke Guidobaldo, and Pope Julius II's visit to Urbino after his successful subjugation of Bologna to papal authority in March 1507. At the start of Book I, Castiglione himself claims that he was in England when the discussions concerning the ideal courtier took place, and he slyly declares that he bases his account on the supposedly faithful recollections of a conveniently anonymous individual (I, 1, 81: "persona che fidelmente me gli narrò"). Later, in Book IV, Castiglione has his characters allude again to his putative absence in England (IV, 38, 496). In both cases, the claim is a fabrication, since Castiglione had in fact

53

returned to Urbino by February 1507, a month before his invented discussions took place; but his slight distortion of history allows him to avoid the indiscretion of participating in his own dialogue. Moreover, just as he builds the historical fact of his trip to England into the fictional frame of his work, so he draws the reader's attention to the historical visit of Julius II at two different places: he mentions it himself at the start of his book (I, 6, 88–89), using the visit to explain the large number of distinguished courtiers and the particularly festive mood at the court; and later, at the end of Book I, he has Francesco Maria della Rovere dramatically interrupt the conversations when he arrives late from having escorted the pope out of the city (I, 54–56, 181–85). By incorporating unimpeachable historical details into his *Cortegiano*, Castiglione provides a kind of historical authenticity for the elaborate fiction he has concocted.

He also gives his dialogues an authenticity of a different but related sort by giving them the appearance of being real discussions carried on by real people. He supplies his characters with carefully differentiated personalities, styles of speech, and points of view, and he shapes their discussions to imitate the relatively unregulated ebb and flow of spontaneous, though not undirected, conversation. There are digressions and interruptions, frustrated debates and exalted monologues, all suggesting the social intercourse real people could conceivably engage in. Occasionally, Castiglione also has his speakers refer most obliquely to events in one another's or their own lives, or to aspects of their physical appearance or personal mannerisms. Sometimes these oblique references, like the one to signor Morello's dyeing of his hair (II, 14, 212), are clarified by Castiglione's text, but others, like Bibbiena's joking allusion to his own baldness and his reference to a trick played on him, (II, 44, 259) are not; this reference is so obscure and personal that modern research has as yet been unable to explain it. The very obliqueness of these scattered and sometimes inexplicable allusions heightens the sense that Castiglione's characters are real, historical individuals, who, having spent a portion of their lives together, naturally allude cryptically to matters that remain impenetrable to outsiders. To be sure, such allusions could become an irritating puzzle to the reader, but Castiglione has the artistic tact to limit their number severely and thus preserve the advantage they entail. Thus, although he does not share later writers' concern for the complex interrelationship between the individual and his environment or conceive of reality as something contained in the minute events and petty details of daily life, Castiglione ultimately does create a work which in its elaborate, historical fiction anticipates the historical novel of many centuries later.

Yet at the same time that he strives to produce an illusion of historical reality, Castiglione leaves no doubt that his vision of Urbino is an ideal fiction. After explaining at the start of Book II (5, 195–96) how each of the participants in the preceding evening's discussions remembered a different version of what was said, Castiglione's own reliance for his account of the ideal courtier upon the supposedly accurate memory of an unidentified individual invites raised eyebrows at the very least, and it underscores the fact that *Il Cortegiano* is a fabrication by directly flouting the laws of probability Castiglione otherwise respects. Castiglione also stresses the fictive quality of his work by unabashedly idealizing his court and its inhabitants. Although his courtiers and ladies have minor character flaws and petty foibles, they are made to appear ideally civilized, perfectly restrained individuals, completely free from serious vices and defects. Although Castiglione may wish to commemorate them as real people, he also consciously wishes to present them as ideal types, as the "onorati esempi di virtù" (IV, 2, 448: "honored models of worthiness"[287]) he calls them in his prologues. Ultimately, Castiglione envisages the court as so far exceeding the limits of normal humanity that he cannot describe its perfection with his limited style, and he modestly asks his readers to use their own imaginations to reach an ideal beyond his eloquence (see III, 1, 336). In all these ways, Castiglione emphasizes the improbability of his fiction and declares that his *Cortegiano* is indeed a work of art.

The feeling that Castiglione is gilding Urbino's lily is confirmed by historical research on the people and events he includes in his book. While such research does not lead to his condemnation on the score of gross exaggeration and falsification, since all the evidence indicates that Urbino was an exceptionally civilized and humane court in an age when many were not, it does reveal that Castiglione did indeed write a most selective history. For instance, Francesco Maria della Rovere receives rather exalted praise:

> . . . in ogni suo movimento mostrava con la grandezza
> dell'animo una certa vivacità dello ingegno, vero prono-
> stico dello eccellente grado di virtù dove pervenir doveva.
> (I, 55, 183)

> . . . in his every movement showed a greatness of spirit
> together with a certain vivacity of temper that gave true

> presage of the high mark of virtue to which he would
> attain.

(84)

Castiglione omits mentioning that just a few months after the
discussions of his book supposedly took place, the seventeen-year-
old heir-apparent to Urbino's dukedom demonstrated his *virtù* by
treacherously stabbing to death his sister's unarmed lover while
Duke Guidobaldo was temporarily out of the palace.[1] Nor does
Castiglione note that Francesco Maria's *vivacità dello ingegno* would
manifest itself throughout his life in a violent brutality that would
lead him to murder Cardinal Alidosi in the streets of Ravenna,
knock the famous ambassador Guicciardini to the ground, and
order his servants to beat to death three Venetian sentries who
challenged his right to bear arms on Venetian soil.[2] Likewise,
Castiglione says nothing of the murders and bloody deeds performed by Febus da Ceva, his brother Ghirardino, and the Unico
Aretino.[3] Nowhere does he provide any hint that the courtiers
and ladies of Urbino fell short of their expressed ideal of perfect
chastity, even though some evidence points to the philandering
ways of Bembo and Bibbiena, and a bastard son born in 1511
offers indisputable proof of the liaison at the court between Giuliano de' Medici and Pacifica Brandono.[4] Castiglione also omits
other details from his history, harmless ones like the fact that both
Ludovico da Canossa and Cesare Gonzaga were his relatives, as
well as some whose inclusion might have adversely affected his
diplomatic activities. Thus he laments Ottaviano Fregoso's demise
at the hands of completely unspecified enemies, because to indict
imperial troops for their shoddy treatment of his friend would
hardly have served the political ends of Castiglione's master, the
pope, who had formed a close alliance with the empire.[5] In general, he clearly felt no need to present a complete picture of
Urbino's history, and he freely suppressed any detail that seemed
irrelevant, indiscreet, or threatened to impair the ideal quality he
wished to transmit in his image of the court and its people.

Because it simultaneously strives to present an illusion of historical reality and unabashedly idealizes that reality, *The Book of the
Courtier* has caused readers a recurrent problem and has divided
them into two opposing camps. Some take the work as a social
document, praising its accurate picture of court life in the Renaissance and its fidelity to the real people it commemorates. While
these readers may recognize the fictional quality of Castiglione's
work, they believe it still offers a valid mirror of its culture.[6] On

the other hand, a different set of critics focuses on the work's unrealistic, idealizing character, and either praises it for its unreal beauty, or condemns it for its distance from real life.[7] While those critics who treat Castiglione's book as a social document generally minimize the difference between its realistic and idealizing goals, the other group stresses their incompatibility. Thus Castiglione's modern readers seem to face an unresolved dilemma: how can his work be both real and ideal, both historically faithful to a particular society and yet the vision of a model civilization?

Such a problem vanishes, however, if Castiglione's "history" of Urbino is placed within the context of its Renaissance culture. His contemporaries assumed that when one wrote history, one created a work of art that was in some measure an ideal reconstruction of reality and not a literal transcription of it. Such a work had to satisfy the criterion of accuracy, but unlike nineteenth- and twentieth-century realists, Renaissance historians did not identify accuracy as the depiction of the minutiae of social life, the *petits faits vrais* of everyday experience, or the idiosyncratic physical and behavioral traits assumed to define the individual. Rather, following the lead of Plato, Aristotle, and other ancient thinkers, the Renaissance thought of the real as the typical, the essence of a thing, or its abstract nature, and did not identify it with those accidental properties to which later ages would give so much attention. Consequently, Renaissance historians would receive praise for accuracy even while they removed facts not consistent with the moral ends of their narratives or eliminated undignified or base persons, actions, and emotions judged incompatible with the dignity of history.[8] A contemporary, for instance, reproached the quattrocento humanist and historian Lorenzo Valla for his graphic realism on the grounds that he lessened the dignity of history by portraying a queen trembling and a king falling asleep during negotiations.[9] Normally historians, exactly like Castiglione, experienced no qualms of conscience when they put historically unsubstantiated speeches into the mouths of their characters or described them in terms so general as to make them into representative types, not particularized individuals.[10] History was written according to models provided by classical antiquity and particularly by the works of Roman historians like Livy and Sallust. It was distinguished by its style and by a set of conventions, including the stereotyped "character" of the military or political leader; set speeches delivered by historical figures, but elaborately concocted by the historian to emphasize the themes of his history; and the rather formulaic description of battle scenes.[11] This artistic, idealized reconstruction of reality in the service of edification was not thought to betray the real, but to reveal its essential character.

Although humanist historical theory and practice thus seem to offer a suitable context for Castiglione's half-realistic, half-idealized vision of Urbino, they do so only in the most general and approximate fashion. *The Courtier* does not employ the third-person narrative form of history, and its subject matter differentiates it completely from the productions of contemporaries who inevitably wrote of political and military matters.[12] Furthermore, Castiglione does not idealize his characters according to the formulas for describing the characters of political and military figures, and although the conversations through which his people reveal themselves have a rather formal air, they by no means resemble the set speeches and formal orations found in Renaissance histories. Since his book differs so profoundly in subject matter and reflects only faintly the principal conventions of the genre, it is singularly appropriate that Castiglione nowhere calls it a history or even hints that it should be interpreted as one. He does, however, provide a different, equally useful, interpretative guide to his vision of Urbino. In a passage at the very start of *The Courtier*, he explains that it is nothing less than a *portrait* of the court of Urbino. He thus puts on the smock of a Renaissance artist and invites Don Michel de Silva, to whom he dedicates the book, to approach it as he would approach a painting.

> E perché voi né della signora Duchessa né degli altri che son morti, fuor che del duca Iuliano e del Cardinale di Santa Maria in Portico, aveste noticia in vita loro, acciò che, per quanto io posso, l'abbiate dopo la morte, mandovi questo libro come un ritratto di pittura della corte d'Urbino, non di mano di Rafaello o Michel Angelo, ma di pittor ignobile e che solamente sappia tirare le linee principali, senza adornar la verità de vaghi colori o far parer per arte di prospettiva quello che non è.
>
> (*Letter*, 1, 71)

> And since, while they lived, you did not know the Duchess or the others who are dead (except Duke Giuliano and the Cardinal of Santa Maria in Pòrtico), in order to make you acquainted with them, in so far as I can, after their death, I send you this book as a portrait of the Court of Urbino, not by the hand of Raphael or Michelangelo, but by that of a lowly painter and one who only knows how to draw

58

the main lines, without adorning the truth with pretty colors or making, by perspective art, that which is not seem to be.

(3)

That Castiglione should conceive his work as a painting rather than a history testifies eloquently to his profound involvement with the art and artists of his own day.[13] Sent to Milan as a youth, he grew up at the court of Ludovico il Moro and was part of the most brilliant society of the later quattrocento. He was educated there for his courtly profession in a world where art and artists enjoyed extraordinary prestige and where he doubtless had the privilege of seeing masterpieces by Leonardo, Bramante, and a host of minor artists. Later, at Urbino, he found another court equally congenial to the arts, whose enlightened rulers had patronized outstanding fifteenth-century artists like Piero della Francesca and the Venetian architect, Laurana. During the last twenty years of his life, Castiglione was drawn increasingly to Rome, where he often lived and worked for long periods of time. He was thus exposed to the stunning achievements of the High Renaissance at the papal court. He frequently associated with Julius II and Leo X, who patronized the greatest artists of the High Renaissance—Raphael, Michelangelo, and Bramante—and who sought to create through art the image of grandeur, glory, and permanence that eluded them in the political and military spheres.[14] Moving in a society that treasured art and admired its creators, Castiglione developed an especially close friendship with Raphael. Raphael was born at Urbino, where Castiglione may have first encountered him, and spent his mature, most creative years in the enlightened circle of humanists, poets, and artists who had flocked to Rome in pursuit of papal patronage and who often counted Castiglione among their number. Castiglione's great grief over Raphael's early death in 1520 bears witness to the depth of their feelings for one another.[15] And Raphael's masterly portrait of Castiglione, which he painted for his friend's marriage to Ippolita Torelli in 1516, demonstrates both the extent of their relationship and the similarity of temperament and sensibility that must have allied them. From the perspective provided by this background, when Castiglione has Ludovico da Canossa prescribe a solid acquaintance with the visual arts for his ideal courtier (see I, 49, 172–73), he does not merely pay lip service to the educational goals of Renaissance culture, but expresses his own deeply held belief in the value of those arts.

Castiglione's decision to label his work figuratively a *ritratto di pittura* is, however, shaped by more than his love of painting or his sincere friendship with Raphael. In part, it can be considered an act of self-defense. Conceivably, a hypothetical Gasparo Pallavicino might object that to describe the court of Urbino in ideal terms and leave out its negative features is a deliberate act of deception, something unworthy an *omo da bene* like Castiglione. In response, the latter might well use the argument Federico Fregoso employs to defend the artifice of his ideal courtier: his book is a work of art, and deception is merely an uncharitable way of labeling the artistry necessary for its creation. Moreover, exactly like his courtier, Castiglione never tries to make his artifice pass as nature, never pretends his idealized image of Urbino is an image of reality. His playfulness about the fictional character of his "history" and his reluctance to supply a completely convincing illusion of reality function as a defense against just such attacks. Note that he never expressly claims that his vision of Urbino is either real or accurate; he never insists that it is literally faithful in every detail. But just to make sure the reader will not be misled, he explicitly compares his book to a painting, symbolically putting a picture frame around his portrait of Urbino which identifies it overtly and consciously as art, something which may epitomize and elucidate life, but should not be confused with it. Thus, at the very start of *Il Cortegiano,* he anticipates and silences the Gasparos by telling them to read it as they would view Renaissance portraits, and to judge its accuracy, its reality, and its truth by the standards used for art, not life.

There is also a more positive reason for Castiglione's decision to commemorate the courtiers and ladies of Urbino by painting their fictional "portraits." In defining the qualities that render his courtier ideal, Castiglione developed a particularly aesthetic view of the personality. The face one presented to others was a consciously shaped image, a visual representation created to suggest a personality possessing the traits admired by one's culture. Appropriately, Castiglione compared this artful creation of a personal image or mask to the painter's creation of a painting. Hence when he confronts the task of reproducing the characters of the courtiers and ladies at Urbino it should hardly be surprising that he solves his problem by conceiving them in the same terms, presenting them as so many carefully, aesthetically fabricated images, portraits of their best selves. As refractions of the ideal courtier, they all doubtless attempted to present themselves in just that way and must have been flattered by Castiglione's treatment of them in his book. And it is his artistry in presenting his friends, rather than their artistry in self-portrayal, that is the main concern of this chapter.

Behind Castiglione's presentation of the people in *Il Cortegiano* as a kind of group portrait lies a large body of theoretical material from the fifteenth- and sixteenth-centuries which identified painting and poetry as the sister arts, labeling as "poetry" everything that could be considered literature in the broadest sense of the term.[16] According to Renaissance theorists, both arts concerned themselves fundamentally with the imitation of human beings and actions of more than common status or significance; their imitations were thus representative and selective.[17] The analogy between painting and poetry was so deeply established that some thinkers even considered the two arts to share the same techniques and methods, although most recognized that writers could not really paint and that painting was but mute poetry.[18] Lacking an ancient tradition of theoretical works about painting, Renaissance writers like Alberti and Leonardo turned instead to the ancient rhetoricians, to Horace, and to Aristotle's *Poetics* in order to elaborate their ideas about painting. Since those ancient thinkers often saw poetry figuratively as a kind of painting, it was quite simple to reverse the equation and completely identify the two.[19] Terms appropriate to one field could be applied readily to the other, and while painters normally called their depictions of historical and monumental scenes *istorie,* historians sometimes received praise as "painters" for their fine descriptive passages.[20] Consequently, in the light of this conventional identification of painting and poetry, Castiglione's assumption of the painter's role by no means contradicts his playing the historian of Urbino, for the two roles could easily be identified with each other. Moreover, if his labeling his book a *ritratto di pittura* appears a less daring and extravagant, though no less functional, simile than it might otherwise have seemed, it compensates for its lack of novelty by indicating precisely that Renaissance aesthetic theory, more than Renaissance historiography, guided his hand as he wrote.

Exactly like its historiography, the aesthetic theory of the Renaissance proclaimed twin goals for the artist, which it felt were completely compatible: fidelity to the real appearances of things, and the simultaneous idealization of those appearances.[21] On one hand, writers argued that the painter should imitate nature and capture the appearance of the world about him, and they praised him for the verisimilitude of his productions.[22] On the other hand, no theorist or practitioner of the arts felt any interest in a literal fidelity to appearances, but believed that only by surpassing nature could he produce a truly beautiful work.[23] A Neoplatonist like Michelangelo might argue that one did so by imitating divine beauty, which the mind could apprehend directly and which nature revealed only imperfectly in its forms.[24] Most theorists, however, followed the lead of Aristotle and told the artist to form his idea of the beautiful by abstracting the essentials from beauties he saw around him and creating from them an ideal beauty.[25] Thus, for Alberti, while the painter began by studying the most beautiful bodies, in the act of painting he added a *bellezza* which was not found in nature and which depended entirely upon his art of composition.[26] In his famous letter to Castiglione, Raphael indicated his own allegiance to this method by reference to an exceptional situation.

> . . . per dipingere una bella, mi bisogneria veder più belle, con questa conditione, che V. S. si trovasse meco a far scelta del meglio. Ma essendo carestia e di buoni giudici, et di belle donne, io mi servo di certa Idea, che mi viene nella mente. Se questa ha in sè alcuna eccellenza d'arte, io non so; ben m'affatico di haverla.[27]

> . . . to paint a beauty, I would have to see many beautiful women, with the added condition, that your excellency would be with me to choose the best. But since there is a lack both of good judges and of beautiful women here, I make use of a certain Idea which comes into my mind. If this has any artistic excellence in it, I don't know; I'm certainly laboring to achieve it.

Castiglione himself even has the Neoplatonist Bembo define beauty in a way that conflates Platonic and Aristotelian doctrine, seeing ideal beauty as a divine influence that selects an already beautiful body in which to make itself manifest (IV, 52, 515), and he has Giancristoforo Romano praise sculpture and painting on the grounds that "l'una e l'altra sia una artificiosa imitazion di natura" (I, 50, 175: "one and the other are artful imitations of nature"[79]). For all these thinkers, the artist's mind refines the impressions of nature so that he may paint or sculpt an ideal beyond nature which nevertheless remains in conformity with it and expresses its laws.[28] Consequently, Castiglione only had to turn to the writings of such theorists to find a fully adequate justification for his half-realistic, half-idealizing mode of presentation in *Il Cortegiano,* and it is hardly surprising that he would have decided to label it a *ritratto di pittura.*

Although Castiglione may have refrained from calling his work an *istoria* in order to prevent readers from expecting a historical narrative, he could have found authority for applying the term to his book among contemporary artists who had a far broader conception of *istoria* than did the historians. For the artists, an *istoria* was a kind of painting that included not just the depiction of historical events, a limitation in subject matter that would only occur in the seventeenth-century French academies,[29] but mythological and allegorical tableaux, and, most broadly, any monumental scene containing a number of characters.[30] The major requirement for such painting indicated by Alberti was that it possess a *copia* of characters, a sufficiently large number to create a rich, dramatic or narrative scene, but not so many as to destroy the harmonious composition of the work.[31] Like all painting, *istoria* had to preserve the dignity of the art by eschewing base characters and unseemly gestures and expressions.[32] Alberti judged such historical painting very highly ("grandissima opera del pictore"), and Leonardo and the rest of the Renaissance shared his evaluation.[33]

Clearly, Castiglione's portrait of Urbino should be considered an *istoria.* Its subject matter is sufficiently broad and grand; its characters are presented in a supremely dignified manner; and it does include quite a *copia* of them, a characteristic of the book which has no precedent among its literary models and may be explained conveniently both as the result of Castiglione's desire to include as many of his friends as possible and as a matter of conforming to the rules of historical painting. Moreover, when Castiglione invokes the names of Raphael and Michelangelo, he provides yet another indication that his book is an *istoria.* Raphael's great fame in the Renaissance rested on the monumental scenes he painted in the frescoes of the Vatican, as well as on his portraits and Madonnas, and, except for the *Doni Tondo,* Michelangelo was strictly a painter of "historical" works, like the frescoes on the Sistine Chapel ceiling. By choosing the names of his two great contemporaries, whose finest achievements were *istorie,* Castiglione not only expresses his self-evaluation in terms all his readers would readily recognize, but he simultaneously indicates, albeit by implication, just what kind of painting his *Courtier* is.

When he invokes the hallowed names of Raphael and Michelangelo, whose exalted heights he modestly refuses to claim he has reached, Castiglione does something more important than indicate the generic affintiy of his work. He decisively places his *Corte-giano* at a particular moment in history, the triumph of High Renaissance art and culture, and he thus forcefully guides its interpretation. Several writers have already shown Castiglione's relationship to the art of his culture, and in particular have demonstrated that the behavioral style of his ideal courtier, defined by concepts like grace and *sprezzatura,* gravity and simplicity, is generally analogous to the style employed by High Renaissance artists and especially by Raphael.[34] But however valid such analogies may be, Castiglione's statement actually compares his *book* and its characters and setting, not his ideal courtier, to the works of the High Renaissance masters. He implies that it shares a common style with them and that he conceived the half-real, half-ideal portraits of his people and their court under the inspiration of contemporary painters or in direct rivalry with them. Thus, he effectively urges his readers to bring the same aesthetic presuppositions and modes of analysis to his *ritratto di pittura* that they would bring to the works of Raphael or Michelangelo; he authorizes them to seek the key to his methods of idealizing character and setting by studying a similar idealization in the sister art of contemporary, High Renaissance painting.

While Renaissance theorists from Alberti on argued that the painter should both imitate nature realistically and idealize it at the same time, it was not always possible to unite these goals in successful, satisfying works of art. During the late quattrocento, especially after 1460, painting moved in two opposite directions, one toward completely naturalistic representation that embraced the ugly and inharmonious as well as the beautiful, and one toward the creation of ideal forms, relatively independent of any concern for realism. This division in style paralleled one in the expression of spiritual meanings. In a realistic painting it became impossible to express a generalized, ideal, spiritual meaning; the particularization of form at best permitted a particularized spiritual effect. Thus, in the paintings of Domenico Ghirlandaio, Antonio Pollaiuolo, and Andrea Verrocchio, spirit could be considered merely a function of matter, and genuine idealization was impossible. It was possible for Botticelli to express a generalized, universal, spiritual state through his figures, but only at the expense of both the rational order of nature implicit in most realistic paintings' perspectival schemes, and of any claim to realistic representation of natural appearances. In Botticelli's Neoplatonic paintings, matter becomes merely a reflection of spirit. To create

Leonardo da Vinci. *Adoration of the Magi.*
Uffizi Gallery, Florence. Photo Alinari-Art Reference Bureau.

works both real and ideal which expressed generalized, universal, spiritual states while possessing rational order—this was the problem that confronted artists at the end of the fifteenth century, the problem that Leonardo, Raphael, and Michelangelo, each in his own particular way, solved, or rather solved again and again, in each new work of art as they created the great masterpieces of High Renaissance style.[35]

Each of these artists solved the general problem of painting an idealized reality by redefining the terms of his predecessors and conceiving anew the art of painting. In their different ways, they all rejected the quattrocento's implicit division between spirit and matter and modified its extreme notions of realism and spirituality. Essentially, they saw painting neither as the embodiment of an ideal realm beyond nature nor as mere imitation of nature, but as a rational reconstruction of it in ideal forms. While they observed

Michelangelo Buonarroti. *Pietà.*
Church of St. Peters, Rome. Photo Alinari-Art Reference Bureau.

nature with a precision their predecessors scarcely matched, they
rejected the practice of placing a number of highly particularized
beings in an additive way upon a perspective grid. To be sure,
such a procedure would provide a rational order for the painting,
but the result would be a perspectival scheme that appeared di-

Raphael Sanzio. *Madonna of the Goldfinch.*
Uffizi Gallery, Florence. Photo Alinari-Art Reference Bureau.

Raphael Sanzio. *Madonna of the Chair.*
Pitti Palace, Florence. Photo Alinari-Art Reference Bureau.

vorced from the ideal figures which would seem arbitrarily imposed upon it. Instead, as early as his *Adoration of the Magi* of 1481, Leonardo began structuring his figures into a tight nucleus of ideal, interrelated, geometrical forms which provided his paintings with a strongly centralized, rational organization. A little later, independent of Leonardo and more classical in inspiration, Michelangelo arrived at a similar solution, shaping the figures of his Vatican *Pietà* and the Bruges *Madonna* into compact, roughly pyramidal masses which had a fundamental simplicity, noble density, and highly idealized beauty of face, body, and gesture. Finally, in Florence during 1505 and 1506, the young Raphael came under the profound influence of the two older masters and assimilated their compositional principles in works like the *Madonna of the Goldfinch* and *La Belle Jardinière*. Like them, he organized his paintings around a central geometric core, although he gave his figures more grace and his compositions a somewhat simpler form than either Leonardo or Michelangelo.

68

The secret of the High Renaissance style, which painters like Sebastiano del Piombo, Fra Bartolommeo, and many lesser artists would eventually understand, was essentially to begin with a nucleus of interrelated, geometrical forms, and then to descend to particulars, rendering just enough detail to create the illusion of nature without sacrificing the rationality and clarity of the basic, ideal design. For instance, study of sketches made by Raphael and Leonardo when just beginning work on a devotional or historical painting shows that they first concerned themselves with organizational problems, which they would solve by the direct use of geometrical forms as the basic elements of design.[36] Then, as the next step in the process, they drew from studio models, over and over again, until they found the right set of postures and gestures to suit the formal design of the whole work and the type of emotion each individual figure was to express. Finally, they added more particularized details, such as beards, costumes, and other identifying characteristics, although these remain unparticularized, in keeping with the idealized structure and expressive content of the work.[37] The resultant figures almost necessarily possess a harmony between their ideal forms and the generalized, ideal spiritual state they express, if only because that ideal state is so largely determined by the disposition and construction of their forms. They thus come to fulfill perfectly the Albertian dictum that the external shapes, postures, gestures, and expressions of figures, which the painter studied through direct observation of nature, should serve as revelations of internal spiritual states. The High Renaissance solved the problem posed by developments in the late quattrocento by fundamentally reshaping both humanity and nature in ideal, generalized forms that simultaneously retained a totally plausible, natural appearance and could express a universalized, spiritual meaning.

Portraits, however, whether of individuals or of large groups posed together in *istorie,* presented a special problem to Raphael and the High Renaissance artists generally, a problem identical with the one facing Castiglione when he sought to immortalize the court of Urbino in his book. Because these works were to contain a faithful record of reality, they had to reflect that reality with some accuracy while at the same time satisfying their High Renaissance aesthetic and achieving ideality of form and meaning. When Raphael chose to paint the portrait of his friend Castiglione, for instance, he could not take the liberties he did in the *Madonna of the Chair,* where he could make the shape and position of the sitter's head and the general disposition of her body conform perfectly

Italian School (possible Vincenzo Catena). *Baldesar Castiglione.*
Widener Collection, National Gallery of Art, Washington, D.C. Photo National
Gallery of Art.

and somewhat arbitrarily to the circular shape of the tondo frame,
and where he could model the skin of mother and child to an
almost unnatural smoothness and softness. One could idealize
more freely when one's subject was ideal to start with, but in painting an actual individual or court the problem of idealizing could
not be solved simply by such radical reconstruction of reality.

Although Raphael's style throughout his life reveals a process of

Leonardo da Vinci. *Mona Lisa.*
Louvre Museum, Paris. Photo Alinari-Art Reference Bureau.

Raphael Sanzio. *School of Athens.*
Stanza della Segnatura, Vatican Museum, Rome. Photo Alinari-Art Reference Bureau.

continual evolution, of ever new and more complex solutions to the problem he faced as an artist, during the period 1514–16 he painted a number of portraits in which the realistic requirements of the genre are perfectly harmonized with the High Renaissance aesthetic goal of idealization. While works created after 1516, such as the magnificent group portrait, *Leo X with the Cardinals Giulio de' Medici and Luigi Rossi,* are intensely realistic and analytical, portraits from the period 1514–16 sacrifice a certain degree of analytical, realistic detail, without distorting the essential appearance of the subject, in order to reach a much higher level of ideal beauty. Among the most dazzling results of this synthesis of realism and idealism stands Raphael's own version of the ideal courtier, the masterly portrait of Castiglione that he painted in

1516 for his friend's wedding (completing it at about the same time that Castiglione was finishing his first version of *Il Cortegiano*). Comparing the features of this portrait with those of Castiglione's book offers striking proof of the shared aesthetic assumptions and techniques as well as the basic similarity of temperament that united these two masters of High Renaissance art.

On examining the portrait of Castiglione, it is immediately apparent that Raphael's solution to the problem of painting an idealized reality here certainly does not involve reshaping the features of his friend into totally arbitrary, ideal forms, which would significantly distort the appearance of reality. Rather, as S. J. Freedberg has observed, Raphael "clarifies the geometry he finds implicit in the form of whole head and of features of the sitter, and in a measure summarizes their appearance from the actuality."[38] Instead of imposing a form upon the details of reality, he recreates that reality around the ideal, geometrical shapes it approximates, a process which is not only a clarification, but a simplification as well. To understand the genius of Raphael's solution, compare his portrait with another one of Castiglione, possibly by Vincenzo Catena, which hangs in the National Gallery of Art in Washington, D.C. Raphael chooses a pose for his subject that allows him to organize his painting about basic geometrical forms.[39] The body of Catena's figure, turned completely in profile except for the head, possesses no distinctive geometrical shape, and the oval of the head is squashed down by the flattening effect of his cap. By contrast, the head of Raphael's figure appears to be a perfect oval, almost a circle, unlike Catena's more elongated form, and its roundness is accentuated by the wide upper edge of Castiglione's beard and the bit of shadow that falls across each temple. Raphael echoes the broad oval of the head in the oval form of Castiglione's hat, whose main axis runs perpendicular to that of his head, and in the roughly oval outline of the body, which would have been clearer if the bottom portion of the canvas had not been removed. Thus in Raphael's portraiture at this point in his career, the transformation of reality into an aesthetically ideal image primarily means choosing just the right pose to permit the simplification and clarification of underlying shapes into a few basic geometrical forms.

Secondly, Raphael's solution also involves the elimination of irregularities and angularities that could destroy or detract from the perception of the simple, underlying shapes. To enhance the clarification and simplification of his figure into ideal forms, Raphael models Castiglione's skin and the material of his clothing

73

with great delicacy and gives his silhouette a definite regularity
and smoothness. The silhouette of Catena's figure also contains
many long, smooth lines, but the irregular protrusions of the hat
create angular interruptions that counter any total effect of harmonious, easy movement. By contrast, in Raphael's portrait the
eye traces a flowing arc from Castiglione's left elbow around to his
collar, fills in the visual gap between collar and hat, and could
either descend from the right side of the hat to the edge of the
right shoulder or jump through two little curves before swinging
gently around the right side of the body in a broad arc, which
symmetrically balances the one it made on the left side. Yet, the
silhouette of Raphael's *Castiglione* appears far less regular when it
is compared with his *Madonna of the Chair,* or with its model, the
Mona Lisa, which Raphael may have seen for a second time in
Rome, just before starting the *Castiglione.* Leonardo, for instance,
eliminates the gap between head and shoulder on the right side of
his figure by means of its freely falling hair, and he surrounds
almost the entire form with a delicate veil, which creates a smooth,
harmonious outline. In the *Castiglione,* Raphael carefully places a
few irregularities, like the gap between collar and hat on the sitter's left, which balances the protruding material on its right side,
in order to avoid the effect of a pure, abstract, and potentially
cold ideality and to enhance the appearance of reality. While it
can be perceived basically as a unity of ideal geometrical forms,
the *Castiglione* has enough carefully calculated irregularities in
outline, in the folds of its garments, and in occasional ornaments,
like the pin in the hat, to insure the illusion of nature.

For the art of the High Renaissance, from the depictions of the
old men in Leonardo's *Adoration* through Michelangelo's athletes to
Raphael's philosophers and theologians in the Stanza della Segnatura, idealization also meant to some degree the identification of
the particular individual as a type. This identification was maintained even in portraiture, for it was the High Renaissance notion
of the best way to achieve a more universal, and hence ideal, meaning. Where a Ghirlandaio, or more strikingly, a Van Eyck in the
North, preserves every individualizing feature and surrounds his
sitters with people, objects, and details meant to affirm their particular identity, Raphael and other painters of the High Renaissance tend to eliminate such particularizing notes from their portraits. Consider, for instance, Raphael's double portrait of his
humanist friends, the scholarly poets Andrea Navagero and Agostino Beazzano (1516), where neither background nor detail of any
sort serves to particularize the subjects, and compare it to the entire

class of paintings representing scholars in their studies completed in the North during this period, of which the most famous is doubtless Holbein's portrait of Erasmus in the Louvre.[40] Less intrigued by the mysteries of nature than Leonardo, Raphael also invents imaginary, rather generalized, nonspecific landscapes for his figures, or places them in an imaginary architecture even when painting a specific historical scene like the *Mass of Bolsena*. For the *Castiglione*, as for many of his portraits, he eliminates background altogether, as well as all distinguishing marks and particularizing objects. With every trace of such idiosyncratic identification removed, only the figure's rich dress proclaims him the member of some more elevated social class. Thus Raphael's picture forces an interpretation in more general, less particularized and purely individual terms. It represents the ideal courtier as much as a specific courtier; Castiglione is both individual presence and representative, universal type.

For the artists of the High Renaissance, ideality not only meant simplification, the elimination of irregularities, and the transformation of individuals into types, but it also meant monumentality and grandeur. This concern is most readily apparent in the heroic giants Michelangelo sculpted in the early years of the sixteenth century and painted a little later on the ceiling of the Sistine Chapel, and it is equally evident in the magnificent, though slightly less immense, specimens of humanity populating Raphael's frescoes, his tapestry designs, and his thousands of sketches. Where quattrocento artists painted ordinary people and even found ugliness or deformity suitable for artistic representation,[41] the masters of the High Renaissance eschewed the common, the base, and the aesthetically unpleasing in order to create a heroic race of supremely dignified men and women whose superbly beautiful bodies and faces distinguished them from the more normal representatives of humanity. The heroic monumentality of these figures is not due, however, simply to muscular development, as was commonly the case in the works of many quattrocento artists like Donatello, Signorelli, and Pollaiuolo. As the transformation of the figure into pure geometrical shapes results from an artfully contrived pose and ornamentation, so the effect of monumentality is due to a number of artistic techniques. For instance, by increasing the relative size of his figures and generally expanding their proportions, Michelangelo turns men into heroes. Earlier in the quattrocento, Mantegna discovered the important secret of altering the perspectival system of his painting so that the viewer seems to look up at giant figures towering above him rather than at human beings on the same plane.[42] Sometimes a symbolic device, such as the table in Leonardo's *Cena*, could seve the purpose of creating a kind of monumentality by establishing a distance between the human viewer and the world depicted in the painting, thus magnifying the superior status of the beings in that world.[43] Raphael, however, like Michelangelo and even more like Leonardo, gave his figures monumentality and a kind of heroic dignity by making them massively solid, compact, and dense. He is normally thought of as the most graceful of painters, and there can be no doubt that his figures show tremendous elegance, delicacy, and ease; but if they are compared with the figures of Botticelli, which were equally renowned for gracefulness, their greater solidity and massiveness become immediately apparent. Their grace has a weightiness, dignity, and slow-moving quality quite alien to that of Botticelli's slender, elegant dream-figures.

To understand just how monumental Raphael's people are, look again at Vicenzo Catena's *Castiglione:* how narrow and insubstantial the chest appears as it is viewed in profile, how delicate, but how slender and inconsequential, the head, topped with a flat, little saucer of a hat! By contrast, look at the great breadth of Raphael's *Castiglione*. In part by virtue of the pose he adapted from the *Mona Lisa*, Raphael gives his subject a seemingly solid, massive body of quite large proportions. Its pose emphasizes Castiglione's broad shoulders and solid chest, both of which are increased even further by the thick folds of material enveloping them, swelling the body out to fill and dominate the picture space. The amplitude of the body is echoed in the head, whose full beard projects roundly to either side of the face and emphasizes its width, whereas the constricted beard on Catena's figure underscores the thinness and slenderness of the face as it tapers down to a point below the chin. Raphael also increases the illusion of breadth in Castiglione's head by means of the hat, whose lower edge provides a strong horizontal movement cutting across the oval of the face, giving it depth and roundness and emphasizing its horizontal axis. Moreover, the ovals of hat and head, whose main axes are perpendicular to one another, interlock in a dense sphere that gives a three-dimensional depth and solidity to the forehead and skull. While Catena's figure has little depth and modeling, Raphael's possesses tremendous density, almost as though it were sculpted.[44] In spatial organization, Raphael's *Castiglione* has roughly the shape of an equilateral pyramid with rounded sides and points. Its front edge is marked by the left arm and sleeve, which push up against the surface of the picture in what is the most notable change Raphael makes in the more open pose he adapted from Leonardo. The right arm recedes back with great foreshortening to reach the far corner of the pyramid, and the head stands solidly at its apex. Not only does the compactness of the implied pyramid augment the effect of massiveness, but, because within its imaginary outlines the figure expands to fill it fully and solidly, its density appears all the greater. The result of this disposition of forms into dense, massive, compact structures is to convey the impression of monumental grandeur in the figure, giving it a substantial dignity and even a feeling of permanence. The goal of both High Renaissance culture and art, the transformation of an imperfect, fleeting, un-ideal life into something grand, stable, and enduring, Raphael accomplishes perfectly in this work. The ideal High Renaissance painter, he portrays being, not becoming.[45]

The effect of massive permanence that Raphael's spatial organization produces would threaten to turn Castiglione completely into a statue were it not for the basically dynamic character of Raphael's design. His figure's solidity of structure is animated by a vital impulse expressed in the slight clockwise rotation of its forms. This movement is particularly enhanced by the scarcely perceptible tilting of the head toward the front and left, which becomes more noticeable when it is compared with the more erect, more upright head of the *Mona Lisa*. Just as the inclusion of certain small irregularities gave a degree of particularity and hence of life to Castiglione's basic, geometrical shapes, so that sense of life is also assured by the dynamism of its design. That dynamism is, to be sure, both extremely moderate and subtle, testimony to a High Renaissance distaste for extremism of any kind, and it is also perfectly harmonious with and contained by the basic geometrical forms whose solidity and seeming permanence remain essentially unimpaired. However strong the dynamic, dramatic impulse becomes in the course of Raphael's career, the ultimate balance, the controlling order, in his painting always remains intact. To the very end, there is always a careful weighing of mass against mass, gesture against gesture, to achieve a final harmony less the result of simple symmetries than of what S. J. Freedberg has called the balance of "differentiated and responsive counterparts."[46]

While Raphael's compositional techniques serve to create an ideal type who also seems a convincingly alive and natural individual, thus satisfying the cultural and aesthetic goals of the High Renaissance, they also insure that the qualities projected by the

77

disposition of the subject's physical forms are identical with, and reveal, the psychological qualities inherent in his character, thus satisfying Alberti's requirement that the shape, gestures, and expressions of the sitter's face and body should declare his mind and spirit.[47] In Raphael's *Castiglione,* compositional techniques achieve magnificently expressive ends. The impression of monumentality created by the compactness and density of the subject's body joins with the rich, but subdued, colors of his costume to substantiate the sense of reserved dignity that characterizes him as a perfect courtier. These qualities are also conveyed through his look and bearing and are further emphasized by the slight forward tilting of the head in what seems a reserved nod of recognition directed at his unknown viewers. The solidity and permanence characterizing the forms of Castiglione's body also harmonize with the sense of composure, the sureness and self-control, and the ease that one perceives in his fixed glance and the carefully composed clasping of his hands. The clarity of Raphael's forms seems to offer a physical counterpart, a symbol, for the clarity and intelligence that shine forth so apparently in Castiglione's face.

Raphael uses more than composition, the disposition and organization of solid masses in space, to achieve his expressive ends. He underscores the clear intelligence of his ideal courtier by his use of light, which clarifies the forms of the body and gleams as a reflection in Castiglione's eyes.[48] Light gives them the appearance of alertness and vivacity which the slight motion of the head also implies, and makes Castiglione, like his own ideal courtier, a figure not only fully composed, but vitally alert. Bright light suffuses the atmosphere surrounding the figure, almost as though the clarity and radiance of the mind projected itself symbolically outward, transforming the world around it in its own image. The lighted atmosphere also functions to emphasize the massive, sculptural quality of Castiglione's body, which seems thrown forward into high relief by the effect of the light around and behind it. Raphael restricts the background of his portrait to this lighted atmosphere, but, nevertheless, the principle determining his use of backgrounds in all his paintings is evident here. Background, like color, composition, and gesture, serves fundamentally expressive ends and is always made consistent with the personalities and structures it encloses. In a sense, Raphael's backgrounds might be considered functions of character—expressions of their essential geometries, symbolic projections of certain traits observable in them, or at least settings consistent in mood with the dominant feelings expressed by the characters. For instance, just as light underscores Castiglione's intelligence and vivacity in this painting, the monumental, regular, yet humanely proportioned architecture of Raphael's *School of Athens* reflects basic qualities in the characters it surrounds and actually seems to derive its proportions from them. The result of all these expressive techniques is a tremendous unity of effect in each of Raphael's works, whereby every detail and aspect of a painting is subordinated to its central concern and underscores its basic theme, while at the same time contributing its own mite of particularizing difference to further the illusion of reality. Unity in multiplicity, a simplified order underlying a host of particularized details, and a sense of monumental permanence qualified by the vital energy of organic movement—these features define Raphael's style, which stands as the most characteristic expression of High Renaissance culture.

Like Raphael's paintings, Castiglione's *Cortegiano* also stands as one of the supreme monuments defining that culture; and his idealization of character and setting reflects, as faithfully as a literary medium will allow, the aesthetic principles and artistic practices of his contemporaries. To create ideal characters, Castiglione, like Raphael, clarifies the essential shapes of real people by simplifying their characterizations to a few essential traits. Then, once the fundamental "geometry" of each person has been made apparent, in order to preserve the illusion of life and nature he adds a limited number of particularizing details which suggest human vitality and historical reality without destroying the simplified, ideal characterization of each person. Castiglione also gives his characters a larger-than-life monumentality by suggesting that they are heroes, while at the same time he has them demonstrate a more approachable humanity in their occasional displays of pettiness, irritation, pompousness, and vanity. To complement these idealized, yet real, characters, he encloses them in an idealized, carefully fabricated vision of Urbino which, like the settings of Raphael's paintings, reflects its characters' chief traits, underscores the themes of the work, and thus allows the artist to achieve a total unity of effect. Because of the difference in their media, analogies between Castiglione and Raphael are sometimes precise and sometimes only general, but in either case they are an unmistakable, eloquent demonstration that the two men shared the aesthetic assumptions and goals of their culture.

The fundamental procedure Castiglione employs to idealize his courtiers and ladies is to simplify and clarify their characters by centering each upon a few essential, easily recognizable traits. This procedure involves giving them all a relatively uniform characterization and set of behavioral responses, making all of them act with ideal grace and decorum as they strive to approximate in themselves the behavior of their ideal courtier and his *donna di palazzo*. Even Gasparo Pallavicino, whose virulent antifeminism might seem to disqualify him from consideration as an ideal courtier, nevertheless dances with the ladies as a good courtier should and is included along with all the others Castiglione praises as noble knights and gentlemen (see I, 5, 87–88 and IV, 1–2, 445–47). Just as Raphael painted his *Castiglione* both to do honor to the individual and to celebrate an ideal type, a representative of nobility and courtliness, so Castiglione depicted characters who are at the same time historical realities differentiated by their personal attributes and ideal types serving to illustrate just how ideal courtiers and ladies behaved. Perhaps a better analogy for Castiglione's procedure might be found in some of Raphael's or Leonardo's paintings of groups whose members share common characteristics, functions, or roles and who were therefore depicted as subtle variants of the same ideal personality type. For instance, all of Leonardo's old men in the unfinished painting, the *Adoration,* possess a common dignity of demeanor and amplitude of body, even though each has his own individualizing features as well.[49] A similar, shared dignity, reserve, and intensity can be seen in the church fathers of Raphael's *Disputa,* who are united as a class of individuals with a common character and who are also subtly differentiated from one another without losing their sense of being members of a class. In essence, when High Renaissance artists and writers had to present a group of individuals who possessed similar characters, functions, or social roles, they took pains to render similar the appearances of all the members of the group, creating a series of individual variations on a single type and thus achieving both an ideal simplicity and a tremendous concentration of artistic effect.

The second procedure Castiglione employs to simplify and hence idealize his characters is to restrict each to having just one or two prominent personality traits which serve to differentiate them from one another. Although in every case he begins with the real and necessarily quite complex personalities of the individuals involved, he always chooses traits that he can present simply and that his readers will readily comprehend. More importantly, he selects just those traits that will allow his characters to be perceived as representative types. Just as Raphael painted the type of the ideal courtier in his portrait of *Castiglione* and created a series of variants on the ideal philosopher in his *School of Athens,* so Castiglione varies his ideal courtiers and ladies by finding simple, stereotypical traits with which to differentiate them and then building their characters around those central traits. Thus while he makes all his people into representative courtiers and *donne di palazzo,* he nevertheless also types Gasparo, Ottaviano, and Niccolò Frisio as misogynists, Bembo as an other-worldly, day-dreaming, impractical philosopher, Bibbiena as a sort of stand-up comedian, Morello da Ortona as a crotchety old soldier, and the duchess as an aloof and revered figure modeled on the "divine" women worshipped by poets in the courtly love tradition. To some extent, Castiglione, like his various spokesmen in his dialogues, thinks of people less as complex personalities composed of a myriad of highly particularized experiences, attitudes, mannerisms, and modes of expression than as collections of overlapping stereotypes. Appropriately, all the participants in *Il Cortegiano* appear to think in this same way. They conceive men and women as having their own appropriately different sexual characteristics, for instance. Castiglione implements stereotyped conceptions by having his courtiers behave with typically "male" forcefulness and virile aggression, while the ladies display a complementary, "female" gentleness, restraint, and delicacy. Similarly, just as he has Federico ascribe energy and impetuousness to youth and characterize old age as possessing the defect of a kind of grumbling incivility (see II, 15, 212), he makes the extremely youthful Gasparo his most impetuous character and has the ancient signor Morello grumble on more than one occasion. To differentiate his people from one another without creating extremely complex characters, Castiglione uses simple, easily comprehended stereotypes which in themselves possess the generality and universality his High Renaissance culture praised as ideal.

With some care, Castiglione organizes his dialogues so that the simple, stereotypical traits characterizing each individual are evident in his first appearance. Thus, Gasparo's initial statements contain an attack on women (I, 6–7, 90); Bembo's show his earnest idealism about love (I, 11, 98–99); and the misogynistic Ottaviano's mock the conventions of courtly love that Bembo takes so very seriously (I, 10, 96–97). Castiglione then proceeds to emphasize these traits repeatedly in each character throughout the four evenings of discussion, thus insuring that the central, core "geometries" of his different courtly ideals will be consistent, unambiguous, and always clearly perceptible. The best example of this consistent underscoring of a character's defining trait is the presentation of Gasparo Pallavicino's misogynism, which is presented on every single evening and is especially prominent because it occasions both the first and last verbal exchanges in Castiglione's book. Gasparo, however, is not the only character presented as a type with such consistency. From first to last, Bibbiena performs as a kind of stand-up comedian, constantly telling jokes, laughing, and making witty sallies, living up perfectly to his definition of man as the laughing animal (II, 45, 260). Even a more minor character like Morello da Ortana is always characterized as the crusty, skeptical, blunt old soldier he apparently was in real life.[50]

In a few cases, the particular stereotypical traits by which Castiglione distiguishes his characters achieve great dramatic impact because they involve individual styles of speech or behavior or striking personal mannerisms.[51] Gasparo, for instance, stands out by virtue of his virulent antifeminism and the tremendous energy with which he constantly questions and challenges all the other speakers. Filled with youthful volatility, he is truly the spirit of eternal contradiction. Similarly, the comic Bibbiena distinguishes himself by his witty speech, and the unworldly, philosophical lover Bembo always wears his heart on his sleeve, mourning the unhappiness of love, complaining about the deception of his beloved friends, and ultimately getting lost in the self-induced ecstasy of his Neoplatonic oration in Book IV. Castiglione even gives the Unico Aretino, a quite minor figure, a distinctive, hyperbolic style which exaggerates his trite, conventionally Petrarchan sentiments. His petulant statements are marked by constant self-dramatization as he strives to monopolize the attention of the group. Though he only plays a bit part, he emerges as one of Castiglione's finest, most memorable, comic creations, a caricature of the pampered court poet whose self-proclaimed sensitivity and suffering make him amusing and ridiculous. Finally, the witty, mischievous Emilia Pia stands out as a distinct personality, constantly taunting her adversaries, teasing the various speakers, and maintaining a careful control over the discussions. In these five instances, Castiglione has truly achieved the goal of immortalizing the court of Urbino by creating memorable images of his friends.

While a striking verbal style or peculiar set of mannerisms sets a few characters apart, the language and behavior of the others remain more or less uniform. In keeping with his belief in a universal courtly language, with the largely intellectual interest of his book, and with High Renaissance aesthetics which did not encourage exaggerated, vivid characterization, Castiglione distinguishes most of his characters more through the opinions they maintain in opposition to one another than through particular styles of speech and radical personality differences. The debate about women in Book III, the contrast between Ottaviano's version of the ideal courtier in Book IV and the earlier ones of Ludovico da Canossa and Federico Fregoso, the conflict over language during the first evening, and the argument about painting and sculpture at the end of Book I— all these confrontations and the issues they raise remain far more memorable than most of the personalities who discuss them and who are mainly identifiable in terms of the positions they take. Castiglione's first two principal speakers, Ludovico da Canossa and Federico Fregoso, are particularly pale characters, perhaps intentionally so in order to allow the reader an unobstructed view of the ideal courtier the two speakers create together. At best, the two emerge as ideal courtiers themselves, showing the social skills in their own behavior that they require of their ideal. As he revised *The Courtier* repeatedly during the two decades preceding its publication in 1528, Castiglione changed not only speeches, but speakers as well, as though to some extent he really did consider some of his characters so similar that he could easily change them about at will.[52] All of them distinguish themselves as ideal courtiers and ladies, but few of them have really distinct personalities, a failing that seems to bother Castiglione only in connection with his beloved duchess, whose virtues he confesses "non avere, non che espresso, ma né anco accennato" (*Letter*, 1, 71: "not even suggested, let alone expressed"[3]).

Just as Raphael eliminates most particularizing details from his *Castiglione* and lets the figure's simple elegance, refined luxury, and dignified self-possession establish his identity as an ideal courtier and nobleman, so Castiglione eliminates most biographical details about his characters that would lessen the sense that they are representative types, idealized variants on the image of the ideal courtier. While it is understandable that he avoids mentioning unsavory episodes in the lives of people he praises, only his High Renaissance interest in creating universal, nonparticularized characters could explain the absolute paucity of details in Castiglione's work. Except for the short sketches of the duke and the duchess, most of his courtiers and ladies receive little more in the way of biographical description than a brief phrase or two in the catalogue at the start of Book IV. The reader knows them simply as *nobilissimi cavalieri* (I, 5, 88) and learns almost nothing about their physical appearances, personal histories, family backgrounds, or military and political activities. What he does learn about them is limited to the various opinions they maintain and to the few stereotyped personality traits they manifest. In fact, whenever Casti-

glione does include elements that seem to pertain to his characters' personal lives and histories, he studiously avoids anything
too idiosyncratic, intimate, or requiring elaborate explanation. He
always chooses details related to a character's age, occupation, or
city of origin, details which allow for convenient stereotyping.
Moreover, he makes his characters perform true to the types involved, even if in reality they might not have done so. Take the
case of the Venetian, Pietro Bembo. Identified explicitly as a son
of Venice in the second book of *Il Cortegiano* (52, 271), he is later
made to behave true to type by arguing for the superiority of the
republican form of government, the kind that his native city possessed (IV, 20, 471). Castiglione has his fictional Bembo act like a
"typical" Venetian, even though the real Bembo apparently pre-
ferred the courts of princes and popes in which he managed to
spend most of his adult life and which he celebrated in his early
dialogue, *Gli Asolani*.[53] The simplicity and easy clarity of Bembo's
ideal characterization depend in part upon such stereotyping;
they would be lost if Castiglione allowed his friend to voice his
true opinion in all its complexity, just as a similar simplicity and
clarity would be diminished had the sculptor Giancristoforo Romano said he thought painting superior to his own art, or Giuliano de' Medici argued against establishing his Tuscan idiom as
the standard language for all Italians. Thus, although Castiglione
retains some indication of his characters' historical identities, he
chooses details that allow him to present them as representative
types and that enhance their depiction as ideals.

While Castiglione parallels Raphael's techniques in idealizing
real people, he also follows his friend's artistic practice in making
sure that his ideal figures possess the illusory appearance of life.
He is not content to present Urbino's inhabitants as a collection of
simple stereotypes, just as Raphael would never think to leave his
subjects depicted as the ovals and pyramids he used in his early
conceptions. Consequently, while both artists carefully establish
the particular central geometries of their ideal figures, they also
supply a limited number of carefully chosen, apparently accidental features and natural details, which produce the impression of
complexity, solidity, and movement characteristic of living beings.
Where Raphael turns to color, light, and modeling and introduces
certain irregularities which give the semblance of life to his perfect forms, Castiglione uses other techniques more appropriate to
his medium. Generally, although he is content to give minor
figures like Francesco Maria della Rovere and Giancristoforo Romano only summary treatment and to have them say next to

nothing during the four nights of discussion, he develops his major speakers much more substantially. First, he builds complexity into their characters by allowing them to speak repeatedly and on a wide variety of subjects. Thus, in spite of Gasparo's consistent presentation as a misogynist and the spirit of contradiction, Castiglione allows him to speak on a broad range of topics and thus suggests a more multifaceted personality and a wider set of interests than might otherwise be apparent. Likewise, the earnest, intellectual Bembo speaks of love, philosophy, learning, and politics, as well as showing himself capable of joking and of engaging fully in the playful banter of every sort of conversation. Even the less memorable Federico Fregoso enters into the debate on language in Book I and expounds a vision of the ideal courtier in Book II, incidentally contradicting his deference to custom and social realities in the second book with his unrealistic preference for speaking archaic Tuscan in the first. By having his characters speak often and on many different subjects, Castiglione is able to suggest something of the complexity and multifaceted quality of real people without having to provide extensive documentation that might destroy the simple clarity of his ideal characterizations.

The second technique Castiglione uses to give a greater semblance of life and nature to his ideal figures is to place similar types together and then to create between them a few subtle, delicate differences, largely matters of tone and nuance. Thus, although Gasparo, Ottaviano, and Niccolò Frisio may all be typed as misogynists when they debate their opponents in Book III, Castiglione takes care to give different emphases to their characters, thereby suggesting slightly different personalities to qualify the basic misogynism each one represents. The mainstay of the debate, Gasparo, speaks with great heat and passion, exploding in a magnificent, though somewhat perverse and morbid, diatribe against women at the climax of the third book. Niccolò Frisio, on the other hand, restricts himself to a few brief shots expressing his uncomplicated, old-fashioned, and simplistic misogynism. Finally, Ottaviano, whose conviction matches Gasparo's, maintains a cool detachment, tactful moderation, and sure sense of the superiority of his position, qualities which suggest the statesman he was in real life and harmonize with the serious vision of the ideal courtier he unfolds in Book IV. Similarly, on the other side of the debate, the two "knights" defending the ladies are subtly differentiated: the enthusiastic Cesare Gonzaga, who literally worships women and considers them the creators of civilization, is paired with the more intellectual, less extravagant Magnifico, who likes to debate about "form" and "matter" and other philosophical notions. Through these fairly small contrasts in character, Castiglione can suggest that his people have significantly different personalities without sacrificing his goal of presenting them as simple variants on the same ideal type.

While Castiglione may satisfy his High Renaissance aesthetic by simplifying and typing his characters without totally depriving them of some suggestion of the complexity and variety of life, in his idealization he is also just as concerned as Michelangelo or Raphael with giving them something of the monumentality of heroes. By virtue of their great self-control, their tact, and their sure command of social processes, he sets his characters apart from and above more ordinary mortals. In their civilized leisure, however, they have no way to display the massiveness, density, and vitality that Michelangelo's and Raphael's figures possess even in repose. Nevertheless, while most of Castiglione's characters do not have the opportunity to behave like heroes, he does suggest that they have the potential to do so, both by thematically linking their self-possession in social situations to the self-possession of the hero, and by specifically celebrating the stoic heroism a few of his people did display in the face of suffering and death. Instead of simply noting the demise of various characters, Castiglione focuses on the heroic, moral struggle they waged against their misfortunes in order to preserve life and dignity. Thus, at the start of his book, he eulogizes the heroic Ottaviano, whose endurance and self-possession even his enemies praised and who is presented as an example of human will triumphing over contrary events, of *virtù* preserving man's dignity in spite of the blows of *fortuna* (*Letter*, 1, 70). The misogynistic Gasparo is also eulogized in similarly heroic terms for his struggle against death and disease (IV, 1, 445), and Cesare Gonzaga adulates the embarrassed duchess for her heroic resolution in enduring great hardship (III, 49, 407). The greatest hero Castiglione celebrates is, however, the one who is conspicuous by his absence from the discussions—Duke Guidobaldo. He is praised as a perfect example of patience and fortitude, a man who bore disease and a particularly malignant fortune

> con tanto vigor d'animo . . ., che mai la virtù dalla fortuna non fu superata; anzi, sprezzando con l'animo valoroso le procelle di quella, e nella infirmità come sano e nelle avversità come fortunatissimo, vivea con somma dignità ed estimazione appresso ognuno. . . .
>
> (I, 3, 83–84)

with such strength of spirit that his virtue was never overcome by Fortune; nay, despising her storms with stanch
heart, he lived in sickness as if in health, and in adversity
as if most fortunate, with the greatest dignity and esteemed of all. . . .

(14)

While the duke's achievement may be conceded to exceed most
men's, and it is true that only a few of Castiglione's friends have
the dubious distinction of living and dying amidst heroic struggles, he allows the reader to infer from the supremely disciplined
social behavior all of them display that such stoic heroism lies fully
within their power.

All Castiglione's art of character portrayal ultimately serves a
single purpose: to make his image of life as it could conceivably
have been lived at the historical Urbino into an image of ideal
civilization defined by social refinement and heroic monumentality. To make Urbino a viable image of an entire civilization, however, he also has to give it a sense of human variety and amplitude. He accomplishes this partially by presenting his characters
as a collection of quite different personality types, significant variants on the single image of the ideal courtier. Thus, he implies
something of the full range of human types to be found in any
civilization. Moreover, he makes his little court into an image of
an entire civilization in a somewhat different way as well; he fills it
with courtiers representing almost every city and region in the
peninsula, effectively suggesting what he doubtless believed, that
Urbino epitomizes, sums up, the entire culture of Renaissance
Italy.[54] Thus from the north he brings the Mantuan Cesare Gonzaga, the Veronese Ludovico da Canossa, and the brothers Febus
and Ghirardino da Ceva of the Piedmont region. Roberto da Bari
travels to Urbino from the southern Italian city after which he is
named, and Morello da Ortona comes from the Abruzzi. The
western shore sends the exiled Fregoso brothers from Genoa, and
the Adriatic, the Venetian Bembo. Florence offers her sons Giuliano de' Medici and Bernardo Bibbiena, while Rome is repre-
sented by Giancristoforo Romano. As his courtiers flock to Urbino
from every region of Italy, Castiglione creates a tremendous impression of human diversity in his little court and renders it, in
spite of its diminutive size, an effective image of ideal Italian
civilization.

Just as all his characters show the principles of civilization operating in their behavior, Castiglione's setting for them likewise re-

inforces his vision of ideal civilization. In this respect also he reveals another affinity with Raphael as he strives to relate his background to the beings it enfolds and to create a total unity of effect
in his work by reinforcing its central theme and mood on several
levels at once. Thus when he describes Urbino's palace and its
surrounding area, he consistently omits particularizing details that
could divert attention from his characters or the themes they em-
body. He never points out, for instance, the features of the landscape, describes the physical appearance of the palace, or explains
where the duchess's chambers were located or what they looked
like. Instead, employing simplified, almost schematic terms, he
presents the palace as an example of civilization using its art to
overcome a wild and unruly nature. He emphasizes that the palace was located on a particularly rugged site, but managed to
triumph over this natural disadvantage, just as his ideal courtiers
use their civilized art to shape their own unruly natures (see I, 2,
82). Castiglione's description underscores the *art* of Urbino's
beautiful palace, which is further stressed in his praise for its fine
adornments and the many treasures it contained. Moreover, Castiglione's description emphasizes both the amplitude and variety
of the civilization it contains as well as the heroic stature of its
people. He praises it for being "non un palazzo, ma una città in
forma de palazzo" (I, 2, 82: "not a palace but a city in the form of
a palace"[13]), and as he contemplates it in his prologues, it
fittingly metamorphoses into the gigantic Trojan horse, its belly
full of heroes (IV, 2, 446).

In his brief description of Urbino, Castiglione also declares,
rather curiously, that it is located at the center of Italy on the
Adriatic side ("quasi al mezzo della Italia verso il mare Adriatico"
[1, 2, 81]). This statement seems at best approximate, but in emphasizing that Urbino stands at the center of Italy, Castiglione
may be less concerned with geographical niceties than with putting his ideal civilization at an appropriate symbolic location. His
deformation of geography serves his artistic purposes, as he
makes Urbino the symbolic center, the very heart of Italian Renaissance culture, to which all the courts and cities in every part of
the peninsula have appropriately enough sent their representatives. Just as the ideal Italian language Castiglione defends is an
epitome of the best language spoken everywhere in Italy, so his
little court, where that language has its home, appears the epitome of all the other courts in the peninsula. Symbolically their
center, it draws to itself all the best they have to offer and appears
the ideal civilization of which they are all merely partial images.

Thanks to Castiglione's simplified, universalized treatment of character and setting, Urbino appears more than merely an *example* of civilization. It is civilization itself, the abstract and universal idea of civilization which Castiglione has distilled from all the courts and courtiers of his experience. Urbino is a model, a paradigm, presented with just enough detail to give its ideal character the illusory appearance of historical reality, and with just enough of the give and take of conversation to supply its activity with the illusory movement of life. The fickle goddess Fortune must have smiled on Castiglione, indeed, in granting him so fine a court that he could transform it into an image of ideal civilization with little significant distortion of reality. And she blessed him even more when she gave that court a name wonderfully appropriate to the character with which Castiglione's art has endowed it.

In a reversal of the old maxim, history here is the handmaiden of art, for Castiglione could not have invented a better, more functional name for his ideal civilization or one more expressive of what he and all the other courtiers and ladies felt about it. *Urbino,* the Italian form of the Latin *Urbinum,* is directly related etymologically to *urbs,* "the city," and its ending would have been perceived by Renaissance Italians as a diminutive, thus making the name a generic diminutive that could be translated as "the little city."[55] The abstract and general character of the name corresponds perfectly to the universal nature of its ideal character; a place that epitomizes civilization could not receive a better label than "the little city." What is more, the Latin *urbs* also had a special, quite suggestive meaning when considered within the context of Castiglione's book and his Renaissance culture. Used without a modifying adjective, *urbs* could also mean "*the* city," Rome itself, the center and epitome of ancient civilization. Thus, for Castiglione and his culture, because of their profound involvement with the classical past, *Urbino,* "the little city," could not fail to suggest another translation making it the new, but "lesser Rome." Such a translation would harmonize perfectly with its symbolic placement at the center of Italy and its presentation as the epitome of contemporary civilization. Its diminutive ending, which affirms its status as the "lesser Rome," also fits the modesty of a writer and a culture which would think it possible to approach, but hardly equal, the achievements of their Roman ancestors, who lived at a time when "gli omini erano di molto maggior valore, che ora" (I, 52, 179: "men were of greater worth than now"[82]). Finally, the diminutive ending also underscores the relatively small size of the city: Urbino was a David among Goliaths, conquering its enemies always against great odds and measuring its grandeur by the excellence, not the number, of its citizens.[56] Thus, the name of Urbino sums up in itself many of the most important qualities defining the ideal civilization Castiglione chose to immortalize in his book.

3/ The Nostalgic Courtier

Throughout the prologues to his four books and the dedicatory letter which prefaces the entire work, Castiglione speaks to his readers *in propria persona,* creating a distinct image of himself as a complex, emotional character who is by far the most real and moving personality in *The Courtier.* Speaking directly to the reader in his own person did not mean for him, or for any other Renaissance author, either indulgence in maudlin confession or romantic self-dramatization. Whether he wrote a treatise or a novel, a satire or an epic, the Renaissance writer obeyed the rules of decorum. Consciously or unconsciously, he adopted an authorial persona, a mask (*persona* in Latin), appropriate both to the genre and the subject matter of his work.[1] When creating this persona, he was not required to exclude totally all details from his personal life; rather, he made a careful selection of feelings, opinions, and experience generally consistent with the generic mask he inherited from tradition and adapted to the particular needs of his work. Moreover, no genre or subject matter restricted him to just a single persona. In writing satire, for instance, he could adopt the more urbane satyr mask of Horace or the rougher one of Juvenal, while in love lyrics he could play the lady's suffering servant along with Petrarch or the detached, erotic ironist with Ovid. Nor was he necessarily prevented from refashioning a traditional mask to suit his own purposes, just as Dante and Milton were to do, in their different ways, with the persona of the epic bard. He might actually combine masks from several different genres, especially if his work, like so many in the Renaissance, was itself a hybrid, the union of many different traditions and genres. For instance, the character of the fisherman in Izaak Walton's *Compleat Angler* derives its features from the pastoral, the georgic, and the philosophical dialogue.[2] Similarly, Castiglione creates a most complex self-image for himself in his *Cortegiano,* a blend of ideal courtier modelled after Cicero's ideal orator, devoted memorialist seeking to immortalize the people of Urbino with his art, and nostalgic shepherd, a role Castiglione knew well from classical and Renaissance pastoral and which allowed him to articulate the profound yearning he felt over the loss of his ideal court.

In the first place, although Castiglione translates Cicero's personal statements from the *Orator* and the *De Oratore* in his first and last prologues, he does not simply ape Cicero's character. Rather, he assimilates it into his own, courtly mask, just as he appropriates many features of Cicero's ideal orator when fashioning his ideal courtier. What he really seems to have learned from Cicero is less a matter of imitating particular features when creating a persona in a philosophical dialogue than the aesthetic desirability of harmonizing that persona with the subject of the work. In the *De Oratore,* Cicero deliberately structured his image to reflect the features of his ideal: he stressed his life-long public role as orator; he supplied evidence from his own life of the encyclopedic learning and public, political involvement prescribed for the ideal; and he demonstrated in his masterful style the desired command of rhetoric. Inspired by Cicero's example, Castiglione presents himself to the reader in the role of ideal courtier, exhibiting in his style, his praise for the men and women of Urbino, and his tactful treatment of Alfonso Ariosto, Michel de Silva, and others, many of the qualities defining the ideal courtier of his book. Fully conscious of the role he chooses to play, Castiglione disclaims in the dedicatory letter that he modelled the ideal after his own image (3, 77), but his modest disclaimer is just more proof that Carlos V accurately pronounced Castiglione "uno de los mejores caballeros del mundo."

That Castiglione makes his mask reflect the qualities prescribed for the ideal courtier is most immediately evident in the carefully controlled, artfully complex, yet clear style with which he speaks. Far from sharing the random movement of real speech or even the relative spontaneity of his characters' exchanges, the statements he makes *in propria persona* are distinguished by quite different stylistic qualities, which begin to manifest themselves from the very first sentence of the book.[3]

> Quando il signor Guid'Ubaldo di Montefeltro, duca d'Urbino, passò di questa vita, io insieme con alcun'altri cavalieri che l'aveano servito restai alli servizi del duca Francesco Maria della Rovere, erede e successor di quello nel stato; e come nell'animo mio era recente l'odor delle virtù del duca Guido e la satisfazione che io quegli anni

aveva sentito della amorevole compagnia di così eccellenti persone, come allora si ritrovarono nella corte d'Urbino, fui stimulato da quella memoria a scrivere questi libri del *Cortegiano;* il che io feci in pochi giorni, con intenzione di castigar col tempo quegli errori, che dal desiderio di pagar tosto questo debito erano nati.

(Letter, 1, 67–8)

When lord Guidobaldo di Montefeltro, duke of Urbino, passed from this life, I together with several other knights who had served him remained in the service of duke Francesco Maria della Rovere, heir and successor to Guidobaldo's state; and as in my mind there remained fresh the odor of duke Guido's virtues and the satisfaction which I in those years had felt from the loving company of such excellent persons, as then frequented the court of Urbino, I was stimulated by that memory to write these books of the *Courtier;* the which I did in a few days with the intention of correcting in time those errors which from the desire of paying this debt quickly were born.

(my translation)

In the first place, Castiglione creates the impression of dignified formality, conscious deliberation, and even solemnity in the slow, measured pace of this sentence, an effect he achieves by placing lengthy subordinate clauses before the main ones, inserting appositive constructions, incidental phrases, and even clauses into the interstices of the sentence, and separating grammatical elements that would normally follow one another closely (e.g., "io . . . restai," "io . . . aveva"). Secondly, his precise use of grammar, tense sequences, and conjunctions keeps the structure of the sentence clear and bears witness to the rational mind behind it. Finally, by expanding the end of each period through the addition of phrases and clauses after the main verbs, he balances the weight of subordinate clauses placed at the beginning, thus giving the sentence a feeling of static balance and equilibrium.

As Castiglione employs similar techniques whenever he speaks *in propria persona,* the slow-paced formality of his style creates the impression of a person who, like the ideal courtier, possesses a reserved dignity. Its fundamental clarity and balance testify to that easy mastery of things the ideal courtier manifests by means of his *sprezzatura.* Again, like his ideal figure, Castiglione uses his style to suggest that he knows a great deal more than he says

directly. Through his constant allusions to classical and contemporary authors, his abbreviated considerations of language and elements of Aristotle's philosophy, and of course, the command of
Neoplatonic doctrine revealed in Bembo's bravura performance,
Castiglione hints at depths of untapped learning while demon-
strating his courtly sense of propriety by avoiding excessively detailed, pedantic expositions. Thus in many ways, and with singular
appropriateness, the courtly author of *Il Cortegiano* shows his
readers how to speak in a courtly style.

Castiglione also uses his prologues as well as his characters'
speeches to perform the courtier's basic act of courting others
through praise and flattery. By stressing the insufficiencies of his
book, which he says he wrote quickly and had little time to polish
(*Letter*, 1, 68–69), he throws himself on his readers' mercy, courting their applause for his literary performance. He makes no
claims for his work's superiority to those who sit in judgment
upon it, nor does he write in an artificially difficult style, which
would challenge the reader to rise to its level and would implicitly
scorn the common herd in favor of a fit, though limited, audience. Like his ideal courtier, Castiglione identifies himself as a
performer who excels in ability but humbly defers to the superior
power and judgment of his audience, thus deflecting their hostility and making them more receptive to the work they are about to
read.

Obviously worried lest praise seem sycophancy, Castiglione
carefully identifies his fundamental motive for celebrating the virtues of Alfonso Ariosto, Duchess Elisabetta, and others not as a
desire for personal gain, but as the love which Federico Fregoso
declares distinguishes the true courtier from the *nobile adulatore*
(II, 18, 216).[4] Moreover, he adopts several strategies to prevent
others from supplying different—and baser—motives for his
praise. For instance, to avoid giving the impression that his praise
is coerced, he distributes it to everyone with an even hand. Where
he has his characters eulogize Henry VIII and François I in an
earlier version of *The Courtier* (*Sec. red.*, III, 38, 225), he adds a
few more sentences about Carlos V in the final text (IV, 38, 496).
Similarly, he praises both Raphael and Michelangelo in the same
breath, although neither would have made such courtly remarks
about the other (*Letter*, 1, 71; I, 51, 176). Most strikingly, Castiglione demonstrates his disinterestedness and freedom when he
lauds Vittoria Colonna's wit and prudence, even though he had
ample cause to chastise her for allowing his manuscript to circu-
late publicly before he wished it to become known (*Letter*, 1, 69).[5]

Note that Castiglione seldom speaks at great length about any character he praises, except those who have died and thus become fit subjects for public eulogies, and that he doles out praise most parsimoniously to those living figures he serves.[6] Castiglione's major strategy for avoiding the charge of being a sychophantic flatterer, however, is to couch all his statements of praise in quite general, thoroughly conventional terms, whose conventionality he underscores through repetition. Rather than narrate the military exploits or civic triumphs of a character he praises, he resorts constantly to general, nonparticularized words, celebrating all of them for their *virtù*, their *ingegno*, their *ottime qualità*.[7] Even when he eulogizes the dead rulers and courtiers of his beloved Urbino, he rarely presents a detailed picture of their accomplishments. Thus, ironically, although *Il Cortegiano* abounds with references to contemporary figures and events, it maintains a constant distance from them and eschews specific details in a way that the realist Machiavelli does not when distributing his own brand of praise and blame in *Il Principe*. By speaking in general, conventional terms, Castiglione avoids endorsing a character's deeds and misdeeds by effectively drawing attention away from the person praised and toward the act of praise itself. As he celebrates a character's "virtue" or "wit" without providing specific, illustrative material to support such generalized praise, Castiglione prevents his statements from being judged primarily as true or false about the character concerned; their form, not their content, becomes their salient feature, or rather, their form simply becomes their content. Thus, Castiglione's statements of praise can only be evaluated as a display of good manners, a sign of their courtly maker's respect for the conventions of society. Sincere gestures of deference and respect, they ultimately have as little specific content, but as much social meaning, as a series of properly performed, graceful genuflections.[8]

Even more than presenting himself in the role of a perfect courtier, Castiglione also undertakes to play the role of memorialist for the court of Urbino. He identifies his primary purpose in writing his *Cortegiano* as a desire to preserve from oblivion the memory of the court and its people, and as he carries out this labor of love, he not only paints a flattering portrait of the court in his dialogues but uses his four prologues explicitly to justify his admiration for it and to extol its virtues and accomplishments directly and unambiguously. Moreover, as he progresses from one prologue to the next, his praise progresses as well, rising to increasingly lofty heights. Thus where the prologue to the first book describes the beauties of Urbino's palazzo and the noble character of its rulers, the prologue to the second argues for the court's superiority in comparison with all courts past and present. The prologue to Book III goes even further, equating Urbino's superior stature to Hercules' superior size and thus actually relating it to the more than human world of heroes. In his last prologue, Castiglione consummates this particular development, as Urbino becomes an epic realm in his imagination and metamorphoses into the Trojan horse, a gigantic receptacle for the greatest heroes of ancient Greece.[9] Appropriately enough, while in the first prologue he merely listed the names of all those courtiers associated with Urbino, in this last one he sings the praises of their "heroic" accomplishments, eulogizing the dead for their dramatic struggle against hostile fortune and celebrating the living for the distinguished offices they held and the noble ranks to which they rose.

Accompanying this gradual elevation of Urbino's image to the heights of heroic grandeur is an increasing insistence on its moral excellence and its value for posterity. In the first two prologues, while Castiglione asserts the superiority of Urbino's inhabitants, he does not do so specifically on the grounds of their *virtù,* but just as Urbino acquires a heroic stature in the last two prologues, its characters turn into paragons of morality at the same time. Thus, in the prologue to Book III, Castiglione tells the reader that if Urbino's pastimes convince him of its excellence, he should be able to imagine easily how much greater the courtiers' virtuous actions were (III, 1, 336). Then, in the last prologue, Castiglione praises the courtiers directly as "omini per virtù singulari" (IV, 2, 446: "men singular in worth"[286]), and he actually envisions the court as a collection of moral *exempla* (IV, 2, 448: "chiari ed onorati esempi di virtù"). Moreover, the court offers its ethical models not only to contemporaries, but to future generations, and Castiglione confesses quite openly in the third prologue that he labors so diligently over his text precisely to "farla vivere negli animi dei posteri" (III, 1, 336: "make it live in the mind of posterity"[202]). Finally, in a burst of optimism, he even goes so far as to imagine that just as his culture looks back with admiration on classical antiquity, so the future will envy his century because Urbino's court existed then (III, 1, 336: "forse per l'avvenire non mancherà chi per questo ancor porti invidia al secol nostro").

Castiglione does not compose his memorial to Urbino simply in order to prove himself an ideal courtier; rather, his book rises out of its author's profound nostalgia for the court of good Duke Guidobaldo's days and from his tragic experience of loss and isolation.[10] His nostalgia and sense of loss color every statement he utters about Urbino and its people, but they are especially strong at the very start of his book, and their presence there effectively establishes them as the most affecting and memorable traits in Castiglione's courtly persona. With great skill, Castiglione begins the dedicatory letter to Don Michel de Silva that opens his book by quietly recounting how, after Duke Guidobaldo's death, he remembered the happiness he had enjoyed at the court and was stimulated by his memories to begin writing (1, 67–68). His first impulse to write, as he recalls it, is unmistakably triggered by his exposure to death and by a nostalgia for the past. As yet, however, there is no suggestion of urgency, no compelling sense of loss that drives him to bring his work to its completion. As he recounts his first decision to write *Il Cortegiano*, the motivation his narrative suggests is simply the wish of a grateful, devoted courtier to pay homage to his fallen lord, and to recall a period he described in earlier versions of his book as "il fior della vita mia" (*Sec. red.*, I, 4, 8). Castiglione continues the narrative of his dedicatory letter, however, in order to explain how Vittoria Colonna's intervention led him to complete his manuscript. He recounts that many years after he had put it aside, he took it in hand again, and was, as he reread it, filled with a much more profound, more total nostalgia for the past.

> ... cominciai a rileggerlo; e sùbito nella prima fronte, ammonito dal titulo, presi non mediocre tristezza, la qual ancora nel passar più avanti molto si accrebbe, ricordandomi la maggior parte di coloro, che sono introdutti nei ragionamenti, esser già morti. ...
>
> (*Letter*, 1, 69)

> ... I started to reread it; and immediately, at the very outset, by reason of the dedication, I was seized by no little sadness (which greatly grew as I proceeded), when I remembered that the greater part of those persons who are introduced in the conversations were already dead. ...
>
> (2)

What Castiglione remembers here is not past happiness as much as the painful *loss* of that happiness through the deaths of so many people. Alfonso Ariosto, Giuliano de' Medici, Ottaviano Fregoso—one by one he mourns for them in a powerful cres-

97

cendo of lament, transforming the opening of his book into an elegy that reaches its climax only when he recalls the greatest loss of all.

> Ma quello che senza lacrime raccontar non si devria è che la signora Duchessa essa ancor è morta; e se l'animo mio si turba per la perdita de tanti amici e signori mei, che m'hanno lasciato in questa vita come in una solitudine piena d'affanni, ragion è che molto più acerbamente senta il dolore della morte della signora Duchessa che di tutti gli altri, perché essa molto più che tutti gli altri valeva ed io ad essa molto più che a tutti gli altri era tenuto.
>
> *(Letter, 1, 71)*

> But what should not be told without tears is that the Duchess, too, is dead. And if my mind is troubled at the loss of so many friends and lords, who have left me in this life as in a desert full of woes, it is understandable that I should feel sorrow far more bitter for the death of the Duchess than for any of the others, because she was worth more than the others, and I was much more bound to her than to all the rest.
>
> (2–3)

In this long opening passage, Castiglione's simple repetitions of *è morto, morto è, morti sono*, and the particular repetitions of *tutti gli altri* in the sentence concerning the duchess, effectively transmit his sensation of living in a universe where the fullness of life he once enjoyed at Urbino has yielded to an all-pervading experience of death and desolation. Community has dwindled away into isolation, and pleasure has turned into pain. More than Duke Guido, an entire world has disappeared, and with it, all the virtue, wit, happiness, and grace Castiglione identified with its inhabitants. By the time this litany is done, his *Cortegiano* has become a plaintive elegy for the dead, a memorial motivated by profound nostalgia for a world he personally has lost, a *cri de coeur* from the bitter loneliness of his *solitudine piena d'affanni* (*Letter*, 1, 71).

Once firmly established at the start of the dedicatory letter, Castiglione's sense of loss, his sad isolation in a universe of death, and his yearning for a happier past exercise a decisive influence on the reader's reaction to all that follows, complementing and magnifying the nostalgic elements that are continually present in Castiglione's response to his experience. Thus his declaration at the start of Book I that he writes in order to renew a pleasing memory (I, 1, 81: "rinovando una grata memoria") takes on an added measure of pathos because of the great losses detailed in the dedicatory letter which have made that happy past all the more distant and inaccessible. Similarly, Castiglione's brooding on the destructiveness of time and the fragility of human life in the prologue to Book II (1, 189) acquires even greater emotional weight because the reader is able to relate these general sentiments to the author's present horror at the devastation death has wrought. Finally, the greater tragedy recounted in the dedicatory letter is balanced by the only slightly less severe tragedy recounted in the prologue to Book IV. Here, Castiglione, directly imitating the last prologue to Cicero's *De Oratore,* briefly recounts the deaths of Gasparo Pallavicino, Cesare Gonzaga, and Roberto da Bari, which have left him oppressed by an *amaro pensiero* (IV, 1, 445) and dismayed by the inevitable misery of man's lot and the frustration of his hopes. To be sure, the last prologue does not linger over the dead, and after a brief, but fitting, tribute, Castiglione turns to praise all those courtiers still alive, celebrating Urbino's continuing excellence and reaching a climax in a fervent wish for the future prosperity of the court and its rulers (IV, 2, 447). The dedicatory letter, written many years after this fourth prologue, poignantly undercuts Castiglione's pious wish and reveals that death has brought about the ultimate deception of his hopes.

As Castiglione's responses in the prologues to *Il Cortegiano* clearly suggest, nostalgia involves more than mere remembrance of things past. It is a sense that the past was qualitatively superior to the present, that it would be desirable to resurrect it, but that, except in the memory, the past is separated from the present by an unbridgeable chasm.[11] Nostalgia originates as a response to a feeling of lost youth and vitality, innocence, and freshness. Characteristically, it projects this yearning into the recollection of the past, envisioning it as a happy, fulfilling world of communal harmony and personal pleasure. Often, since nostalgia involves a fundamental feeling of loss, it goes beyond mere yearning for a supposedly more perfect past and generates a strong contrast between that past and a distinctly diminished present. Consequently critics have claimed, with some justice, that nostalgia underlies the myths of a paradise lost and a vanished Golden Age, and that it is the typical emotion behind the pastoral, manifested in the shepherd-poet's longing for that strange and distant, yet familiar and satisfying realm which Virgil immortalized as Arcadia.[12]

Although he does not use the word "nostalgia," when he is

defending his claims for Urbino's superiority at the start of his second book Castiglione nevertheless demonstrates a genuine understanding both of nostalgia's pyschological origin and the characteristic way it shapes each individual's perceptions of past and present. As he attacks the old men for condemning the courts of the present indiscriminately while praising without qualification those of their youth, he describes perfectly how nostalgia operates in shaping one's memory of the past.

> né dei passati piaceri riserva [l'animo] altro che una tenace memoria e la imagine di quel caro tempo della tenera età, nella quale quando ci ritrovamo, ci pare che sempre il cielo e la terra ed ogni cosa faccia festa e rida intorno agli occhi nostri, e nel pensiero come in un delizioso e vago giardino fiorisca la dolce primavera d'allegrezza.
>
> (II, 1, 188)

> . . . and [the mind] retains of past pleasures merely a lingering memory and the image of that precious time of tender youth in which (while we are enjoying it), wherever we look, heaven and earth and everything appear merry and smiling, and the sweet springtime of happiness seems to flower in our thoughts as in a delightful and lovely garden.
>
> (90)

Castiglione goes on to berate the old men for not realizing that it is they who have changed, not the courts, that they mourn their own loss of youth, power, and vitality without realizing it, and that their powerful feelings of nostalgia make them misperceive the truth about both past and present.

If Castiglione denounces the old men's nostalgia, isn't he equally vulnerable to the same criticisms? Doesn't his own nostalgia for Duke Guido's court lead him to a distorted presentation of its image? To some degree, it certainly does, for even a reader unfamiliar with the real history and people of Urbino may suspect that Castiglione sees his all-too-ideal court through rose-colored glasses. Nevertheless, his nostalgia differs from that of the old men in two major ways. First, Castiglione establishes an implicit set of contrasts between his own character and that of the nostalgic old men he attacks. Where they are presented as giving in to their feelings and irrationally condemning the present without exception, Castiglione presents himself as a much more balanced and reasonable judge who wisely contends that no age, past or present, can be wholly good or wholly evil (II, 2, 191–92). Where the old men attack mere changes in customs as signs of moral degeneration, Castiglione shows himself able to discriminate between morally indifferent matters like dress and things of real, moral significance (II, 3, 193–94). Finally, where the old men are scolded for being unaware of how their nostalgia affects their perceptions of past and present, that very scolding demonstrates Castiglione's own self-consciousness about it. The effect of all these contrasts is not to deny the latter's nostalgia, which colors his entire work from its powerful, affecting first pages, but to show that it has not blinded him to reality or perverted his judgment. Castiglione places his nostalgia within the context of a reasonable, discriminating, self-conscious personality and thus makes himself a difficult target for the mockery and censure he directs at the old men.

Castiglione's nostalgia differs from theirs in yet another respect. While both he and they yearn for a more beautiful, fulfilling past, he refrains absolutely from projecting his sense of loss into a moralistic condemnation of the present. Instead of contrasting Urbino's past glory with its subsequent decline, he chooses to contrast it with his own very personal isolation, and he refuses to interpret the separation between his past and his present as a symptom of moral decay or historical degeneration. As a result, his nostalgia differs substantially not only from that of the moralistic old men, but from that of the more historically oriented Cicero, who offered Castiglione at least a partial model for his nostalgia in the prologues to the *De Oratore*.

In their prologues, both Cicero and Castiglione celebrate historical figures whose supposedly real conversations their dialogues record and whose deaths they eloquently mourn. Both authors also firmly establish their own personal relationship to the figures and events described, and both depict themselves as looking back from an unhappy present to a happier world in the past. Here, however, the resemblances cease, for Castiglione seems much less concerned with the complex, concrete historical situation of his beloved Urbino when compared to Cicero, who carefully relates the characters and events he describes, as well as his own situation, to the larger developments of Roman history. The latter specifically sets his dialogues at a crucial turning point in Roman history, a time just before the first serious explosions of violence and revolution that would eventually lead to the Augustan *imperium*. Thus Cicero ironically praises one of his protagonists, Lucius Crassus, for having the good fortune to die of natural causes just before the Republic was swamped by violence and the old moral order destroyed.

> Non vidit flagrantem bello Italiam, non ardentem invidia senatum, non sceleris nefarii principes civitatis reos, non luctum filiae, non exsilium generi, non acerbissimam C. Mari fugam, non illam post reditum eius caedem omnium crudelissimam, non denique in omni genere deformatam eam civitatem in qua ipse florentissima multum omnibus praestitisset.
>
> *(De Oratore, III, ii, 8)*[13]

> He did not see Italy ablaze with war, the Senate inflamed with passion, the leading citizens arraigned for nefarious crime, his daughter's grief, her husband's exile, the utterly lamentable flight of Gaius Marius, the massacre unparalleled in savagery that followed his return, nor in fine the utter corruption in every respect of a country in which at the period of its supreme prosperity he had himself held by far the highest position.

Moreover, Cicero recounts how the historical catastrophe that followed Crassus's demise engulfed all the other speakers in his dialogue: Quintus Catulus was forced into exile and suicide; Antonius was murdered; Cotta became an exile; and Sulpicius betrayed his friends and then fell victim himself to a change in the political situation (see III, iii, 8–10). Note also how Cicero places himself as a character within the historical scheme he has established. He opens his first book by complaining that the normal career of public office followed by a dignified retirement which Roman patricians previously had enjoyed was denied him by the civil strife that plagued Rome since the death of Crassus in Cicero's boyhood. He then goes on to describe how he himself became involved in those political struggles:

> Nam prima aetate incidimus in ipsam perturbationem disciplinae veteris; et consulatu devenimus in medium rerum omnium certamen atque discrimen; et hoc tempus omne post consulatum obiecimus eis fluctibus, qui, per nos a communi peste depulsi, in nosmet ipsos redundarunt.
>
> *(De Oratore, I, i, 4)*

> For in my early years I came just upon the days when the

old order was overthrown; then by my consulship I was drawn into the midst of a universal struggle and crisis, and my whole time ever since that consulship I have spent in stemming those billows which, stayed by my efforts from ruining the nation, rolled in a flood upon myself.

Cicero finishes this paragraph by describing himself snatching a few moments of leisure for writing this book while in the midst of the continual political warfare still troubling the state. His nostalgia for the more peaceful time of his youth, a time firmly fixed in the sweep of Roman history, could not be more understandable.

By contrast, Castiglione ignores much of Urbino's history and is especially vague when alluding to historical events involving its relationships to other Italian states. He never explains what enemies Duke Federico triumphed over or who was responsible for Duke Guidobaldo's many misfortunes. Moreover, he selects a date just after Pope Julius II's visit in 1506 as the time when his dialogues supposedly took place, not because he wishes to call attention to its historical significance, but because the visit allows him to account for the particularly festive mood of his courtiers' conversations.[14] Finally, where Cicero has an intense, personal involvement in historical events, Castiglione says nothing about his own historically quite significant diplomatic activities, which brought him into direct contact with the most powerful European rulers of his age. He also remains somewhat vague about what happened to the court of Urbino during the time he was writing and revising his *Book of the Courtier,* and he is equally vague about his own personal relationship to it. The dedicatory letter raises a series of puzzling questions: Did the court of Urbino cease to exist when the duchess and her courtiers died? Is Francesco Maria no longer its ruler as he was when Castiglione composed the prologue to Book IV? Has Castiglione himself left the duke's service, and is he still in Spain as he was when he sent the manuscript of *Il Cortegiano* to Vittoria Colonna? To all these questions concerning his own and Urbino's history, Castiglione's reply is silence. Deprived of any historical framework, his separation from what he might call his sweet, springtime garden of Urbino becomes a mysterious process: a mythical fall from innocence, an inexplicably sinless expulsion from a paradise of delights into a bleak universe held thrall to death.

Castiglione's mysterious separation from Urbino as well as his nostalgic lament over death and loss also suggestively invoke similar elements in the pastoral tradition that may well have strongly influenced him as he wrote his book. The courtly society to which Castiglione belonged and which he celebrated in his *Cortegiano* particularly affected the pastoral. In works of that literary mode, courtly poets could fabricate an illusory world of innocence and nature which was simultaneously and paradoxically extremely sophisticated and artificial. Utilizing the most transparent allegories, they could flatter the powerful by making shepherds and shepherdesses sing the praises of figures easily identifiable as their lords and ladies. Thus, Renaissance poets from Poliziano and Sannazaro to Sidney and Jonson wrote pastoral verse, masques, plays, and novels in which the roles of shepherd and courtier merged and the pastoral world was supplied with all the aristocratic hierarchies, urbane manners, and sophisticated characters associated with the court. Castiglione himself, with his cousin Cesare Gonzaga, wrote a pastoral masque called *Tirsi* for the carnival of 1506 at Urbino. While its characters are "simple" shepherds, they are clearly disguised courtiers; their manners are refined and graceful, and their language is highly sophisticated, a pastiche of translations from Virgil and quotations from Poliziano and Sannazaro. Moreover, not only do its characters speak like courtiers, but they are actively engaged in courtship during their performance, one singing a love complaint to an obdurate nymph, and the other hymning the praises of the shepherds' goddess, an allegorical figure representing the duchess Elisabetta Gonzaga. The contrast between these two courtship songs is a contrast between inferior courtship directed at an unsuitable object and superior courtship directed at a stable, benevolent figure; and it thus provides the theme of Castiglione's work, which is a revelation of the nature of true courtship. *Tirsi* offers a clear demonstration of the total interpenetration of courtly and pastoral worlds in the minds of its author and the members of his society. Consequently if Castiglione, like most of his contemporaries, felt no reluctance to transport the court into the pastoral bower, he could also simply reverse the process in his *Courtier* and give its courtly world and his own courtly role some of the chief characteristics of pastoral.

In a brief article, Rosalie Colie suggestively labelled *Il Cortegiano* an "urban pastoral" and drew a large number of parallels between the world of the pastoral and the one Castiglione creates in his book.[15] To be sure, most traditional pastorals define their world fundamentally in contradistinction, if not in hostile opposition, to that of the city or the court,[16] but Renaissance courtly pastoral frequently wedded the two, and *The Courtier* cannot be said to be unpastoral just because it emphasizes urban values like sophistication, wit, and polished manners rather than the natural simplicity and spontaneity of shepherds and goatherds. Moreover, even many of the characteristic qualities that traditionally define the pastoral world find their way into Castiglione's book. For instance, although its discussions do not take place in a pleasance, a meadow, or even a garden, the countryside around Urbino, which makes two significant appearances framing the courtly conversations in Urbino's palace (I, 2, 81 and IV, 73, 544), is the same benevolent natural world, abounding with food, fresh air, and melodious birdsong, that poetical shepherds traditonally enjoyed. Also, like the pastoral pleasance, Castiglione's court is a place of pleasure and freedom, of *otium,* not *negotium,* and like many a band of fictional shepherds, its inhabitants cheerfully while away the hours with singing and dancing, games and contests, enjoying the substantial rewards of good fellowship in their small, egalitarian community. Both pastoral grove and urbane court are detached from the world of everyday affairs, and both are characterized by a harmony between art and nature and a freedom from any sense of sin or guilt. In short, though no sheep may graze in Urbino's halls, Castiglione hangs the trappings of pastoral about his palace just as he and others used to do for the pastoral plays and masques they presented there during carnival.[17]

If Castiglione's court has a bucolic air about it, that air might even more appropriately be labelled "Arcadian." Virgil invented the half-mythical, half-real world of Arcadia as the setting for his *Eclogues.* He took a real place whose geography was harsh and unpleasant, but which was conveniently far away from Rome, and transformed it into a "spiritual landscape," an imaginary realm which turned its back on historical actualities and combined the simple features of humble, everyday country life with other features clearly the result of psychological projection: a totally benevolent nature, a life of complete leisure, simple shepherds able to compose songs in the most sophisticated language, and a mythical merging of human figures into the landscape.[18] In the Renaissance, Sannazaro gave new currency to Virgil's mythical realm in his *Arcadia* (first edition, 1502; second, 1504), an immensely popular work with which Castiglione was surely familiar.[19] Like Virgil's Arcadia, Sannazaro's is half real and half imaginary, sometimes seeming like the countryside around Naples and sometimes like a strange, remote realm whose mood combines idyllic content with elegiac longing. Divorced from the realities of the contemporary, historical world, it is a realm of art and poetry, a dream of life as it ideally should be. Perhaps without consciously intending to do so, Castiglione nevertheless makes his court of Urbino into yet another variant of Arcadia. As the comparison with Cicero has shown, Castiglione takes a real court which played a significant, if minor, role in Renaissance Italian history, and presents it in such a way that although its characters frequently allude to historical figures and events, it shares the strange remoteness from reality, the a-historical quality characterizing Virgil's and Sannazaro's Arcadias. Like them, Urbino is simultaneously a real place, where historical figures engage in credible conversation, and a mythical, ideal realm of total leisure, social harmony, and simple, yet sophisticated art.

Both Castiglione's nostalgic yearning for the sweet garden of Urbino and the mysterious character of his apparent separation from it also fit the Arcadian nature of his work. The figure of the sad shepherd, nostalgically mourning for a lost pastoral world from which he has been expelled or separated, was familiar to Castiglione from Virgil's first eclogue and especially from Sannazaro's *Arcadia,* in which nostalgia has become a central feature of the shepherd's mask. At the start of his *Arcadia,* Sannazaro himself appears disguised as the sad, solitary Sincero, a Neapolitan nobleman who has travelled to Arcadia and become a shepherd there, learning to love its simple, innocent pleasures, its freedom, and its poetry. While he never abandons his urbane and courtly character, he nevertheless becomes profoundly attached to the imaginary, pastoral world where he and the other shepherds sing songs of love-longing and laments for the dead, poems filled with a gentle, elegiac nostalgia for a happier world. At the end of *Arcadia,* Sincero-Sannazaro is definitively and unwillingly separated from his mythical realm of poetry in a mysterious, allegorical journey that returns him to his friends at Naples and leaves him filled with nostalgia, mourning for the Arcadian world he has left behind.

Although *Il Cortegiano* contains many features that link it to Sannazaro's *Arcadia* and to countless bucolic works from classical antiquity and the Renaissance, Castiglione's brooding response to death, which has overwhelmed his Arcadian Urbino, involves a fundamental horror that profoundly differentiates his work from the entire pastoral tradition. To be sure, death lurks in the shades of shepherds' bowers just as it does in Urbino's halls, but there it is treated as a fact of nature, part of the natural cycle that offers the mourning shepherd the consolation of seasonal, if not personal, rebirth, and thus softens death's potentially brutal impact. Death is transmuted into an affirmation of the wholeness and inviolability of nature, and by providing material for the shepherd's enjoyable, sad songs, it even becomes an ally of pleasure in his bower.[20]

At some points in his *Book of the Courtier*, Castiglione seems to embrace this pastoral view of death; he seems to imagine time moving through an organic cycle in which death occupies the last phase as a fitting and natural terminus of life and guarantees some form of rebirth and renewed existence. Although *Il Cortegiano* contains no detailed treatment of history and does not adumbrate an explicit scheme for it, there are many indications that Castiglione implicitly shared with his humanist predecessors and contemporaries a basically organic, cyclical view: culture flourished in antiquity, faded and died in the Middle Ages, and was reborn in the time of Dante, Petrarch, and Boccaccio, reaching its new maturity during Castiglione's own age.[21] Thus, when addressing himself to the old men who attack contemporary courts, he insists on the progress that has been made in civilized life when early, crude beginnings are compared to the heights reached at Urbino, where the best men and customs were in flower ("fiorirono" [III, 1, 336]). Castiglione develops his organic, cyclical view of history most fully in his discussions of the Italian language, which first grew as a tender, new *fiore* in Tuscany and has since then begun to grow from time to time ("nascendo poi di tempo in tempo") in many places throughout Italy (I, 32, 137). Note, moreover, the particularly revealing images used in the following passage:

> Ma delle parole son alcune che durano bone un tempo, poi s'invecchiano ed in tutto perdono la grazia; altre piglian forza e vengono in prezzo perché, come le stagioni dell'anno spogliano de' fiori e de' frutti la terra e poi di novo d'altri la rivesteno, così il tempo quelle prime parole fa cadere e l'uso altre di novo fa rinascere e dà lor grazia e dignità, fin che, dall'invidioso morso del tempo a poco a poco consumate, giungono poi esse ancora alla lor morte; perciò che, al fine, e noi ed ogni nostra cosa è mortale.
>
> (I, 36, 145)

> But among words there are some that remain good for a time, then grow old and lose their grace completely, whereas others gain in strength and come into favor; because, just as the seasons of the year divest the earth of her flowers and fruits, and then clothe her again with others, so time causes those first words to fall, and usage

brings others to life, giving them grace and dignity, until they are gradually consumed by the envious jaws of time, when they too go to their death; because, in the end, we and all our things are mortal.

(58)

Like the pastoral poet, Castiglione here softens the potential horror of death, which devours men and their works, by imagining it as the final phase in a natural cycle that offers the specific consolation of rebirth. In fact, the effect of death is even further muted by his emphasis on the balanced way some words die while others are born and grow in force, and by his emphasis on the gradual character of the entire process ("a poco a poco"). As a result, his last clause ("perciò che . . . ") seems to capture perfectly, albeit fleetingly, the mood of pastoral nostalgia, a calm, sad acceptance of natural inevitability in which time can be granted the trust implied in Castiglione's repetition of the old adage that "time is the father of truth" (see *Letter,* 3, 78).

In spite of these strivings for a comfortable perspective, Castiglione is finally unable to share the pastoral poet's complacency about time and death; for the most part, he does not place them within the consoling context of natural processes, and he is usually filled with bitter thoughts about death rather than calm resignation over its inevitability. Thus, although he occasionally depicts time as an agent of growth and improvement, he more characteristically stresses its destructive effects. Not only has it shattered the frail lives of men, but it has toppled empires and buried languages in oblivion. Ironically, while the courtiers and ladies of Urbino are never seen at the convivial banquets they must have enjoyed together, time is depicted as a strong-jawed monster (*tempus edax*) who feeds off the living and parodies their convivial communion by devouring the communicants themselves. In an even more powerful image, Castiglione presents time as a turbulent sea, a power that is irresistible and ultimate—and likewise devours its victims.

> . . . noi con la nave della mortalità fuggendo n'andiamo l'un dopo l'altro per quel procelloso mare che ogni cosa assorbe e devora, né mai più ripigliar terra ci è concesso, anzi, sempre da contrari venti combattuti, al fine in qualche scoglio la nave rompemo.

(II, 1, 189)

. . . one after the other we in our ship of mortality go

scudding across that stormy sea which takes all things to itself and devours them; nor are we ever permitted to touch shore again, but, tossed by conflicting winds, we are finally shipwrecked upon some reef.

(90)

The most direct evidence of Castiglione's discomfort, his horror, in response to death is that while he rarely couples it with nature and nature's illusory but reassuring regularity, he frequently links it to fortune, which he always characterizes as a fickle goddess whose arbitrary, irrational, uncontrollable, and omnipotent nature inevitably frustrates man's hopes for order and justice in the universe.[22] If Castiglione manifests a certain ambivalence about time, characterizing it both as the benevolent father of truth and as a devouring sea, he expresses no ambivalence whatsoever about fortune, which he hates and fears as a destroyer. For instance, at the start of the fourth book, when he reworks his image of man's life as a fragile ship, he not only identifies the tempestuous ocean with fortune rather than time, but he presents the ocean of fortune as a force that actively seeks to destroy its victim, whereas the ocean of time in his earlier passage was slightly less antagonistic and man himself was seen as at least a party to his own demise ("al fine in qualche scoglio la nave rompemo").

> Pensando io di scrivere i ragionamenti che la quarta sera dopo le narrate nei precedenti libri s'ebbero, sento tra varii discorsi uno amaro pensiero che nell'animo mi percuote e delle miserie umane e nostre speranze fallaci ricordevole mi fa; e come spesso la fortuna a mezzo il corso, talor presso al fine rompa i nostri fragili e vani disegni, talor li summerga prima che pur veder da lontano possano il porto.

(IV, 1, 445)

> Thinking to record the discussions held on the fourth evening following those reported in the preceding books, I feel amidst various reflections one bitter thought strike upon me, making me mindful of human miseries and of our vain hopes: how often Fortune in midcourse, and sometimes near the end, dashes our fragile and futile designs and sometimes wrecks them before the port can even be seen from afar.

(285)

More than man's opponent in bringing about his death, fortune obstructs his plans to achieve material security, fame, and earthly immortality. Castiglione attributes to fortune, again imagined as a storm (le procelle), the responsibility for Duke Guidobaldo's gout and military misadventures (I, 3, 83–84), Ottaviano's sufferings (Letter, 1, 70), and the duchess's many adversities (I, 4, 86).[23] In a phrase, Castiglione sums up what he feels about the fickle goddess: "la fortuna, come sempre fu, così è ancor oggidì contraria alla virtù" (Letter, 1, 70: "fortune, as she ever was, is, even in these days, the enemy of virtue"[2]).

In an ironic way, however, fortune does serve man's best interests, for it gives him the opportunity to display his virtues as he triumphs over its opposition, albeit his triumph is at best an extremely limited one. Alberti confidently predicted that the exercises of virtù would bring man worldly success and prosperity, and Machiavelli cautiously declared that a vigorous, clear-sighted prince could reach some of his political goals since virtù could defeat fortuna at least half the time.[24] By contrast, Castiglione nowhere envisages virtue achieving such substantial material or political results. When the duke and duchess, Ottaviano, and others triumph over fortune, they do so spiritually, as the following description of Duke Guidobaldo's victory illuminates:

> . . . benché in esso fosse il consiglio sapientissimo e l'animo invittissimo, parea che ciò che incominciava, e nell'arme e in ogni altra cosa o piccola o grande, sempre male gli succedesse: e di ciò fanno testimonio molte e diverse sue calamità, le quali esso con tanto vigor d'animo sempre tollerò, che mai la virtù dalla fortuna non fu superata; anzi, sprezzando con l'animo valoroso le procelle di quella, e nella infirmità come sano e nelle avversità come fortunatissimo, vivea con somma dignità ed estimazione appresso ognuno. . . .
>
> (I, 3, 83–84)

> . . . although he was very wise in counsel and undaunted in spirit, it seemed that whatever he undertook always succeeded ill with him whether in arms or in anything, great or small; all of which is attested by his many and diverse calamities, which he always bore with such strength of spirit that his virtue was never overcome by Fortune; nay, despising her storms with stanch heart, he lived in sickness as if in health, and in adversity as if most

fortunate, with the greatest dignity and esteemed by all. . . .

(14)

In Castiglione's world, the true hero is the stoic, who despises the slings and arrows of outrageous fortune and maintains his personal integrity in the face of inevitable suffering and defeat.

The fundamental experience of death to which Castiglione was exposed and which he records in *Il Cortegiano* is clearly not the pastoral vision of natural consummation; for him, death is a sudden, unexpected interruption of life. Unnatural, arbitrary, irrational, and unjust, it did not allow the inhabitants of Urbino to grow to maturity and then slip gently away into the peaceful sleep of eternity, but struck them down without warning just when they were beginning the most productive phases of their careers. For instance, throughout the litany of his dedicatory letter, Castiglione stresses the unnaturalness and injustice of death: Alfonso Ariosto died when still a *giovane* (1, 69); Giuliano de' Medici's "bontà e nobil cortesia meritava più lungamente dal mondo esser goduta" (1, 70: "goodness and noble courtesy deserved to be enjoyed longer by the world"[2]); and death took many others "ai quali parea che la natura promettesse lunghissima vita" (1, 71: "to whom nature seemed to promise very long life"[2]). In the prologue to his last book, Castiglione similarly weeps for those who were taken before their time, and here, as in the dedicatory letter, he emphasizes the opposition, not the cooperation, between death and nature. Note, for instance, his lament for Gasparo Pallavicino, who "in *età molto immatura* fornì il suo *natural* corso" (IV, 1, 445; my italics: "finished his *natural* course *at a most unripe age*"[my translation]).[25] Arbitrary, perverse, irresistible, death and fortune are the ultimate powers in Castiglione's universe; they reduce cosmos to chaos and negate the very possibility of forming any scheme, any order at all. The tragedy of Urbino is thus not simply that its inhabitants have died, but that their premature deaths have destroyed Castiglione's sense that any universal form of order and justice exists in the world about him.

While Castiglione's horrified vision of a universe overwhelmed by the absolute tyranny of death and fortune separates him from the pastoral tradition, it also helps explain why he refused to follow Cicero's lead and establish a historical scheme in which to embrace the deaths of his protagonists. For Castiglione, man's life is not lived within the framework of history, but rather in the context of his personal struggle against the universal forces of time, fortune, and mortality. Instructively, although Cicero also laments the deaths of his protagonists in the *De Oratore* as examples of the power and mutability of fortune ("vim varietatemque fortunae" [III, iii, 8]), such general reflections hardly prevent him from carefully relating those deaths to the tragic development of Roman history, from claiming that when a certain Gaius Julius died, the Republic died with him (III, iii, 10: "ille . . . et vixisse cum republica pariter et cum illa simul exstinctus esse videatur"). Castiglione, on the other hand, when imitating Cicero in the prologue to his last book, avoids altogether duplicating Cicero's historical scheme and adapts from him just those passages that fit his own particular, tragic vision of life. Thus, although he begins by translating the opening words of Cicero's third book, he jumps immediately to a later passage from that same book where Cicero utters one of his two complaints about the power of fortune and the futility of human effort.

Instituenti mihi, Quinte frater, eum sermonem referre et mandare huic tertio libro, quem post Antonii disputationem Crassus habuisset, acerba sane recordatio veterem animi curam molestiamque renovavit. (III, 1, 2)

Pensando io di scrivere i ragionamenti che la quarta sera dopo le narrate nei precedenti libri s'ebbero, sento tra varii discorsi uno amaro pensiero che nell'animo mi percuote e delle miserie umane e nostre speranze fallaci ricordevole mi fa; . . .

When I set about recalling and embodying in this Third Volume the discourse of Crassus that followed the remarks made by Antonius, I confess, brother Quintus, that the recollection was painful to me, renewing as it did an old sorrow and distress.

Thinking to record the discussions held on the fourth evening following those reported in the preceding books, I feel amidst various reflections one bitter thought strike upon me, making me mindful of human miseries and of our vain hopes: . . .

O fallacem hominum spem fragilemque fortunam, et inanes nostras contentiones, quae medio in spatio saepe franguntur et corruunt et ante in ipso cursu obruuntur quam portum conspicere potuerunt! (III, ii, 6)

e come spesso la fortuna a mezzo il corso, talor presso al fine rompa i nostri fragili e vani disegni, talor li summerga prima che pur veder da lontano possano il porto. (IV, 1, 445)

Ah, how treacherous are men's hopes, how insecure their fortunes! How hollow are our endeavors, which often break down and come to grief in the middle of the race, or are shipwrecked in full sail before they have been able to sight the harbour!

how often Fortune in mid-course, and sometimes near the end, dashes our fragile and futile designs and sometimes wrecks them before the port can even be seen from afar. (285)

Note that where Cicero recalls a specific historical event to which he attaches reflections of a general nature, Castiglione's "bitter thought" is not the recollection of a particular event, but his paraphrase of Cicero's more general reflection. It almost seems that Castiglione inverts Cicero's procedure: where the latter begins with the historical event and only later comments on it generally, the former begins with a general reflection and then narrates the deaths of his three fellow courtiers from Urbino, a narrative which provides examples illustrative of the generalization with which he began. Moreover, where Cicero speaks of murders, massacres, and assassinations, thus seeing the deaths of his protagonists as the work of human agents involved in history, Castiglione characteristically speaks simply of death itself or imagines his fellow courtiers succumbing to the hostile, universal force he calls fortune. In essence, Cicero contemplates a historical vision of Roman patricians engaged together in a tragic struggle for the survival of the state. By contrast, having been deprived by death of the human community he once knew at Urbino, Castiglione envisions a universe of individuals, each fighting essentially alone against the impersonal forces of time, fortune, and death, for the sake of personal survival and personal dignity.

Although Castiglione does not share either the pastoral poet's complacency or Cicero's historical vision, it might be expected that, faced with the horror of death and the chaos it makes of human life, he would turn to Christianity, just as Milton did in *Lycidas,* and seek in the order of an eternal, heavenly existence some compensation for the inadequacies of this earthly one. In fact, such a compensation must have suggested itself to Castiglione in his life, for he was a serious, pious Christian whose decision to take holy orders in 1521 testifies to the depth of his religious concern.[26] Nevertheless, in response to the horrors of death, nowhere in *Il Cortegiano* does he hold out clearly the possibility of Christian redemption.[27] Strikingly, in his vision of the human condition as a frail bark helpless before the destructive storms of fortune, he actually constructs a sort of Christian commonplace *manqué*. In a fully Christian version of the commonplace, man may be buffeted about by the storms of time and fortune, but he also has a sure port in heaven toward which he can successfully steer his course. In the first passage where Castiglione develops this image (II, 1, 189), the only port mentioned is the one left behind at the journey's beginning, and in the second (IV, 1, 445), while he does speak of a port to which man attempts to sail, the context makes it clear that that port is an earthly harbor of material success and worldly fame. In neither case is there any hint of a pious hope that heaven awaits man as his true port, a secure haven after the storms and sufferings of his earthly journey. To be sure, Castiglione's passages do not specifically exclude Christian readings, and there is every reason to believe that the man who was awarded the bishopric of Ávila would approve pious interpretations. Nevertheless, he completely refrains from inviting them himself, and throughout *Il Cortegiano* he presents a stark and tragic vision of the human condition which renders his nostalgia for the vanished Arcadia of Urbino all the more poignant and understandable.[28]

In response to the horror of death, which swallowed up all of Urbino's gentle shepherds and shepherdesses, Castiglione does more than simply yearn nostalgically for the happy, innocent world from which he has been cut off definitively. As he contemplates his Arcadian landscape littered with the tombstones of those he loved so well, he does what he did when Falcone, the friend of his youth, died: he sets out to write an elegy, to compose a fitting and enduring memorial for the dead. Rather than brood passively and helplessly about the past, Castiglione is spurred into action by his recollections, and like Cicero in the *De Oratore*, he recreates the vanished world of the past, making his book into a monument for those who left behind them few traces of their earthly passage.[29] Castiglione would save his friends from the ultimate anonymity of *mortal oblivione* (III, 1, 336), from remaining nameless and unremembered throughout the brief duration of human history. Like that greater master of nostalgia, Marcel Proust, Castiglione also turns to art, not religion, in his attempt to recapture lost time, to resurrect a dead past, and to achieve for himself, perhaps, a momentary intimation of immortality. Cast into a solitary universe of death, the nostalgic courtier engages himself and his art in a heroic struggle to create a sense of meaning, justice, and order in life which untimely death has denied. In this desperate battle against the forces of time and fortune, only art has a chance of prevailing. Even so, there can be no real certainty of success in Castiglione's enterprise, only the hope beyond hope that he can transform the painful recollection of his vanished past into the enduring memorial of his art.

4/ Un Ballo in Maschera

At a critical turning point towards the end of Book II, when the discussions of that evening are drawing to a close and the selection of a new speaker for the next evening has not yet been made, Castiglione interrupts the conversation with a delightful bit of action. Before it occurs, Bernardo Bibbiena has already turned from telling jokes to defending women against the attacks of the group's leading misogynist, Gasparo Pallavicino. Noticing that the ladies sit silently while the men debate about them, Bibbiena seizes the opportunity to free himself from the speaker's role by egging the ladies on to assume the burden of their own defense. He slyly interprets their silence as a sign that they do not care whether anyone insults them, and in reply to his taunt, they make a surprising and effective physical gesture.

> Allora una gran parte di quelle donne, ben per averle la signora Duchessa fatto così cenno, si levarono in piedi e ridendo tutte corsero verso il signor Gasparo, come per dargli delle busse, e farne come le Baccanti d'Orfeo, tuttavia dicendo:—Ora vedrete, se ci curiamo che di noi si dica male.
>
> (II, 96, 328)

> Then, at a sign from the Duchess, many of the ladies rose to their feet and all rushed laughing upon signor Gasparo as if to assail him with blows and treat him as the bacchantes treated Orpheus, saying the while: "Now you shall see whether we care if we are slandered."
>
> (193–94)

By no means intimidating signor Gasparo, this unexpected bit of action serves a useful, dramatic function: it rouses courtiers—and readers—from any lethargy that Bibbiena's lengthy series of jokes may have induced, and it intensifies the debate on women,

117

which continues for the few remaining paragraphs of Book II and which the duchess then selects as the principal subject for the next evening.

> Così, tra per le risa, tra per lo levarsi ognun in piedi, parve che 'l sonno, il quale omai occupava gli occhi e l'animo d'alcuni, si partisse; ma il signor Gasparo cominciò a dire: —Eccovi che per non aver ragione voglion valersi della forza ed a questo modo finire il ragionamento, dandoci, come si sol dire, una licenzia braccesca.
>
> (II, 97, 329)

> Thus, partly because of the laughter and partly because all had risen to their feet, the drowsiness which by now was in the eyes and mind of some seemed to be dispelled; but signor Gasparo began to say: "You see that because they are in the wrong, they wish to resort to force and end the discussion in this way by giving us a Braccesque leave, as the saying goes."
>
> (194)

Yet if the ladies' clever gesture startles everyone awake, it no more offends the other members of the group than it offended Gasparo, and all admire it as a decorous, witty action.

The ladies' preservation of decorum becomes all the more striking when their action is contrasted with the only other incident occurring in Castiglione's work in which someone rises up from his seat before the duchess has officially terminated the discussions for the evening. That other incident takes place in Book I toward the end of the debate on language. Consistently frustrated in his attempt to defend his views and ordered by Emilia Pia to end a discussion long since grown tiresome, Federico Fregoso cannot repress a desire to make a final reply to his opponent, and he creates an embarrassing situation by rising up out of his seat in order to speak.[1] Although merely to continue the debate would have appeared indecorous in itself, Federico's standing while everyone else remains seated magnifies his faux pas. His intended reply is immediately cut off by Emilia, who commands again that they stop debating and tactfully turns everyone's attention back to the subject of the ideal courtier, which the debate on language interrupted some time before. While the reader cannot know what happened to Federico, he can assume that the unfortunate fellow had sufficient savoir faire not to remain on his feet, making an unseemly spectacle of himself, but that he took advantage of Emilia's redirection of the conversation in order to sit down as quickly and inconspicuously as possible. By contrast, there is absolutely no embarrassment when Castiglione's "bacchantes" rise up from their seats in order to feign an attack on Gasparo. Their gesture is initiated by a nod from the duchess, who generally promulgates the standards of decorum for the group and would never encourage anything unseemly, while Gasparo interprets the simulated attack as just another move in the debate about women and replies to it with a witty rejoinder. Consequently, where Federico appears a bit ridiculous in standing up, the ladies' action is an example of the witty, decorous behavior that has led so many to sing the praises of Castiglione's Urbino.

While the ladies' action may appear both clever and appropriate, explaining why they behave that way and how their action can be both wittily surprising and socially decorous involves quite complex questions concerning the dynamics of social life at Urbino. In the first place, their behavior not only contains unmistakable aggression, but Castiglione underlines its aggressiveness by comparing his tender *donne di palazzo* to the ferocious bacchantes who dismembered Orpheus. Both their action itself and Castiglione's description of it explicitly confirm his awareness of human aggression but simultaneously raise questions both about the character of his awareness and about the role aggression plays generally in the operations of Urbino's ideal society. Secondly, though its aggressive character is apparent to author and reader, the ladies' simulated attack on Gasparo is neither intended nor perceived as an expression of genuine hostility and hatred; perfectly decorous, it does not create social tensions that disrupt the flow of courtly life. But exactly how does Castiglione's ideal society avoid those dangers? How do the men and women of Urbino deal successfully with aggression that could potentially produce embarrassment, tension, and disruptive conflict? To answer all these questions about aggression and the social mechanisms used to handle it is to illuminate the basic paradox that distinguishes Castiglione's society from the ideal worlds of contemporaries like More, Erasmus, and Rabelais. It is to understand how laughing bacchantes and combative misogynists can live together with genuine harmony in Urbino's house of mirth, or, as Castiglione himself calls it, "il proprio albergo della allegria" (I, 4, 85).

The pages of *Il Cortegiano* repeatedly document its author's awareness of human aggressiveness. At one point, he declares that

119

men are more willing to censure the errors of others than to praise things well done (II, 7, 198), and, at others, he stresses the unprovoked slander and gossip to which women are exposed, especially if it is known that they are in love (III, 4, 341–42; III, 43, 397–99). As a result of the envy and malice, which it is assumed will be directed even at the ideal courtier, many aspects of his dress and behavior are described as though they were defensive weapons. For instance, a prominent justification for his chief virtue, *mediocrità*, or moderation, is that it functions as a shield against envy (II, 41, 254: "grandissimo e fermissimo scudo contra la invidia"). In all these cases, Castiglione and his spokesmen point directly at the basic hostility and totally unprovoked malice that seem to characterize all human intercourse. They agree heartily with their contemporary, Machiavelli, that man's nature predisposes him to transform human life into continual war.

While Castiglione chooses to focus his dialogue exclusively on Urbino as an ideal society exemplary for its social harmony, peace, and freedom, this decision does not imply that he naively thought the rest of contemporary Italian civilization was equally ideal. In fact, without drawing attention away from his ideal court or diminishing the brilliance of its image, he does manage to tuck into the less conspicuous corners of his book a few reminders of the grim realities outside Urbino's protecting walls. The stories in Book III, for instance, which celebrate women's courage and virtue, include a few that document the existence of violence, rape, and murder in contemporary Italian society (III, 47, 404–5; III, 48, 406). His characters' intermittent lament over the "Italian wars" and the invasion of Italy by "barbarians" also underscores a most unpleasant reality (I, 2, 82; I, 32, 136–37; II, 26, 230–31; IV, 4, 450). Moreover, when Calmeta insists that only presumptuous, wicked courtiers succeed in contemporary courts, Federico Fregoso's qualified reply, that not all princes are so stupid or evil as to reward such men, really seems to support Calmeta's—and Castiglione's—low estimation of the age (II, 21–22, 222–24). Finally, in the prologue to Book II, when Castiglione defends Urbino from the attacks of old men and implicitly from all those critics who throughout the Renaissance condemned the miseries of life at court, he begins by actually endorsing their condemnation of his age.

> In somma riprendono infinite cose, tra le quali molte
> veramente meritano riprensione, perché non si po dir che
> tra noi non siano molti mali omini e scelerati, e che questa

età nostra non sia assai più copiosa di vicii che quella che
essi laudano.

(II, 2, 191)

In short, they censure a multitude of things, among which
there are many actually deserving of censure, for it cannot
be denied that there are many evil and wicked men
among us, or that our times abound much more in vices
than the times they praise.

(92)

In short, Castiglione and his characters seem to share Benvenuto
Cellini's unblinking vision: they live in an age dominated by constant rivalry, lawless violence, and brutal aggression.

Nevertheless, Castiglione's view of his world is rather more balanced than are those of Machiavelli, Guicciardini, and Cellini.
Thus he continues the passage cited above, explaining that good
and evil, civilization and aggression, are really inseparable in the
world, and that they balance one another precisely, increasing
together or decreasing together according to the changing levels
of vitality animating a culture. If the ancient world possessed
more than human talents and totally divine virtues, it also necessarily contained vicious men who would surpass in evil anything
the present could produce. Similarly, Castiglione argues, like
many contemporary and modern commentators, that the brilliant
civilization of Urbino and other Renaissance Italian courts is
matched by the manifest evils of the age (II, 2, 191–92). In fact,
through his presentation of Urbino's model society, Castiglione
will show that its elegant civilization and aggression are inextricably intertwined.

Set against a backdrop of war, destruction, cut-throat competition, and unprovoked malice, Urbino seems indeed the very
house of mirth. Free from hatred, jealousy, and personal animos-
ity, the court resounds with the continual laughter of its "amata e
cara compagnia," who behave like affectionate brothers and sis-
ters, united to one another as well as to the duchess by a chain of
love (I, 4, 85–86). Although they may all have definite political
and military involvements in the grim world outside their castle
walls, within those walls life passes merrily on amidst dancing,
singing, conversation, and games. Yet while Urbino is blessedly
free from violence and the more destructive manifestations of
aggression, it is hardly a garden of innocence from which human
aggressiveness has magically disappeared. To be sure, the lion

does not devour the lamb in Castiglione's house of mirth, but that does not mean they will lie down together. Rather, in the sophisticated, cultured world of Urbino, lions and lambs restrict their aggression to roaring and bleating, and if they refrain from attacking one another with tooth and claw, their mockery, sarcasm, and witty debate are, in their own terms, exceptionally "biting."[2]

Il Libro del Cortegiano is filled with verbal aggression, which is most directly apparent in the constant teasing and mockery the courtiers and ladies direct at one another. Morella da Ortona, a lusty old man who feels he still possesses youthful vitality, is twitted at one point for trying to look young by using cosmetics and at another for being something of an incontinent old lecher (II, 14, 212; IV, 55, 520). The marchese Febus da Ceva from the Piedmont, who had spent much time in France, must bear the brunt of jokes about the French (II, 37, 248–49). Bibbiena twists Emilia's last name around so that she becomes "Emilia Impia" (II, 61, 280). And when Emilia chooses Ludovico da Canossa as the first to present his ideas concerning the ideal courtier, she indulges in a bit of mockery by explaining that she chooses the count only so that everyone else will be moved to speak in order to correct what he says (I, 13, 101). What is more, neither the count nor any other character sits idly by while being mocked without attempting some sort of witty reply to his attacker, just as Gasparo, set upon by the bacchantes, fires back the stinging retort, his verbal equivalent of the ladies' simulated physical aggression.

Witty repartée is not, however, the only form verbal aggression assumes at Urbino, for it also manifests itself consistently in exhibitionistic self-display. Though held together by a chain of love, the courtiers and ladies are not expected to behave as though they were merely interchangeable links. Every individual is allowed—in fact, expected—to display his knowledge and judgment as he expounds his point of view and dominates the conversation for a given period. Implicitly, such dominance could be interpreted as a matter of aggression directed at all the others, and there is no question but that it involves rivalry as each man strives to speak so eloquently that he matches the courtly ideal of the group. Sometimes the charge to speak actually comes as a direct challenge to the speaker, as when, at the end of Book III, the duchess orders Ottaviano to justify taking up the subject of the ideal courtier again by making him even more perfect than others have made him (III, 77, 442). Moreover, while a single individual may be allowed his moment of glory at the center of the group's attention, the competitive character of such a procedure is underscored by having all the others function not as passive listeners, but as active participants in his performance. They are expected to question, challenge, and disagree with the speaker, an arrangement Emilia Pia explicitly endorses when she justifies her choice of Count Ludovico as the first to speak.

The courtiers' sacred right to question and challenge one another leads to the other most explicit form that aggression assumes in Castiglione's book—debate. Count Ludovico has hardly spent two minutes explaining his conception of the ideal courtier when Gasparo Pallavicino objects to his requiring noble birth for the ideal, thus opening the first of countless debates which are still in progress as Castiglione's work comes to an end. Countering the monotony that might result from uninterrupted exposition, debates spring up every few pages on every conceivable topic: arms and letters, painting and sculpture, the importance of dress, the superiority of monarchy as a form of government. The longest digression in the work consists of the debate on language in Book I, and argument totally dominates the third book. Only when Bibbiena and others tell jokes during the second half of Book II and when Bembo flies off into Neoplatonic rapture at the end of Book IV does debate disappear into the harmless, enjoyable exhibitionism of the comic entertainer and inspired orator. Moreover, when caught up in a clash of views, far from presenting their arguments as cool, disinterested, dispassionate analyses, the courtiers mingle the aggression of repartée with the aggression of debate, repeatedly descending to oblique, never really savage, but always biting, arguments ad hominem directed at their opponents. Ludovico, defending a universal Italian language, mocks Federico indirectly by ridiculing those who make a religion out of speaking and writing the Tuscan dialect and who thus sound affected and unnatural even to a Tuscan (I, 37, 150). Gasparo explains the Magnifico's intellectual arguments in defense of women as merely an attempt to ingratiate himself through flattery with the women present (III, 11, 351). Even the ladies are not above ridiculing their opponents by attributing their misogynism to lack of success with the fair sex (II, 69, 292; II, 92, 323).

The recognition that repartée and wit, exhibitionism, and debate constitute forms of aggression may seem particularly "modern," but Castiglione shared this insight. First, while Bibbiena's analysis of wit and jokes explains that humor derives from incongruity and the unexpected, his insistent description of wit as "biting" or "stabbing" focuses unmistakably on its aggressive character (e.g., II, 66, 289; II, 80, 305). In fact, he recognizes its

123

aggressive character so well that he inserts repeated cautions about the dangers of directing it at certain people or institutions (II, 46, 262; II, 50, 268). When delivering brief gibes and witty remarks, declares Bibbiena,

> devesi guardare il cortegiano di non parer maligno e velenoso, e dir motti ed arguzie solamente per far dispetto e dar nel core; perché tali omini spesso per diffetto della lingua meritamente hanno castigo in tutto 'l corpo.
>
> (II, 57, 277)

> the Courtier must take care not to appear malicious and spiteful, and not to utter witticisms and *arguzie* solely to annoy and hurt; because such men often suffer deservedly in all their person for the sins of their tongue.
>
> (157)

Secondly, Castiglione's courtiers show an awareness of the aggression contained in debate by referring to it in terms of knightly combat and warfare as well as in terms of litigation.[3] Finally, there is one passage that underscores the element of personal competition involved in conversation at Urbino by contrasting it with the much less competitive, more relaxing activity of dancing. At the end of Book I, when the discussions have effectively reached a conclusion, Calmeta declares:

> Signori, poiché l'ora è tarda, acciò che messer Federico non abbia escusazione alcuna di non dir ciò che sa, credo che sia bono differire il resto del ragionamento a domani; e questo poco tempo che ci avanza si dispensi in *qualche altro piacer senza ambizione.*
>
> (I, 56, 184; my italics)

> Gentlemen, since the hour is late and in order to give messer Federico no excuse not to say what he knows, I believe it's a good idea to defer the rest of our talk to tomorrow and to spend the little time remaining in *some other pleasure free from ambition.*
>
> (my translation)

In this context, *ambizione* means desire for success and personal glory, and it implies rivalry and competition; it identifies a tension of will and intellect which is animated by each person's strong, aggressive drives as he seeks to distinguish himself from his equally talented and aggressive peers. Federico Fregoso remarks on the next evening that *ambizione* presents especially grave problems for the ideal courtier, since it often prevents him from recognizing the errors in behavior and judgment he is making (II, 6, 197). If Castiglione's courtiers see *ambizione* as a powerful drive in their ideal, surely they share Calmeta's awareness of it as the force animating them and their discussions.

The most extensive display of competiton and rivalry in Castiglione's book occurs in the recurrent debate concerning the nature, place, and value of women. It is the only debate that is not considered a digression from the main subject being presented; and where all the other arguments tend to be brief and to occupy just a small portion of a single evening, this one surfaces in every book and consumes the third in its entirety. Its opening shots are heard at the very start of Book I, as Emilia slyly selects her old antagonist Gasparo to propose the first game, and he accepts the assignment while muttering a complaint about how women always seem to escape hard work (I, 6–7, 89–90). More volleys fly back and forth during the second evening as Gasparo continues to make disparaging comments about women (II, 35, 244–45; II, 69, 292). Finally, a full-scale battle erupts at the end of Book II, raging on until the end of the next one, and pitting the misogynists Gasparo, Ottaviano, and Niccolò Frisio against the ladies and their champions, Cesare Gonzaga and the Magnifico, Giuliano de' Medici. Even in Book IV Gasparo cannot refrain from making at least one misogynistic comment in passing (IV, 30, 485), and Ottaviano's presentation of his ideal courtier can be interpreted as an attempt to justify his own misogynism. Finally, in the last pages of his work, Castiglione heavily underscores the centrality of this subject for the on-going life of his society. Instead of ending the book on the high note of Bembo's speech or the courtiers' discovery that a magnificent day has dawned, he allows Gasparo to reintroduce his favorite topic by means of one last disparaging remark. Castiglione then concludes *The Courtier* inconclusively, as Emilia Pia's final challenge to her enemy anticipates renewed skirmishing on the next evening—and on countless evenings after that.

The debate about women stands out from all the others not only because of its extensive development in Book III and its insistent intrusion into the discussions of every evening, but for two other reasons as well. First, Emilia Pia and the duchess, the women's chief representatives in the group, assume a relatively active, participatory role in it. During all the other discussions, they sit in fairly passive attitudes while the men talk, and they intrude only to terminate boring digressions and to restrain the men from indecorous behavior. In the debate on women, which affects them directly, they intervene frequently, mocking their attackers and urging their defenders on to ever greater efforts. The debate is nothing less than war between the sexes, and to emphasize its difference from all the other debates, Castiglione uses a special set of metaphors to label it and define its singularly aggressive character. Essentially, his characters view their debate as a chivalric combat in which misogynists are tagged the "enemies" of women and the Magnifico is summoned as a knight to defend women's honor by defeating their opponents. These metaphors do not originate with Castiglione; they have a long history in connection with the *questioni d'amore*, often sophistical debates about love and the relationship between the sexes which formed the staple of conversation in courtly society during the High Middle Ages and the Renaissance.[4] Castiglione departs from the tradition by strikingly shifting the debate away from the intricate problems of love relationships and aiming it at the more fundamental question that underlay those other debates, that of women's nature, place, and value. As a result of this shift, his debate on women receives yet more emphasis, and its central importance in *The Book of the Courtier,* where it is second only to the question of the ideal courtier, is well established indeed.

Although Castiglione clearly sides with the Magnifico and Cesare Gonzaga in their defense of women, since he hands them arguments sufficient to defeat their opponents at every turn, nevertheless, by giving so much prominence to these debates, he betrays a definite concern with the questions they raise. He reveals a seeming nervousness about the particular role women play in courtly society, for while he might judge the misogynists' reaction perverse, he does subtly support them at times. For instance, he gains sympathy for them by placing them in an unfair situation in which those they attack, namely Emilia and the duchess, are also vested with the authority to command and judge their attackers. Moreover, Gasparo tells the Magnifico not to use technical terms lest the ladies fail to understand their debate, and just two pages or so later Emilia interrupts them to protest against this use of technical language, thus seeming to confirm the misogynists' low evaluation of women's intellectual ability (III, 15, 356; III, 17, 358). But the most important indication that Castiglione takes the misogynists' attacks seriously and does not insert them simply to liven up the discussions is that he allows the reader to relate those attacks directly to the inversion of traditional social roles at the court of Urbino. However much the misogynists may suffer from a perverse view of women, their opinions rest upon a clear perception of the social order operative during their discussions, and their arguments can thus be interpreted as a real protest against what they see as a flagrant violation, an inversion, of the normal hierarchy of their world. The simple fact is that women, not men, rule the court of Urbino in Castiglione's book, from which the leading male figure, Duke Guidobaldo, is conspicuously absent. In the real world of Italian Renaissance society and in the real world of Urbino, such an inversion must have occurred only on the most purely social occasions and even then only to a limited extent. Castiglione, however, chooses to focus his *Cortegiano* exclusively on the leisure activities of the court and to present it as though women really played the exalted roles that several centuries of courtly literature had granted them. In a sense, he gives concreteness and reality to what was for the most part only an intellectual and artistic ideal in Renaissance society, and he displays his awareness of the antagonism that many in his male-dominated culture must have felt toward this ideal, not only by including his misogynists' persistent, vehement complaints, but by granting them a limited respectabiltiy and an unmistakable foundation in realtiy.

The substance of the misogynists' arguments is quite conventional: women are the irrational daughters of Eve; they are led by passion, appetite, and their bodily needs; they have less strength, courage, and virtue than men (e.g., III, 19, 362; III, 28, 376; III, 37, 390; III, 39, 392). Yet as the misogynists, and particularly Gasparo, trumpet these banalities, their speech betrays an underlying emotion quite distant from self-confidence. Especially as the battle begins in earnest at the end of Book II, they see themselves in a defensive position and deliver their statements with a querulous tone. Rather than beginning with an attack, Gasparo's opening shot is a protest against Bibbiena for being too partial to women and unfair to men. Why, he asks, should men be expected to show more respect to women and refrain from joking about them when the same consideration is not extended to men (II, 90, 321–22)? A little later, Gasparo again complains that women are being favored over men, that the Magnifico wants them to rule cities in place of men, and that their real desire is to become men themselves (II, 92, 323; III, 10, 349–50; III, 15, 356–57). It seems clear that Gasparo's and the other misogynists' hostility to women is motivated less by a confidence in the male's continuing supremacy than by a desperate urgency to fight what seems a losing battle. Where women rule and men acquiesce in such an inversion of traditional social roles, Gasparo and his fellows would understandably feel on the defensive. While they may tolerate that inversion at Urbino as an exceptional instance, they clearly feel frustration and resentment because of it and express their feelings in the aggressive attacks they make on women generally. Rather than court and worship women as the other men do, they seek to destroy the thrones from which Emilia Pia and the duchess rule over them with absolute, and even arbitrary, tyrannical, authority.[5] But as long as they can only attack women generally and are restrained by their social positions as guests and retainers at the court of Urbino from launching out directly at those particular women who rule over them, they inevitably fall short of success. Smoldering with frustration, they inevitably and repeatedly blaze up, expressing their antagonism in antifeminist gibes and provocative debates.

The misogynists' hostile rection to women's social power also reveals a definite fear of female sexuality. If women are considered inferior because they are more irrational, passionate, and carnal than men, they are also dangerous for the same reasons. Note how they are denounced as lecherous Eves and emasculating Cleopatras whose sexual powers allow them to enslave their weak, male prey (III, 19, 362; III, 37, 390). For Gasparo especially, love is synonymous with the loss of male dignity and autonomy (III, 64, 427–28). In fact, he and the other misogynists betray something close to paranoia when they interpret their opponents' claims for women's equality as claims for superiority (e.g., III, 21, 366). As the debate progresses through Book III, this paranoia almost seems justified when the Magnifico and Cesare turn equality into superiority and exalt ideals as idols (III, 51–52, 410–13).[6] In response, Gasparo burns silently as the others discuss the proper sort of courtly love and then explodes suddenly and unexpectedly in a denunciation remarkable for its fearful magnification of women's sexual power over men. Women, he cries,

> . . . procurano quanto più possono d'aver gran numero d'innamorati e tutti, se possibil fosse, vorriano che ardessero e, fatti cenere, dopo morte tornassero vivi per morir un'altra volta; e benché esse ancor amino, pur godeno del tormento degli amanti, perché estimano che 'l dolore, le afflizioni e 'l chiamar ognor la morte, sia il vero testimonio che esse siano amate, e possano con la loro bellezza far gli omini miseri e beati e dargli morte e vita come lor piace;

onde di questo solo cibo se pascono e tanto avide ne sono, che acciò che non manchi loro, non contentano né disperano mai gli amanti del tutto; ma per mantenergli continuamente nelli affanni e nel desiderio usano una certa imperiosa austerità di minacce mescolate con speranza, e vogliono che una loro parola, uno sguardo, un cenno sia da essi riputato per somma felicità. . . .

(III, 74, 438–39)

. . . seek to have as many lovers as they can and would have all of them burn (were that possible) and, once they were in ashes and dead, would have them alive again so that they might die a second time. And even though they are in love, still they relish the torment of their lover, because they think that pain and afflictions and the constant invocation of death is the true sign that they are loved, and that by their beauty they can make men miserable or happy, and bestow life and death upon them as they choose. Hence, they feed only on this food, and are so greedy of it that in order not to be without it they neither content their lovers nor reduce them to utter despair; but, in order to keep them continually in worries and in desire, they resort to a certain domineering austerity in the form of threats mingled with hope, and expect a word of theirs, a look, a nod, to be deemed the highest happiness. . . .

(278–79)

In Gasparo's imagination women become demonic, vampire-like creatures who suck the life out of their victims without totally killing them, reducing them to a pleasureless life-in-death.[7] This long and remarkably savage outburst terminates the debate on women in the third book and prompts Ottaviano to urge moderation on all sides as he changes the subject back to the question of the ideal courtier. But Gasparo's extreme statement nevertheless reveals most strikingly the sexual fear of emasculation that lies behind his, and perhaps the others', hostility toward women. In light of this fear, the image Castiglione used for his ladies at the end of Book II acquires a new resonance: for the paranoid misogynists, women really do seem a group of raving bacchantes ready to descend upon the hapless Orpheus and tear him apart.

While the misogynists' attacks can be explained as hostile reactions to sexual and social inversions, they can also be interpreted as hostile reactions to civilization itself. Even more than most societies, the courtly world of the High Renaissance purchased its civilization at the price of personal restraint and limitation.[8] Although it granted the individual a right to self-expression, it restricted the sphere in which his self-expression could operate, excluding profoundly personal, emotional, and even intellectual experience from its bounds. Soaring passions, deeply probing philosophies, the excesses of both vulgar and exalted human experience had no place in High Renaissance society, and they have no place in Castiglione's Urbino, which seems even more insistent than the real courts of its day upon limiting the range of forms its inhabitants' self-expression could assume. To be sure, such limitation does permit an infinite refinement of sensibility and subtlety of expression; it allows for the delicacy and precise control of a Raphael. But as it excludes the ugly, the grotesque, the explosive, and the unrestrained, it also excludes the excitement and fervor of a Tintoretto. Moreover, Urbino also places outside its bounds most of the serious, practical activities important for everyday life in the Renaissance. Thus although the ideal courtier and many of Castiglione's characters consider arms their principal profession, throughout four nights of discussion there is scarcely a word concerning how one handles weapons. Castiglione and his spokesmen show the reader how to court his peers and superiors, not how to lead an army, manage a treasury, or administer a town. The courtiers at Urbino are thus bound by two sorts of limitation and potentially suffer a double frustration. First, because their sphere of action is greatly reduced at court, they cannot engage in the activities that traditionally provide men in their society with a sense of identity. They can behave as knights only metaphorically, and as long as they are engaged in courtly games like those depicted in *Il Cortegiano* they neither rule states nor make policy. Secondly, the rules of their games, enforced by the duchess and Emilia Pia, limit their range of emotional expression and intellectual exploration. They can continue debates only to a certain point; they cannot criticize friars; they ultimately do not control the very discussions they are nevertheless expected to carry on. Women can readily serve as symbols for both forms of limitation, since they establish and enforce the rules of social intercourse, and, what is more, since their ardent champions explicitly identify them as the source and hence the symbol of civilization (III, 51–52, 410–13). While most of Urbino's inhabitants must find that the controlled intensity and subtle refinement of their experience justify such limitation, it is understandable that some men would

bridle at it and would direct their hostility at the women supposedly responsible for the very civilization they resent.

Hostility between women and their attackers is just one more
facet of the aggression which, in one form or another, is the rule,
not the exception, in Castiglione's ideal society. Yet, its presence
does not mean squabbling, vituperation, or jealous vendettas, for in
Urbino at least, aggression proves itself compatible with social
peace and harmony. In part, this accomplishment is due to the
personal qualities of the court's inhabitants; it offers eloquent testimony to Castiglione's belief that at least some human beings can be
trained to cooperate in order to create a viable, humane civilization. Just as important as individual self-control and good will,
however, are the particular social mechanisms and processes that
Castiglione's courtiers and ladies use, not to eliminate potentially
destructive aggression, but to tame it and harness its energies so
that they animate conversation and do the constructive work of
civilization. As much as the superiority of its people, what raises
Urbino above other societies is its inhabitants' maintenance of a
high level of controlled, sublimated aggression, which is responsible for the exuberant wit, the vigorous intellectual interaction,
and the constant hilarity that make their court a model civilization.

While Castiglione agrees with Machiavelli that human beings
are intensely aggressive creatures, he shares neither his great contemporary's scorn for them nor that Machiavellian pessimism that
refuses to believe men capable of sustained cooperation or humane concern for one another and the common good.[9] At his
most negative, Castiglione has his characters condemn men's totally unprovoked, malicious slander of women, but generally,
even where he detects "una certa innata malignità" (II, 7, 198: "a
kind of innate malice"[97]) in human beings, he speaks of it in
matter-of-fact tones, without bitterness or anger. He simply identifies man's promptness to blame others sooner than praise them
as an aspect of reality which must be accepted and which he
accepts without grave complaints. Castiglione does not lose faith
in man because his fallen character makes him prone to evil.
Quite the contrary, he maintains a firm optimism that even the
worst men can be led to behave decently. Thus although women
are frequently slandered without reason, he feels that because
they can control the impression they make on others, "non è omo
tanto procace ed insolente, che non abbia riverenzia a quelle che
sono estimate bone ed oneste" (III, 5, 344: "there is no man so
profligate and so forward as not to have reverence for those
women who are esteemed to be good and virtuous"[208]). Messer

131

Niccolò might condemn such optimism as naive, but Castiglione advocates a more balanced position: if men feel aggression, they can also be socialized to respond to other emotions and commitments of a more elevated character. From observing men's behavior, he concludes that such socialization is relatively effective, at least as a check on vicious tendencies. Consequently, he does not fear to construct his ideal society partially upon his faith that most men can be so trained that they will want to behave in a moral, socially correct, and humane manner, and that at least some of them will be able to consistently achieve such a behavioral goal.

The most direct expression of Castiglione's optimism about human beings occurs in Ottaviano's redefinition of the ideal courtier in Book IV. Like many humanist educators, Ottaviano assumes that most children are morally neutral at birth, and that because they are malleable and capable of training, they can reach great heights of physical, intellectual, and moral development.[10] Even though the courtiers wonder whether virtues are innate or acquired, in either case they implicitly accept the possibility of man's potential for moral improvement. Similarly, Bembo's Neoplatonic doctrines assume that man is mutable and capable of self-development through discipline and learning. Finally, the very fact that Castiglione writes his book argues for a positive assessment of human potential; the ideal courtier may be a moral superman, and no individual may rise to his heights, but certainly many men can be taught to shoot their arrows close to such a mark (see *Letter*, 3, 77).

Because Machiavelli feels a profound pessimism about men and their boundless, unquenchable desires, he concludes that their normal condition is the scramble of a free-for-all. He accounts for the emergence of civilization by something like the contract theory, which Hobbes would consciously formulate more than a century later: in order to escape the constant warfare of his natural state, man cedes a certain amount of his power to others in exchange for guarantees of security and protection, which permit him to enjoy his desires in relative peace. This situation is unstable, however, because man's desires are infinite, but at least it permits civilization to exist for limited periods of time.[11] In Castiglione's analysis, on the other hand, civilization wears a much more attractive face. As revealed in Urbino, it has both negative and positive features, both restraints and freely given cooperation, both laws and love. Because men are aggressive and often stupid and destructive, Urbino provides rules for social intercourse and arbiters who enforce them. But positive factors are just as important for the success of this society: tolerance, cooperation, mutual respect, and love. In *Il Principe* Machiavelli insists that the chain of love that links men together snaps apart at the slightest blow from self-interest or desire.[12] Castiglione, in contrast, believes that such chains can be forged to hold fast despite the worst buffetings they are exposed to and that men really are capable of loving their fathers more than their patrimonies, their friends and masters as much as themselves.[13]

Machiavelli might justly dismiss Castiglione as another one of those fuzzy-headed Utopians he condemns in *Il Principe*,[14] if the latter really believes that an enduring civilization could be founded upon love alone in the face of men's desires and aggression. But Castiglione clearly does not base his ideal society merely upon his belief in men's better impulses. Through the complex image of social life he creates in his book, he shows a definite relationship between its success as a civilization and the existence of certain social mechanisms that operate to minimize or eliminate the dangers posed by men's irrepressible aggression. Where Machiavelli sees aggression as a force that is profoundly opposed to civilization's laws and institutions and that will ultimately, inevitably, subvert them, Castiglione recognizes the existence of social processes by which civilization can control aggression's destructive potential. For Castiglione, these mechanisms include the stylization of social behavior, a certain kind of verbal exaggeration, and a striking use of laughter as an accompaniment for witticisms and repartée, mechanisms which do not destroy aggression but control it and utilize its energies by making it part of the game of life played at Urbino. Through these means, Castiglione's characters transform the ceaseless movement of social intercourse into graceful, decorous gestures of a perennially entertaining masked ball.

For social activity to be stylized, it must fulfill two conditions: it must fall into patterns which are recognizable and allow for repetition; and it must be structured to encourage symbolic rather than literal interpretation. To some extent all social life shows stylization in the thousands of formulaic gestures and statements used repeatedly when people address one another, take leave of one another, change the subject of conversation, and so on.[15] What distinguishes the group of courtiers and ladies at Urbino from other groups is the extensive amount of stylization that transforms their social life into a graceful dance from beginning to end. While Castiglione divides his work into four books and uses a large number of speakers partially in order to create variety and facilitate comprehension, his procedure also gives him ample means to establish the patterned, stylized nature of social life at Urbino. He tells the reader how the group meets each evening, "all'ora consueta . . . al solito loco" (III, 2, 337: "at the usual hour and place"[202]);[16] they always sit in the same circle of chairs, the men alternating with the women; and after their discussions they inevitably relax with dancing and singing. Moreover, when each speaker begins or finishes expounding his views, he repeats a series of stylized gestures, varied to suit his taste and the situation and to display his masterly ability to manipulate the formulas of politeness, but always having essentially the same basic form and function. This comprehensive stylization of behavior serves as a general counter-balance to the potential disruptiveness of aggression, for with every repeated gesture or phrase it symbolically reconfirms the social order. Stylization gives the group a sense of the continuity and stability of its mode of organization by structuring present activity in terms of a pattern which is derived from the group's past experience and which anticipates a hypothetical future. It provides the group with a visible means by which to symbolize and reassert its identity, giving it a sense of coherence every time its patterns are repeated.

Among the stylized patterns governing social life at Urbino, the most immediately striking ones, and the ones most useful in dealing directly with aggression, are the "deference rituals" employed by all of Castiglione's characters.[17] Throughout their speeches, they defer to one another by repeatedly declaring their ignorance and inadequacy and by constantly requesting relief from the burden of speaking, which they claim goes beyond their abilities.[18] Moreover, when Count Ludovico in Book I begins his exposition of the ideal courtier's qualities, he prefaces it by saying that he cannot fashion *the* ideal, merely *his* conception of it (I, 13, 102), and in Book III the Magnifico repeats this stylized formula as he claims only to advance *his* vision of the ideal *donna di palazzo* (III, 8, 347). In each case the speaker presents his opinion as nothing more than his opinion, not as the truth which other characters would be obliged to believe or reject. Thus he defers to them implicitly by refusing to claim a special authority or status for his views. Through such stylized gestures he courts their good will and blunts the aggression they may feel towards him.

The most notable, most consistently repeated, and yet most subtly varied deference ritual is that which each of Castiglione's major speakers uses as a preface before beginning to expound his views. The initial speaker in Book I, Ludovico da Canossa, establishes its two-stage pattern: first, he expresses his inadequacy to discuss the topic assigned and indicates his reluctance to speak; and then he agrees to do so, justifying his decision on the grounds that he does not wish to break the rules of the group or show disrespect to Emilia (I, 13, 101). Later that same evening, Federico Fregoso repeats in expanded form this two-stage pattern of refusal and acceptance. At first he expresses his reluctance to speak by praising the count and asking him to continue. In response, Emilia reiterates her command that Federico hold forth, and this time Federico acquiesces (I, 55, 183–84). Again, about midway in the discussions of the second evening, Bibbiena is asked to discuss wit and jokes. Faithful to the well-established pattern, he first tries to weasel his way out of the task assigned him by pointing to the lateness of the hour. Then, when the others protest, he agrees to speak, justifying his decision with a variation of the familiar formulas: although he claims to sit amidst a group of men and women as knowledgeable as he on the subject of humor, he will obey Emilia's command in order to give the others no excuse to refuse to carry out their own speaking assignments in the future (II, 45, 259–60). This same pattern also holds for the speakers of the third and fourth nights.[19] Thus, by using stylized gestures of deference throughout their speeches, Castiglione's characters deflect the hostility others might feel and continually reconfirm the value and order of the group.

These deference rituals communicate symbolically in a complex way. When Count Ludovico refuses to speak by claiming that he is not qualified to discuss the ideal courtier, he makes a statement that neither he nor the others believe is literally true. Likewise, Bembo and Bibbiena are recognized authorities on the subjects of Neoplatonism and humor, and their statements of insufficient competence cannot be intended as accurate self-appraisals. Not offered as assertions of fact, such statements really demand a symbolic interpretation; the individual affirms the value of the other members of the group through a symbolic act of self-humbling which is performed to compensate for his prominence as the major speaker before the group. Moreover, these stylized gestures of insufficiency also invite a complementary and equally symbolic response. When one person deprecates his own abilities, the others are expected to insist that he go ahead and speak. Thus they reaffirm his abilities and value, symbolically indicating that he does indeed deserve the special position granted him. In effect, the other members of the group raise up the deferential speaker with their praise, counter-balancing his act of self-humbling. The deferential person tells the others through his gestures not only that he respects them individually but also that he will behave conventionally, thus affirming the conventions of the group and putting his aggressive, exhibitionistic drives at its service. The group's positive response tells him that his act of deference is appreciated, and, by complementing it with their praise and acceptance, they balance his affirmation of the group with an affirmation of the individual himself.

To say that the activities of Castiglione's ideal society are stylized into repeated patterns is to say that his society is governed by rather elaborate, formalized sets of rules. Compared with most groups, the lords and ladies of Urbino are remarkably self-conscious about the rules governing their interaction; they consciously establish them at the start of the first evening, allude to them frequently throughout their discussions, and at times challenge and modify them. Although they never speak literally of "rules" or "regulations," they do refer to *la forma ordinata* (I, 15, 106) for their activities, which Emilia Pia established at the start and which they sometimes use as the ultimate justification for assuming the burden of speaking.[20] Their clearest acknowledgment that rules guide their social intercourse occurs when Cesare Gonzaga asks that they be changed.

> Certo . . . non si dovria già impedir il corso di questo ragionamento; ma, se io tacessi, non satisfarei alla libertà ch'io ho di parlare, né al desiderio di saper una cosa; e siami perdonato s'io, avendo a contradire, dimanderò; perché questo credo che mi sia licito, per esempio del nostro messer Bernardo, il quale per troppo voglia d'esser tenuto bell'omo, ha contrafatto alle leggi del nostro gioco, domandando e non contradicendo.
>
> (I, 23, 119–20)

> Certainly . . . no one ought to interrupt the course of this discussion; but if I were to remain silent, I should neither be exercising the privilege I have of speaking nor satisfying the desire I have of learning something. And I may be pardoned if I ask a question when I ought to be speaking in opposition; for I think this can be allowed me, after the example set by our messer Bernardo who, in his excessive desire to be thought handsome, has violated the laws of our game by asking instead of gainsaying.
>
> (39–40)

After some playful banter between Cesare, Emilia, and the duchess, he at last receives permission to ask a question rather than make a challenge. Thus his departure from the *leggi* governing social interaction actually reconfirms them as they widen out to embrace the new form of social intercourse he has introduced. Finally, a whole series of details—the formal establishment of Emilia Pia as the duchess's *locotenente* (I, 6, 90) with authority to enforce the rules, the courtiers' constant chiding of one another for going out of bounds (e.g., II, 42, 256; III, 4, 341), and their occasional, playful use of judicial and legal metaphors for their social activity (IV, 42, 500; IV, 73, 544)—all point to their consciousness of the rules they use to govern their social interaction.

In no case should Urbino's rules be thought of as rigid principles requiring mechanical obedience; Castiglione's courtiers are not mandarins in a decadent emperor's court. Though formal, consciously structured, and necessarily limited, their society can nevertheless embrace Bembo's impassioned monologue, Bibbiena's performance as a comic entertainer, intense debates on women and language, and fairly serious, straightforward, though not unchallenged views of the ideal courtier. While the rules prescribe that men and women sit in alternate seats around the circle, they may move to different chairs on different nights, and while the rules forbid interrupting a speaker in mid-sentence, they do permit many sorts of interruptions at the appropriate moment. Nor do Castiglione's courtiers allow themselves to be tyrannized by the rules: consciously aware of them, they use them and abuse them, manipulating them to suit their own ends. The rules of Urbino's society actually encourage each individual to give his speech the stamp of his personal style, while he nevertheless remains in harmony with the group, a participant in the brilliant dance of conversation, now lively and energetic, now slow and stately, which gives their social life order and coherence.

When Castiglione's courtiers speak of the rules governing their social life, they do so because they conceive of that social life fundamentally as a game. Castiglione himself labels it a game when he praises Urbino for the brilliance of the *giochi* he describes in his book (III, 1, 336). More importantly, his courtiers themselves repeatedly identify their social activity as a game which operates according to a prescribed form. Emilia Pia, for instance, begins the discussions the first night by making a game of designing new games to be played (I, 6, 89), and not only does Federico Fregoso label his proposal to fashion the ideal courtier a *gioco* (I, 12, 100), but Emilia employs the term repeatedly as she briefly outlines the rules by which that game is to proceed (I, 13, 101). Whenever the courtiers and ladies refer to the *leggi* governing conversation or speak of its *forma ordinata*, and whenever they consciously stylize their behavior, they effectively tell one another, "we are still playing our game."

Because in Urbino's society aggression operates continuously at a high level of intensity and manifests itself in a variety of forms ranging from the drives animating debate to the small eruptions of wit and repartée, that society makes use of other social mechanisms besides stylization both to avoid destructive hostility and to turn life into an elegant, civilized game. The first, less widely distributed mechanism involves the self-conscious exaggeration of metaphors indicating aggression that occurs whenever the debate on women flares up. Almost as though they recognize the issue's potential explosiveness, Castiglione's characters self-consciously employ the terms of chivalric combat, calling attention to the aggressive element involved in an exaggerated manner which thus helps to defuse it. The other technique used much more extensively to control aggression is the laughter with which the courtiers and ladies of Urbino preface and accompany their witty gibes and retorts. For instance, when Count Ludovico tries to define the ideal courtier's nonchalance by making a comparison with women's use of cosmetics, Costanza Fregoso laughs as she rebukes him for attacking the fair sex (I, 40, 154). Similarly, in Book IV the duchess laughs as she asks Morello da Ortona why an old man should seek love if it causes one to be so unhappy (IV, 55, 520), and at the end of Book II, when Castiglione's bacchantes rise up to attack Gasparo, they do so amidst gales of laughter. Moreover, laughter also accompanies those actions that single out one individual for preferential treatment, as when the duchess makes Emilia Pia her lieutenant and when Emilia selects Ludovico as the first speaker (I, 6, 90; I, 13, 101). As Castiglione's characters laugh whenever they make gestures that could be interpreted as aggression directed at other individuals, they make *Il Cortegiano* ring with the sounds of merriment from beginning to end.

The purpose of using exaggerated metaphors and of laughing as one makes a witty remark is to establish a "frame," to use Gregory Bateson's term, for the action or statement involved.[21] These techniques are related to what they accompany the way that a picture frame is related to a painting: it sets up bounds which separate the painting from the wall and identify it as a painting even if it is only a bit of string pasted to a piece of canvas. What is equally important, in doing so, the frame strictly structures the response that the perceiver will have to what he sees, telling him not only that he is looking at something intended to be taken as an art object, but that he should also respond to it in an appropriate fashion, that is, aesthetically. In the same way, exaggerated metaphors and laughter are frames in the sense that they provide interpretational signals to the perceiver, informing him that what he sees or hears should be interpreted in a certain way. In the first place, they limit his interpretation of the other's motives, telling him not to interpret the aggression involved as hostility or desire for personal preponderance at his own expense, but rather as a deferential wish simply to participate as a player in the game they have all been playing. Secondly, the interpretational signal structures and limits the perceiver's own reaction to what he has seen and heard. To reply with open hostility or resentment to what others do as they play the game is to become a spoilsport, to behave indecorously by refusing to obey the rules of the game when one's opponent has signaled that he does. In this situation, the perceiver's desire to please his audience is crucial, for while he may not share in the mirth obtained at his expense, the others' laughter effectively checks his potentially angry response by implicitly endorsing the way the game has been carried on. Fortunately, the victim of a joke need not sit there in frustrated silence; he retains the option of making a witty retort to his attacker, just as Gasparo responds to the bacchantes who have set upon him and just as all of Castiglione's characters do continuously. The rules of the game played at Urbino encourage this sort of quid pro quo exchange, and the members of Castiglione's society are sufficiently good diplomats to remain satisfied with the simplified form of justice involved.

While metaphorical exaggeration and laughter neutralize the potential danger of social disharmony that might result from displays of aggression, smiles and laughter are also the typical response to those displays and testify to the high level of satisfaction everyone, except perhaps the victim of a joke or the loser of a particular debate, receives from them. Freud's analysis of wit and jokes suggests one reason for this satisfaction.[22] Like Castiglione, Freud assumes that men possess powerful aggressive and exhibitionistic tendencies, and he demonstrates convincingly that those tendencies are expressed in the jokes they tell. In those jokes and witty remarks, however, the aggressive impulse does not appear in its pure form but is distorted in an instantaneous, unconscious process which disguises or masks it. These disguises assume many forms as they render the aggressive or exhibitionistic content of a joke relatively harmless and unnoticeable. Freud identifies them with the disguising mechanisms observable in dreams, and he holds that they derive from childhood forms of playing with words and ideas—free association, nonsense phrases, illogicality, irrational rhyming, etc. In his analysis, the joke is essentially regressive, masking its dangerous tendencies with the play forms that delighted the child during the early stages of his development. As a consequence of successful disguising, those who listen to a joke can laugh rather than feel the indignation or resentment that a brutal, unmitigated display of aggression would provoke. Freud explains that because people would normally have to use their own psychic energy to repress their aggressive tendencies in such a situation, the successful disguising of the aggressive content of a joke permits them to release that energy in profoundly satisfying laugher. In reality, they laugh neither at the aggressive impulse itself nor at its disguises, but at the impulse that has been disguised as play. To return to Bateson's concept, one does not respond separately to painted canvas and frame, but to both as a unity, to the painted canvas transformed into a work of art by the presence of its surrounding frame. Consequently, the merriment of Castiglione's society can be explained as resulting from its inhabitants' ability to make aggression wear the mask of play.

There is another way of explaining the continual gaiety of Castiglione's society which also accounts for the intense pleasure experienced by its members even when they are not laughing at jokes and witticisms. By playing social life as a game according to consciously articulated rules, they do more than give it a sense of order and continuity. Because games, however complicated, are still necessarily simplifications of life, and because they operate by excluding large segments of life as simply irrelevant to the activities involved, they permit the players to concentrate their attention to a tremendous degree and to engage themselves with great intensity in the game.[23] In a sense, the structuring and simplifying rules give them freedom, releasing them from most normal concerns and allowing them to channel their energies completely into the game they play. From this perspective, the limitations of activity and experience characteristic of Urbino and High Renaissance society generally should not be interpreted entirely as loss, for those limitations make possible an experience that is powerfully intense and satisfying, but simultaneously safe and controlled. The transformation of social life into a game thus effectively deals with aggression not by eliminating it, but by delimiting the field in which it operates and using it to produce a

greater personal involvement, excitement, and pleasure than ordinary experience in society would otherwise involve. Thanks to
their ability to turn life into play, the inhabitants of Urbino can
enjoy an orderly, decorous existence and at the same time reach
heights of exuberant hilarity and unalloyed pleasure that few
societies could rival.

It should be observed that while the social intercourse of Castiglione's characters is both exuberant and intense, it also seems to
tolerate only a particularly mild and sublimated form of joking,
repartée, and debate. If characters twit one another, they often do
so indirectly, as when Ludovico attacks those who make a "religion" out of speaking Tuscan, thus implying most indirectly that
his opponent Federico performs just such a silly, sacrilegious act.
When they attack directly, they often choose to single out personal traits about which a character feels no special weakness or
exposure, or issues on which little value is placed. For instance,
when Gasparo and the other misogynists are teased for their lack
of success with the fair sex, such a comment may cut, but it is
clearly not a matter of deep concern for those particular individuals. Thus although the sallies and attacks of Castiglione's characters may involve "biting" or "stabbing," they rarely bite deeply
or stab to the heart.

For the particularly mild, sublimated form that aggressive humor and exhibitionism take in Castiglione's society, there is a
simple explanation. The social situation at Urbino is a notably
informal one which allows its participants great freedom of personal expression. While requiring that certain deference rituals
and orderly procedures be performed, its rules encourage spontaneous, albeit properly timed, interruptions, witty gibes, taunts,
and even occasional outbursts. Precisely because of the high level
of informality characterizing this situation, its participants must
refrain from anything more than extremely sublimated and disguised forms of humor and aggression. Were more direct forms
allowed, the level of aggression might rise too sharply for such a
relatively informal social situation to contain with its very open
rules. The result might be hostility, wounded feelings, and disruptive arguments and fights. The limitations that Castiglione's society places on the direct expression of aggression and exhibitionism can be beter understood if its joking is compared with that of
oratory and debate. In trials, rhetorical exercises, debates, and
written exchanges, more vehement forms of argument had their
place and more violent and directly aggressive joking and personal attacks would be tolerated. The orator, or debater, defend-

ing his vision of the truth, was not expected to moderate his convictions or qualify his opposition to his opponents. One need only think, for instance, of the vehement, personal attacks in Elizabethan and Puritan pamphlets, which sometimes went to the point of open slander, in order to understand just how mild and sublimated the ridicule and repartée are in Castiglione's *Cortegiano*. The fundamental reason orators and debaters have such latitude in displaying personal hostility and joking, sometimes savagely, at their opponents' expense is that they operate in extremely formal and tightly structured situations and hence are less easily shaken by relatively undisguised aggression. Moreover, such joking and attacks are an accepted convention within that situation; they are perceived as *part of the game* and not as unseemly, offensive outbursts. On the other hand, in Urbino's less tightly structured, more informal environment, such directly aggressive statements would be distinctly out of place and would render the social situation absolutely intolerable.[24]

However, because Urbino's informal society does in fact contain a great deal of aggression, and because the game its inhabitants play does produce intense emotional involvement, there is a constant danger that aggression will explode out of its self-imposed limits, that sublimated repartée will degenerate into direct insult and lead to a violent shouting match. On several occasions, the competitive game played in Castiglione's ideal but by no means perfect society threatens to become a free-for-all. On those occasions, the courtiers exceed the bounds of propriety with desperate attempts to win arguments; they allow real hostility to show through their statements; or they strike a raw nerve unintentionally with their repartée. For instance, when Federico Fregoso rises to his feet at the end of the language debate in Book I, he does so because he wants to win so badly that he ignores the rules of decorum that require him to remain seated and not pursue an argument against the wishes of the ladies. Again, Gasparo's violent outburst against women at the end of Book III is openly hostile and socially unattractive. Bembo's Neoplatonic rapture in Book IV can also be considered indecorous, for although the self-absorption involved in his speech hardly angers or offends any particular individual, it threatens the very game of social intercourse itself as it reduces dialogue to monologue and then finally to the silence of mystic contemplation. One of the most striking instances of failure to disguise aggression adequately as play occurs when Ludovico da Canossa takes advantage of a momentary pause in Bembo's oration and ruffles Morello da Ortona's feathers with an overly moralistic, almost condescending attempt at repartée.

> Disse il conte Ludovico ridendo: —A voi forse paiono crudeli perché non· vi compiacciono di quello che vorreste; ma fatevi insegnar da messer Pietro Bembo di che modo debban desiderar la bellezza i vecchi e che cosa ricercar dalle donne e di che contentarsi; e non uscendo voi di que' termini, vederete che non saranno né superbe né crudeli e vi compiaceranno di ciò che vorrete—. Parve allor che 'l signor Morello si turbasse un poco, e disse: — Io non voglio saper quello che non mi tocca; ma fatevi insegnar voi come debbano desiderar questa bellezza i giovani peggio disposti e men gagliardi che i vecchi—.
>
> (IV, 55, 520)

Count Ludovico said, laughing: "Perhaps they seem cruel to you because they do not grant you what you want; but be instructed by messer Pietro Bembo as to how old men ought to desire beauty, and what they ought to seek in women, and with what they ought to be satisfied; and if you do not go beyond those limits, you shall see that they will be neither proud nor cruel, and will grant you what you wish."

Then signor Morello seemed a little annoyed, and said: "I have no wish to know what does not concern me; but be instructed yourself as to how this beauty ought to be desired by young men who are less vigorous and sturdy than their elders."

(341)

Even though Ludovico laughs as he speaks and Morello responds by matching insult with insult, undisguised aggression nevertheless threatens to destroy the game and turn play into open warfare.

For game playing really to satisfy, it must excite intense personal involvement in its participants and in its spectators as well. That involvement, however, properly remains within the limited sphere of play, distinct from the wider realm of social life and incorporating those facets of normal social roles that are manageable by the game's rules. In essence, those rules dictate that during the game people are supposed to be intense less as people than as players. As such, in Castiglione's informally structured society they can express their aggression, exhibitionistic drives, and enthusiasms, but only in the mild and sublimated forms that their game allows. Maintaining the nice distinction between oneself as a player and as a person is extremely difficult, however, primarily because of the powerful emotions concerned, and in the instances where hostility momentarily breaks through in Castiglione's book it is precisely his characters' intense emotional involvement that is at fault. It prevents them from sufficiently sublimating and disguising the forms of their aggression and exhibitionism, from establishing frames to indicate they are playing, from perceiving the frames others adhere to, and, consequently, from acting as players and treating social intercourse as a game. It seems as though a kind of madness, an emotional seizure, suddenly takes possession of them, making it impossible for them to keep the roles they assume as players distinct from the larger roles they play in everyday social life. While this blindness may not bother the individual afflicted with it, for the group as a whole such behavior generates embarrassment, tension, and a genuine fear that chaos threatens. For a horrifying moment, the gay mask that civilization wears seems nothing more than a polite fiction helpless before the powerful forces of human passion and aggression.

That ugly scenes do not develop in all these instances at Urbino is due to the quick-wittedness and tact of Castiglione's characters as they resort to certain stylized procedures that enable them to restore social order. Ideal in their ability to understand and manipulate social processes, they easily grasp the meaning of the framing devices employed to disguise aggression as play, and they quickly recognize the dangers that threaten when those disguises are abandoned or fail. To deal with such crises, which particularly plague informally structured societies like Urbino, Castiglione's characters immediately take recourse to a standard social operation designed to enable the offending party to save face: some member of the group, serving as its symbolic representative, intervenes in the discussion and deflects it away from the point of contention; he provides a distraction which allows the individual who has lost control of himself to recover his composure and disguise his hostility once again as play.[25] Thus, when Ludovico da Canossa and Morello da Ortona are about to grab one another by the throat, Federico Fregoso spots the danger at once and immediately intervenes to change the course of the conversation. By virtue of his intervention, he serves as the symbolic representative, the public spokesman, for the other members of the group, and he not only prevents Ludovico from making a retort that would lead to worse insults, but he praises Morello, thereby publicly restoring the respect Ludovico's mockery implicitly denied.

Quivi messer Federico, per acquetar il signor Morello e divertir il ragionamento, non lassò rispondere il conte Ludovico, ma interrompendolo disse: —Forse che 'l signor Morello non ha in tutto torto a dir che la bellezza non sia sempre bona, perché spesso le bellezze di donne son causa che al mondo intervengan infiniti mali, inimicizie, guerre, morti e distruzioni. . . .

(IV, 56, 521)

Here messer Federico, in order to calm signor Morello and to change the subject, did not let Count Ludovico reply, but interrupted him and said: "Perhaps signor Morello is not entirely wrong in saying that beauty is not always good; for women's beauty is often the cause of countless evils, hatreds, wars, deaths, and destructions in the world. . . ."

(341)

The success of Federico's intervention is clear, both because Morello remains silent, and because Ludovico restricts his hostility to a subordinate clause in the comment he makes when endorsing Federico's return to the question at hand. Similarly, in response to Federico's own faux pas in Book I, Emilia Pia does not merely interrupt him, but turns the group's attention away from him; she changes the subject of conversation and allows him a moment to cover his embarrassment and silently resume his seat. At the end of Book III, Ottaviano employs the same technique to divert attention from Gasparo's vitriolic remarks about women while at the same time he utters a few words of praise for his fellow misogynist. Thanks to the wit and tact of other members of the group, characters who temporarily lose control of themselves and cast off the civilized masks they wear can put them on again. They are granted a merciful moment to regain that simultaneous detachment from themselves and intense emotional involvement in playing which constitute the paradoxical essence of participation in every game, including their own.

Castiglione's insistence upon the existence of human aggressiveness and his celebration of Urbino's techniques for transforming it into play separate his vision of the ideal society from those of his contemporaries. In contrast, More's *Utopia,* Erasmus's colloquy *The Godly Feast (Convivium religiosum),* and the concluding chapters

of Rabelais's *Gargantua* describing the Abbaye de Thélème all depict ideal societies from which human aggressiveness has been
banished. Erasmus imagines his ideal society as a group of lay
theologians set apart from the world in a morally purified, pro-
tected environment, who spend their time earnestly discussing
philosophical and religious matters. They engage in a joint quest
for truth and rarely halt their journey for disagreements or quar-
rels. On the other hand, Rabelais's Thélèmites do play games,
and, consequently, some aggression would have to be involved in
their society. Rabelais's emphasis, however, falls almost completely
on their superb ability to cooperate freely with one another, a
cooperation that leads them, before long, to dress alike and to
engage in exactly the same activities together (see chapters 56 and
57). For Rabelais, ideal cooperation really means ideal uniformity.
Unlike Erasmus and Rabelais, who do not discuss the problem of
aggression, More explicitly worries about it and consciously designs the institutions of Utopia to minimize, if not eliminate, it.
Lest they become aggressive beasts, Utopians cannot hunt or
butcher animals, and they must take every conceivable precaution
to avoid personal involvement in war. The entire aim of their
extensive education and systematic supervision even as adults is to
eliminate the aggressive exhibitionism More condemns as pride.
As a result of eliminating aggression, their society enjoys peace
and harmony, but More's Utopians, like Rabelais's Thélèmites and
Erasmus's lay theologians, appear to be faceless entities in a
crowd, undifferentiated and undistinguishable from one another,
all dressed alike in the same monotonous, grey uniform.

Where all his contemporaries condemn aggression and strive
mightily to eliminate it, Castiglione not only accepts it as an ines-
capable human reality, but makes his ideal society actually encourage its display and arrange certain institutions to insure its continuing presence. Thus the rules governing the game they play both
allow individuals to indulge their exhibitionistic tendencies to the
full and simultaneously require that objections and challenges be
directed to each speaker. On the more basic level of social organization, Urbino divides power unequally between the men, who
almost totally dominate the conversation and direct its flow, and
the women, who serve as umpires and judges, presiding at times
like petty dictators over the discussions. The result is an institutionalized tension between men and women, a social instability
insuring that the battle of the sexes will go on eternally in some
form at Castiglione's court. Moreover, all the inhabitants of Urbino tease and mock one another, egging their enemies on to

debate and encouraging their friends to leap to their defense. Even the duchess and Emilia Pia, whose function is usually the passive one of setting limits for aggressive display and keeping the peace, frequently provoke the men with mockery and challenges and are especially energetic in promulgating the war fought in their defense throughout Book III. Finally, Bibbiena notes a fundamental fact about repartée, that witty sallies really have no grace at all unless they "bite" (II, 43, 257: "né senza quel poco di puntura par che abbian grazia . . . "). Granted Castiglione's belief that certain social mechanisms can control the destructive potential of human aggression, his people nevertheless do seem determined to pile fuel on a fire that frequently flares up and threatens to consume their house of mirth.

In explaining why they constantly stoke the fire of aggression, the lords and ladies of Urbino would simply affirm that to put out the fire that might consume them is to put out the fire that gives them light and warmth. Without it, life in their *albergo della allegria* would be cold and dead indeed. Aggression can provide the satisfying release of laughter only because it also produces the tensions that make such release necessary and possible. Aggression gives the courtiers' game of conversation the excitement of personal involvement, and it provides the dynamism and movement that come from challenge and response. In fact, when justifying her selection of Ludovico as the first speaker, Emilia Pia indicates clearly just how important the tensions and instabilities produced by the aggression contained in arguments and challenges are for the on-going life of her society.

> Adunque, per non perder più tempo, voi, Conte, sarete quello che averà questa impresa nel modo che ha detto messer Federico; non già perché ci paia che voi siate così bon cortegiano, che sappiate quel che si gli convenga, ma perché, dicendo ogni cosa al contrario, come speramo che farete, il gioco sarà più bello, ché ognun averà che respondervi; onde se un altro che sapesse più di voi avesse questo carico, non si gli potrebbe contradir cosa alcuna perché diria la verità, e così il gioco saria freddo.
>
> (I, 13, 101)

> So, in order not to lose more time, you, Count, shall be the one to undertake this task in the way messer Federico has said; not indeed because we think you so good a Courtier that you know what befits one, but because if you say

> everything contrariwise, as we hope you will do, the game
> will be the livelier since everyone will have something to
> answer you; whereas, if another with more knowledge
> than you had this task, nothing could be objected to him
> because he would speak the truth, and so the game would
> be tedious [lit., cold].
>
> (26)

Rather than moralistically condemn aggression and the tension it necessarily generates as the source of social discord, Castiglione values it as the essential, vital force that animates his and all societies, giving meaning and movement to discussions that might otherwise stagnate in endless repetition.

Appropriately enough, the name of the game that Castiglione's courtiers play is the game of courtship. In it each participant competes to win the favor of the duchess by behaving as an ideal courtier and serving both the whole group generally and the duchess specifically. The prominent deference rituals noted earlier allow each speaker to mask his display of wisdom and opinion as a gesture of deference offered the entire group, so that even while he occupies a privileged position above them, he simultaneously appears to court their favor. Similarly, the two least interrupted speeches, those of Bibbiena in Book II and Bembo in Book IV, are presented as a kind of entertainment and thus can be interpreted as a matter of courting the applause of those who listen. Generally, all of Castiglione's courtiers strive to please the duchess, competing in their speeches less to triumph over their opponents than to show their worthiness before her, to reveal their love and respect for her, and to receive her favor. As courtiers, performers, and entertaining wits, they all strive primarily to do her reverence, thus transforming aggression into worship or courtship before her throne. Aggression not only provides animation for social intercourse, but by assuming the form of reverent worship, it actually provides a powerful, affective unity for Urbino's ideal society as its courtiers strive to play the same, ideal role and to reach an identical goal. When Castiglione identifies reverence as the emotion linking all the courtiers and ladies together to the duchess in a chain of love, he clearly does not think of merely passive affection, but of a tremendous, cohesive force which is a carefully channeled and controlled form of aggression. Ironically, the aggressive energy that Machiavelli thought would blow apart the fragile chain of love actually serves to bind its links all the more firmly together. As it is harnessed, aggression metamorphoses into the servant of love and guarantees the order and unity of Urbino's society.

By utilizing aggression in the dynamic game of courtship, Castiglione's characters save their world from the diseases that seem endemic to most ideal societies—boredom and anonymity. Castiglione implicitly recognizes the problem of boredom when he notes that people are always desirous of new things (*Letter,* 1, 69) and that they tire easily when exposed to repetition without variation (II, 8, 201–2; II, 12, 207–8). Thanks to the institutionalized, controlled disruptions of aggression, the inhabitants of Urbino will never succumb to ennui. Nor will they be victims of that faceless anonymity that results from the complete elimination of exhibitionism in utopian works. Castiglione's society is founded on respect for the individual, his opinions, and his personal sense of worth, and it organizes its competitive game of courtship so that each person can exhibit his talents without lessening the value of others. Where More's people are grey and faceless, Castiglione's wear attractive garments, not flashy and vulgar, but rich and elegant, testimony to the dignity of the individuals wearing them. Where other ideal societies take upon themselves the futile task of eliminating aggression, Castiglione's ideal court more realistically accepts it, and with real genius domesticates it, harnessing its vital energies to give social intercourse intensity, movement, and cohesion.

As the courtiers and ladies gather night after night in the duchess's chambers, their constant repetition of stylized gestures, verbal formulas, and ritual laughter transforms the movements of social life into the elegant harmonies of dancing. As Castiglione's dancers trip merrily through a *bassa,* or glide with stately ease through a *roegarze* (I, 56, 185), they never cease to perform as ideal courtiers and ladies, continually disguising aggression under the mask of play and courtship. Their masking does not deny or petrify the individual's nature, but transfigures it so that he can appear the beautiful, socially decorous, ideally civilized person he would like to be. Unmistakably, an enormous gulf yawns between this *ballo in maschera* and the more famous, later one by Giuseppe Verdi. In Verdi's opera, the masked ball is condemned as a matter of mere façade: the beautiful costumes of a superficially brilliant court simply cover over the treachery, sensuality, and violence that lie beneath and that eventually manifest themselves, bloodying the masks and silencing the music. Castiglione's masked ball, on the other hand, is not a lie which perverts reality, but the ultimate polite fiction which uses art to make the most out of life by turning aimless, unstructured movement into graceful dancing in brilliant costumes.

Because the inhabitants of Urbino are obliged to wear figurative masks and to dance according to the rules, their social conformity does not transform them into mechanical dolls. Quite the contrary, Castiglione's book suggests that true freedom for a society, as for an ideal courtier, lies not in an ultimately futile rejection of rules and conventions, but in recognizing and mastering them. Urbino's society reveals how to transform social intercourse into a brilliant game that both satisfies the individual's need for vital experience, recognition by others, and self-expression, and simultaneously promotes the harmony and coherence of the group. While everyone must come to dance at the masked ball of civilization appropriately and beautifully disguised, each person freely chooses his own distinctive costume as well as the dances he will dance, and the entire group freely selects together the music it wishes played. Such an arrangement must have seemed so profoundly satisfying to Castiglione that he could not help wishing for its eternal continuation. As an expression of his wish, he purposefully ends *The Book of the Courtier* by interrupting Gasparo and Emilia in a final exchange as they begin to circle about in their old, familiar dance once again. As Castiglione concludes his last page, he thus makes it seem that his dancers have only paused for breath, and that on the next evening—and on countless evenings after that—they will once more don their beautiful masks and swirl across the floor in their ever more graceful, expansive, exhilarating dance of life.

5/ A Festive Symposium

Castiglione's decision not to write a treatise, but to expound his ideas on courtliness by recounting the *ragionamenti* his friends had held during four evenings at Urbino, would hardly have shocked his contemporaries. From the dawn of the Renaissance until well after its close, the dialogue served many writers as a favored vehicle for literary display and philosophical speculation. In part, their preference was dictated by the prestige the dialogue enjoyed in antiquity and by the brilliant use to which esteemed writers like Plato and Cicero had put it. More profoundly, the form served the idealism of the age, its belief in the word as the creator of civilization and as the chief educator of its human ideal.[1] Not to speak was to be less than human; not to speak well, not to display a solid command of languages and rhetoric, was to be profoundly uncivilized. Many Renaissance men felt that to talk with urbanity, wit, and refinement was the supreme human accomplishment, and they often naively seemed to think that the achievement of such verbal distinction would entail a similar achievement of moral and intellectual excellence.[2] Their faith in the civilizing word led them to dream of an ideal life spent in a garden under the shade of trees, where good friends could converse together freely and urbanely on every conceivable subject.[3] They sometimes tried to realize their dream in retreats like the Medici's Careggi, the "Paradiso degli Alberti," and the courts of Urbino, Mantua, and Ferrara. For the most part, however, philosophers, poets, and courtiers from Petrarch to Izaak Walton were content to realize their dream in the urbane, civilized conversations of the dialogue.

In his *Dialogus* (1401), which he addressed to the great humanist educator Petrus Paulus Vergerius, the Florentine chancellor and historian Leonardo Bruni suggests yet another, equally important reason for the popularity of the dialogue during the Renaissance. Bruni's work recounts how Coluccio Salutati, the fourteenth-century Florentine chancellor and humanist, rebuked a group of younger men who had come to visit him and had made no effort to carry on a discussion. Bruni has Salutati deliver an eloquent defense of conversation, praising it primarily for its ability to instruct its participants and listeners. Conversation, or disputation, is valuable because it shows how the process of reasoning operates when individuals are forced to defend their opinions, attack their opponents, and clarify their assertions. Moreover, in this congenial dialogue about dialogue, Bruni has Salutati celebrate conversation for the wide range of topics it can handle and the diverse points of view it can bring together.[4] Using similar arguments, Alberti has characters in his *Libri della famiglia* (1432–43) praise conversation because it can treat of many different subjects with great freedom; eschewing the rigor of philosophy and the formality of oratory, it instructs in its own less systematic way.[5] Alberti's comments might be inscribed on the banner of an age marked not by the inclusive, harmonious systematizing of the *Summa Theologica,* but by the self-conscious syncretism of a Pico della Mirandola; it was an age for which the dialogue clearly presented an ideal form for the expression of multiple points of view and the accommodation, if not the reconciliation, of competing systems of thought. In a dialogue the writer could give dramatic, concrete expression to his ideas on every conceivable subject and could vividly present a number of different opinions on matters whose truth was often relative or about which the author was undecided.

One final consideration helps to explain the appeal of the dialogue during the Renaissance. While the form could be used polemically as the means to refute the ideas of one's opponent or to educate the reading public in one's own prejudices, it could also be used much more subtly as a means to reveal some notion of one's true opinion at the same time that one simultaneously concealed it or at least prevented its easy and certain identification. Since most Renaissance writers were the subjects of dukes or princes or popes, the direct expression of unpopular or unconventional ideas could have resulted in fines, imprisonment, or worse. Fully aware of such unpleasant realities and accepting the virtue of discreet indirection, men like More, Erasmus, and Castiglione all denounced the "Stoic philosopher," the uncompromising idealist who blurts out his notion of the truth without regard for circumstances or consequences; and Rabelais plays the clever fool in his prologues in order to throw the dogs of worldly power and intolerant authority off his scent.[6] The dialogue saved some writers from the dangers of direct pronouncements and at the same time spared them an often awkward, always unsatisfying silence. As More showed in his *Utopia,* dialogue could be used with such subtlety that scholars still argue whether Hythloday or the character More represents the author's true opinions. Tasso used dialogue similarly in his *Malpiglio overo de la corte* to contradict subtly and almost unnoticeably the notion that courts, like the one at Ferrara where he was imprisoned, really provided a home for merit.[7] And Castiglione found in dialogue a way to express reservations he felt about such matters as hereditary nobility, the value of women in society, and the superiority of monarchy to republican forms of government, while still giving the appearance of conformity to conventional wisdom.

If Castiglione was prompted to cast his thought in the mold of the dialogue because of the prestige it enjoyed in his culture, that culture offered him not one but an almost bewildering variety of dialogue forms as the models for his work. Renaissance writers could find in the treasure house of antiquity shelves of dialogue forms ranging from the philosophical debates of Plato through the rhetorical performances of Ciceronian dialogues to the satiric exchanges of Lucian's colloquies. Even within the opus of Plato they could discover works as diverse as *The Republic* and *The Symposium,* the *Phaedrus* and the *Parmenides.* Writing an essay on the dialogue, Tasso surveys the wide variety of forms the genre could assume and divides dialogues into no fewer than nine categories in an attempt to account for them all. Although he praises as superior to all others the Socratic style, by which the teacher enlightens his pupil by constantly questioning him, Tasso recognizes the existence of other styles and hence acknowledges the complexity attending the form as a whole.[8] To complicate matters even further, when the Renaissance turned from theory and study to practice, it often hybridized the forms it inherited, combining the didactic dialogue with the symposium, as Alberti did in his *Cena familiaris,* or the philosophical debate with Lucianic satire, as More did in the first book of his *Utopia.* In short, when Castiglione sat down to compose his *ragionamenti,* his culture set before him a sumptuous banquet of subtly different dishes to nourish the growth of his genius; it offered him an endless succession of dialogues imitating the ever-varied patterns of human intercourse. The question, however, remains: from that rich banquet, of what dishes did Castiglione partake to nourish himself as he labored to bring forth his *Cortegiano?*

Castiglione himself suggests an indirect, though somewhat misleading, answer to this question when he places his work in the same camp with Xenophon's *Cyropaedia,* Plato's *Republic,* and Cicero's *De Oratore,* on the grounds that all of them describe ideal characters or societies, just as Castiglione's book does.[9] Xenophon's work, however, could not have offered a pattern for Castiglione to follow, simply because it is not a dialogue at all. On the other hand, both Cicero and Plato composed dialogues which, upon examination, reveal a number of formal similarities to elements in *The Book of the Courtier.* In particular, ample evidence has led some writers to see the *De Oratore* as the direct model for Castiglione's work.[10] In the first place, both works maintain the fiction of dialogue from start to finish and have their principal characters express themselves in a highly formal and rhetorical manner. Secondly, Castiglione's concept of the ideal courtier corresponds in many basic features quite closely to Cicero's ideal orator; both figures are supposed to be masters of language, will have received comprehensive, liberal educations, and will involve themselves in the political and social life of the state. Thirdly, Castiglione's original plans called for a work in three books, an indication that he may have been thinking of the three books of Cicero's dialogue, and his use of prologues as well as the elegiac character of his last one strongly recall the *De Oratore.* Finally, Castiglione filched Bibbiena's theoretical discussion in Book II concerning wit and humor directly from the work of his Roman ancestor. Nevertheless, while all this evidence supports fully the contention that Castiglione kept Cicero in mind as he composed his *Courtier,* it does not really establish a formal similarity between the two works.

From the perspective of its distinctive form, Cicero's *De Oratore,* like its model, Plato's *Phaedrus,* must be classified as an educational or didactic dialogue. That subspecies of dialogue divides its characters into two quite different groups: teachers who deliver themselves of their opinions ex cathedra, and pupils who literally or metaphorically sit at their feet, listen with rapt attention, and ask questions only for the sake of gaining enlightenment. In Cicero's work, Antonius and Crassus, like Socrates in the *Phaedrus,* speak at great length for the purpose of educating the young men who attend to their expositions with frequent expressions of enthusiasm and whose questions are usually requests for clarification and additional information.[11] While Castiglione's dialogue certainly has an educational purpose and allows characters temporarily a podium to expound their ideas, it does not divide them into two clearly differentiated groups of teachers and pupils whose main

154

purpose in coming together is the pursuit of wisdom. Rather, it portrays a group of friends enjoying their leisure together, discussing the ideal courtier primarily as a means of entertaining themselves and only secondarily out of concern for the knowledge involved. They see their festive gathering in the duchess's quarters as a game and view one another as witty competitors in the sport of conversation. Gasparo Pallavicino and Morello da Ortona could hardly be considered, and certainly do not consider themselves, the pupils of Giuliano de' Medici and Ottaviano Fregoso, and the questions they ask are more than schoolboy requests for enlightenment. In fact, it is precisely these questions that permit Castiglione to distinguish the kind of dialogue he is writing from a didactic work like the *De Oratore*. By having characters like Gasparo and Morello use questions as a means to *challenge* the principal speaker, Castiglione parodies the form of the educational dialogue, which tolerates questions only for the sake of information and clarification. In *Il Cortegiano,* questioning is a means to assert the importance of the questioner, not the person who is questioned, and it serves as a corrective for the slight social elevation implied when a person is made principal speaker, for it reminds him forcefully that he and his ideas are not sacrosanct and above criticism. Such questioning thus prevents any character from really speaking ex cathedra, and it separates the form of *Il Cortegiano* definitively from that of the educational dialogue.

Castiglione's work is also quite distant in form from the philosophical debate that occupies the first two books of *The Republic,* and there can be no question of any resemblance to the essentially uninterrupted monologue Socrates delivers in the last eight books of that work. The difference between the form of *Il Cortegiano* and Plato's philosophical debates needs some commentary precisely because Castiglione's book, from beginning to end, is filled with debates on subjects like language, women, nobility, and political systems. In Plato's works, the philosophical debate involves a basic conflict concerning the nature of truth between opposed and often hostile characters; it is marked by great intensity and involvement; it is carried on rigorously, almost invariably by means of Socratic questioning; and it dominates exclusively the dialogue or portion of a dialogue in which it occurs. By contrast, the debates in Castiglione's *Courtier* involve conflicts of opinion often left unresolved when they end and open to future discussion, at least in the minds of the participants. They are considered a form of entertaiment as much as an effort to resolve the issues involved, and they are carried on by means of anecdotes, stories, and elabo-

rate, highly rhetorical speeches, all of which are part of the orator's bag of tricks Castiglione inherited from Cicero and his
fifteenth-century imitators. Finally, the debates in *Il Cortegiano* are
just one of the many ways in which Castiglione's characters converse with one another, and, with the exception of the extensive,
inconclusive series of exchanges about women, all the debates are
presented as digressions from the main subject being discussed.

Just as Castiglione distinguished his work from the didactic dialogue by parodying its use of questions, so he separates it from
the philosophical debate by explicitly rejecting that style.
Specifically, he has Emilia Pia intervene to terminate the two most
extensive debates in *The Courtier*, the debates on language and
women, just as the speakers are beginning to employ the style of
the philosophical debate. Representing the norms and tolerances
of Castiglione's courtly society, Emilia Pia accepts the arguments
about women in Book III as long as they are carried on through
elaborate, rhetorical speeches which rely on anecdotes and tru-
isms for proof. She objects, however, when the more philosophi-
cally inclined Magnifico begins to debate by using terms like "matter" and "form," which he has derived ultimately from Aristotle.

> Allora la signora Emilia rivolta al signor Magnifico,—Per
> amor di Dio,—disse,—uscite una volta di queste vostre
> "materie" e "forme" e maschi e femine e parlate di modo
> che siate inteso. . . .
>
> (III, 17, 358)

> Then signora Emilia turned to the Magnifico and said:
> "For Heaven's sake, leave all this matter and form and
> male and female for once, and speak so as to be under-
> stood. . . .
>
> (218)

Essentially, Emilia is objecting here to the technical, specialized
vocabulary which the philosopher employs in order to make
subtle, rigorous distinctions, and in rejecting such language, she
also implicitly rejects, on behalf of Castiglione's dialogue form, the
kind of philosophical debate normally associated with it.

Emilia's other intervention, which terminates the debate on language in Book I, provides an even more striking rejection of the
style employed in philosophical debate. For most of their argument over whether to speak archaic Tuscan or contemporary,
courtly Italian, Federico Fregoso and Ludovico da Canossa have

debated by exchanging fairly lengthy speeches conforming to the particularly rhetorical style of debate approved at the court of Urbino. All of a sudden, however, their style changes dramatically, and for a brief moment the spirit of Plato becomes a moving presence in their debate.

Allor il Conte,—Dubito,—disse,—che noi entraremo in un gran pelago e lassaremo il nostro primo proposito del cortegiano. Pur domando a voi: in che consiste la bontà di questa lingua? —Rispose messer Federico: —Nel servar ben le proprietà di essa e tôrla in quella significazione, usando quello stile e que' numeri che hanno fatto tutti quei che hanno scritto bene. —Vorrei,—disse il Conte,— sapere se questo stile e questi numeri di che voi parlate, nascano dalle sentenzie o dalle parole. —Dalle parole,— rispose messer Federico. —Adunque,—disse il Conte,—a voi non par che le parole di Silio e di Cornelio Tacito siano quelle medesime che usa Virgilio e Cicerone, né tolte nella medesima significazione? —Rispose messer Federico: —Le medesime son sì, ma alcune mal osservate e tolte diversamente. —Rispose il Conte: —E se d'un libro di Cornelio e d'un di Silio si levassero tutte quelle parole che son poste in altra significazion di quello che fa Virgilio e Cicerone, che seriano pochissime, non direste voi poi che Cornelio nella lingua fosse pare a Cicerone, e Silio a Virgilio? e che ben fosse imitar quella maniera del dire?

(I, 38, 151–52)

Then the Count replied: "I fear that we shall enter on a wide sea and depart from our first subject of the Courtier. Still I would ask you, in what does the excellence of this language consist?"

Messer Federico replied: "In respecting its proprieties, employing it so, and adopting that style and those harmonies which all who have written well have used."

"I should like to know," said the Count, "whether this style and these harmonies that you speak of arise from the thought or from the words?"

"From the words," replied messer Federico.

"Then," said the Count, "do you not think that the words of Silius and of Cornelius Tacitus are the same as those which Virgil and Cicero employ? Are they not used in the same sense?"

157

> "They are indeed the same," replied messer Federico,
> "but some of them are not preserved well and are used in
> a different sense."
>
> The Count replied: "And if from a book of Cornelius
> and from one of Silius all those words were removed that
> are used in a sense different from that of Virgil or Cicero
> (which would be very few), then would you not say that
> Cornelius was the equal of Cicero in language, and Silius
> the equal of Virgil, and that it were well to imitate their
> manner of speech?"
>
> (63)

At this point, before the count can lead his opponent to what
seems the inevitable conclusion—that literary excellence depends
on far more than a writer's vocabulary—Emilia Pia interrupts
them: "A me par . . . che questa vostra disputa sia mo troppo
lunga e fastidiosa; però fia bene a differirla ad un altro tempo" (I,
39, 152: "It seems to me that this debate of yours has now become
too long and tiresome; therefore it would be well to postpone it to
another time"[63]). What has become tiresome for her is nothing
other than the only example of Socratic argument in Castiglione's
work. The style Tasso praised as supreme in the dialogue Emilia
here rejects for making a social situation tedious, and her rejection reinforces the formal distinction between *Il Cortegiano* and
the kind of philosophical debate Plato triumphed in writing.

Just as Castiglione's work shares the intellectual interest that
predominates in didactic and philosophical dialogues, but possesses a strikingly different form, so it also bears a limited resemblance to the colloquies of Lucian and Erasmus. Like them, it has
an interest in the relatively realistic depiction of character and
situation, and it strives to create the effect of genuine conversation in the give and take of its speakers' exchanges. Where educational and philosophical dialogues to some extent subordinate
character to theme, colloquies reverse the balance, and in *Il Cortegiano* Castiglione clearly feels as great a concern for portraying his
people as for presenting his concept of the ideal courtier. The
colloquy, however, has a basically satirical perspective which Castiglione's work does not share. In fact at one point, when the
Magnifico begins a tirade against wicked friars, Emilia Pia commands him to stop, effectively silencing the only satirical outburst
in the work. Even more, *Il Cortegiano* must be distinguished from
the colloquy because the social situation it depicts is fundamentally different. Typically, the colloquy presents a chance en-

counter of two or three people who halt for a moment to talk after coming upon one another in the street. Castiglione's book, on the other hand, while it preserves a degree of informality by permitting questions, interruptions, and playful banter, nevertheless depicts a simultaneously much more formal situation which has been arranged in advance and is treated as a special, festive occasion. Whereas conversations in a colloquy begin and end with seeming spontaneity and as they progress try to reflect the randomness of free, unstructured talk, the festive conversations in *Il Cortegiano* present a paradoxical kind of formal informality. While they range over a wide variety of topics, Castiglione's characters formally structure the movement of their talk: they employ opening and closing ceremonies and verbal formulas of all sorts; they have a formal process for selecting speakers; and they recognize the duchess and her lieutenant, Emilia Pia, as judges empowered to enforce the rules that govern their intercourse and to which they all bow. And even though they do offer spontaneous questions and interrupt one another, they carefully make both questions and interruptions subject to their code of rules and thus formalize the informality involved.

While the festive ceremoniousness, the formal informality, of Castiglione's dialogue distinguishes it from the colloquies of Lucian and Erasmus, it also identifies *Il Cortegiano* with another subspecies of the dialogue, one which combines in itself both the intellectual interest and formal situation of didactic and philosophical works and the interest in character and informal situation of the colloquy. That other form of the dialogue is the symposium, or, to use its more suggestive Latin name, the convivium.[12] This dialogue form was recognized as a separate genre in antiquity and was written in imitation of the real symposia that played such an important role in the social life of the ancient world.[13] Symposia were formally arranged social gatherings which normally involved heavy drinking and which took place after, not during, a meal. They had a conventional seating arrangement and a conventional, ceremonial opening which involved pouring out a libation to the gods. Nevertheless, although formally arranged and formally managed, symposia were simultaneously informal affairs at which people could freely and comfortably talk and drink together, listen to flute players or watch acrobats, and engage themselves as a group in guessing games and riddle contests. Sometimes weddings and holiday celebrations became occasions for symposia, but the Greeks and Romans did not need that sort of pretext to arrange for such festive drinking and conversation together. For both cultures, the symposium offered a formalized mode of social relaxation, a ceremonious and yet exhilarating release from the routines and burdens of normal social life.[14]

According to ancient literary critics like Athenaeus and Hermogenes, the literary genre of the symposium was written in prose in imitation of such real festivities and was distinguished primarily by the serious level of its conversations, which replaced games and other diversions as the chief entertainment of the group.[15] Especially because of Plato's brilliant, philosophical *Symposium* and Xenophon's slightly later, less purely intellectual imitation, the genre was characterized from the first not only by a social situation that mingled formal ceremonies and informal banter, but also by serious conversations pursued in a gay and playful manner. Ancient thinkers considered the symposium a matter of *serio ludere,* serious festivity, and throughout antiquity, from Plato and Xenophon, through Plutarch's *Banquet of the Seven Sages* and Macrobius's *Saturnalia,* down to Athenaeus's encyclopedic *Deipnosophists,* it engaged the imaginations of countless creative artists and philosophers. Its conventions were so well established and it was so readily recognizable as a literary form that writers like Horace, Lucian, and Petronius could easily use it for purposes of satire and parody. With the end of the Roman empire in the West, however, the literary symposium essentially disappeared until the beginning of the Renaissance. Dante's *Convito* is the exception that proves the rule, for although its title suggests a symposium, it is a treatise on his own poetry and not at all the representation of men engaged in festive conversation. Influenced by a long tradition that saw Scripture as a banquet of wisdom, Dante offers his book to the reader as a dish filled with table scraps the author has collected while sitting beneath the feast of the angels.[16] In a brilliant transformation of the symposium concept, his book itself becomes a metaphoric meal shared by writer and reader in a convivial act of communion. Nevertheless, the *Convito* clearly bears no formal resemblance to the situation, characters, and mood of the symposium as it was cultivated by classical authors like Plato, Xenophon, and Plutarch.

Erwin Panofsky has argued that a defining trait of the Renaissance is its reintegration of classical form and classical content, and nothing could better illustrate his contention than the many symposia written by Italian humanists in the fifteenth and sixteenth centuries.[17] Renaissance writers demonstrate a consciousness of what constitutes a literary symposium at least as early as 1401, when Bruni ends his *Dialogus* by having one character invite the others to continue their serious discussions over dinner, a "duplex convivium" to refresh both body and soul.[18] Later, in the fourth book of his *Libri della famiglia,* Alberti has his characters appropriately enough discuss *amicitia* over a dinner which they amusingly discover, all of a sudden, must be one of those *conviti filosofici* which Plato, Xenophon, and Plutarch described.[19] The symposium was not merely recognized as a genre but was frequently employed as a vehicle for philosophical and moral speculation: in the early years of the quattrocento, the Greek scholar Filelfo produced a series of dialogues he entitled *Banquets;* Alberti wrote a short work called the *Cena familiaris,* as well as his books on the family; and in 1474 and 1475 Ficino produced his *De Amore.* This symposium commemorated a real feast held in 1474 by the members of the Florentine Platonic Academy in order to celebrate Plato's birthday, and it consisted of speeches forming an extensive commentary on Plato's original *Symposium.* By the time Castiglione began to think of his *Cortegiano,* the classical conception of the symposium was fully recognized as a form of the dialogue, and he had before him a wide variety of models, both ancient and contemporary, for his own work.

It should consequently not seem surprising that *Il Cortegiano,* which admittedly abounds with reminiscences of Cicero's *De Oratore,* also recalls Plato's *Symposium* and the symposium genre generally. It does so especially at the end when Bembo delivers his speech in praise of love, which is strongly influenced by Socrates' speech in the *Symposium.* Likewise, when Emilia Pia tugs at Bembo's robe and brings him back down to reality after his climb to the heights of love, her gesture recalls the entry of the drunken Alcibiades at the end of Socrates' speech, which also marks a return to reality after an ecstatic vision of love.[20] Moreover, where Plato starts his *Symposium* by having Eryximachus urge that the normal, less intellectual pastimes enjoyed at most contemporary banquets be rejected in favor of speeches in praise of love, Castiglione opens his symposium by having Emilia Pia pass over and reject the courtly games that formed the standard recreation of her society.[21] Instead, she formally approves Federico's proposal that they all give speeches on the more serious topic of the ideal courtier. Perhaps also recalling Plato and other writers of symposia as well, Castiglione includes certain recurrent characters in his book: Bibbiena is the writer of comedies who entertains the group with his wit; Francesco Maria della Rovere, the late-comer whose entry interrupts the discussions; and the duchess, the host who plays a prominent role in directing the festivities.[22] In a more profound way than such superficial similarities and continuities might suggest, however, Castiglione's book captures the essential qualities defining the symposium as it duplicates the basic social situation, mode of characterization, setting, and mood that define the genre. To be sure, there is no tippling in *Il Cortegiano,* but the absence of such a detail can be explained in large part by the social practices of Castiglione's age, whose society did not follow its meals with all-night drinking bouts as the Greeks did. What is more important, ancient writers, who speculated about the genre, did not feel that the depiction of eating and drinking was its defining characteristic, but conceived it in rather broad terms as a paradoxically formal, ceremonious situation in which individuals carry on relatively serious conversations, but in an informal atmosphere and a festive mood.[23] On the basis of such authority alone, Castiglione's book deserves a place beside the works of Plato, Xenophon, and Plutarch, Alberti, Ficino, and Erasmus. There are, however, many other reasons as well to read *Il Cortegiano* as a brilliant reworking and extension of the symposium genre.

Because the symposium basically depicts a special, festive occasion, it is distinguished by having its own special time and space, which are different from the time and space of ordinary, everyday activities. Effectively, it creates a separate realm dominated by its serious, yet festive mood, a realm established temporarily within the confines of the workaday world, but separated from it by means of its special setting. From Plato's work on, practically every symposium takes place inside an enclosing structure, in a room or house or walled garden; unlike the discussions depicted in colloquies and philosophical dialogues, its conversations could not take place out in the open on street corners or along roads. Moreover, the seclusion of the symposium world within its surrounding walls is further dramatized by the spatial arrangement of its participants, who sit around a table or on the periphery of the circle formed by their chairs. They thus face inward and look at one another, while turning their backs, literally and symbolically, on the world outside. The surrounding walls of their room join with the circle of their chairs to create a concentric set of boundaries which powerfully distinguish the world of society outside the symposium from the one inside it. So powerful is this distinction in Castiglione's book that it infects the language his characters use and leads them to speak in spatial metaphors, to identify behavior, for instance, less as good and bad, than as being within bounds and out of bounds. Thus Bibbiena cautions his friends to respect the proprieties in telling jokes and not to go beyond *i termini* (II, 42, 256). The courtiers frequently chide one another when they digress for wanting to go out of bounds (III, 37, 390: "uscire de' termini") of their discussion. Appropriately, they speak continually of "entering" and "leaving" discussions, and when Emilia Pia reprimands the Magnifico for his philosophical debate about women, she commands him to "come out" (*uscite*) from such a discussion, almost as if he had withdrawn into himself, into private regions of personal knowledge and interest, and had to be urged to return once again to the public space of discussion symbolized by the physical arena enclosed in the courtiers' and ladies' circle of chairs. Finally, it should also be noted that in *Il Cortegiano* virtue itself is defined in Aristotelian terms as the mean between the two extremes; finding it is compared to finding the center of a circle, and departing from it, consequently, involves a metaphorical going out of bounds.[24] The creation of a bounded, secluded world for the symposium also helps account for the way Castiglione's society excludes or ignores large areas of human feeling and activity. It explains why that society stigmatizes and rejects displays of overt aggression, moodiness, and volatility, as well as overly personal and technical discussions, for all are considered part of the outside world and have no place within the magic circle of chairs inside Urbino's palace walls. And it is precisely to maintain the distinction between what is in bounds and what is not that Castiglione has his characters all willingly defer to Emilia Pia and the duchess, who are aptly considered *umpires* for the game that is being played.

The symposium's establishment of boundaries that seclude it from the outside world also helps explain a peculiarity attending its themes. Although they are potentially concerned with every topic people could discuss at a festive gathering and are often quite encyclopedic in scope, symposia frequently discuss themselves, the principles underlying them, and the rules they select for their successful operation. Plato, Xenophon, Alberti, Ficino, and Erasmus all produce symposia that treat of love, the force binding their characters together during their conversations. Plutarch and Athenaeus write symposia at least partially about symposia. And Castiglione has his courtiers discuss courtliness, the principle animating their society, as well as love, the force that holds it together. In short, there is a self-involvement, a turning inward, almost a solipsism, characterizing the symposium, which its participants aptly symbolize by sitting with their backs to the outside and their eyes on one another. Where the gaze of characters in a colloquy could be described as centrifugal, as they look out at the world about them in order to anatomize it, and where the characters in a work like *The Republic* stare off into the realm of ideas, the gaze of participants in a symposium should surely be described as centripetal. Neither satirical of the outside world, like colloquies, nor critical of its premises and modes of operation, like most educational and philosophical dialogues, the symposium simply turns its back on society's values and concerns. This eloquent gesture does not imply rejection as much as a temporary indifference, for the symposium assumes and depends on the continuing existence of that outside world. Although it has temporarily set that world aside, its characters come from that world and will eventually return to it. The symposium thus has an extremely paradoxical relationship to the society around it, simultaneously independent and dependent, both setting aside the social order and yet nowhere directly challenging it.

The singular nature of the symposium world emerges more clearly when it is compared to its distant relative, the world of utopias. Unlike symposia, utopias are openly critical of society. Often they contain elements of direct satire, but even when they do not, they are always and everywhere an implicit rejection of a social order they mean to replace. Consequently utopias are not imagined as temporary festivals for participants, but as permanent homes for inhabitants. Where symposia ignore the practical concerns of society simply because they assume that society will continue to operate in its normal way, utopias set out to create brave, new worlds and devote their fullest attention to the necessities of life. Utopias erect political structures, plan economies, establish judicial systems, and draw up schemes for ideal educations. By contrast, although symposia occur in secluded spots, they are not set at the ends of the earth, surrounded by inaccessible mountains and impassable seas, as most utopias are. Rather, the walls around symposia are filled with doors that permit people to come and go at will, and if the doors are closed to keep out riff-raff, they are often opened to admit an uninvited or unexpected guest. Moreover, when the feast is done, it and its boundaries simply dissolve and cease to exist, while the rock walls of utopia protect it from the rest of the world throughout its imaginary eternity.

The symbolic boundaries established in the seating arrangement and setting of the symposium play an important role in generating the special sort of behavior its participants display. Like most dialogues, symposia often use historical characters, presented with some fidelity to human psychology and respect for biographical detail. At the same time, the creator of a symposium often belies his realistic characterization by making his people behave with a tolerance, mutual respect, and sense of community that render them human and social ideals. According to its rules, the symposium, unlike the society around it, is a time set aside for festivity and collective harmony, and as soon as a character has crossed its magical boundaries, he is asked to modify the behavior he normally displays and to become another person. To be sure, he still continues to retain his identifying personal, historical, and cultural traits, but he also becomes an ideal representative of civilization. He strives to behave with civility, courtesy, and charity, and the symposium brilliantly allows him to discharge his dissident, aggressive feelings and his desires for personal preponderance in the socially acceptable and controlled forms of wit and repartée, games and contests. As he enters the symposium world, he subjects himself to its formal set of rules, which stylize his behavior and insure social harmony and order. In effect, by participating in a symposium, he becomes a masker, temporarily wearing the figurative mask that is the image of his most civilized self and that permits him to affirm his own humanity and sociability as well as the fundamental value of community.

The individual transformations produced as characters cross the magical boundaries of a symposium result in a collective, social transformation. For at least a temporary period, a group of otherwise disparate individuals, each egocentrically pursuing his private ends, becomes an ideally harmonious community. No wonder the feast had such a sacred character for the Greeks! Always more than mere eating and drinking, it was a communion to which the gods were ceremoniously invited, and to profane it with unseemly behavior was to be profoundly uncivilized and irreverent, as swinish as the horde of suitors who descended on Odysseus's home during his absence.[25] While Castiglione's book does not literally celebrate a feast and generally does not characterize the festivities at Urbino in religious terms, his characters do flirt playfully with the notion that it is a "sin" to break the rules of decorum by criticizing wicked friars or asking questions when one should raise objections (see III, 20, 365 and I, 23, 120). Moreover, he repeatedly stresses the communal sentiment that unites the courtiers and ladies in Urbino's house of mirth. All are attached to the duchess by a "catena che tutti in amor tenesse uniti" (I, 4, 85–86: "chain that bound us all together in love"[16]); they form a grand family held together by a truly fraternal affection. It is hardly surprising that in his Neoplatonic oration Bembo should

165

follow Dante's lead and imagine heaven as the *convivio degli angeli* (IV, 70, 541), a fitting complement for the earthly convivium being celebrated continuously in Urbino's palace.

If the festive society that forms inside the symposium's walls turns its back on the normal concerns of the world about it, like all festivities it also ignores the social structures and hierarchies of that world. Where society thrives on making status distinctions, the symposium is markedly egalitarian, a fact it underscores through the particular spatial arrangement of its participants. Seated around the edge of a table or on the periphery of a circle, the characters in every symposium, including Castiglione's, are all theoretically equidistant from the center of the space they share in common, and they all possess equal portions, literally and symbolically, of the festivities. During the symposium, its particpants effectively abandon the status and privileges conferred on them by their society. By the rules of their community, all are entitled— even expected—to speak with equal freedom, and it would be judged extremely indecorous—the gaucheness Petronius satirizes in Trimalchio—for any one of them to "pull rank" on his social inferiors. Since all its participants are equals, the symposium traditionally had its characters direct their witty barbs at the host, an attempt to compensate for the slight preponderance his special position conferred upon him.[26] Similarly, if Castiglione's duchess is too "sacred" a figure for his courtiers to tease, her surrogate, Emilia Pia, certainly has to put up with teasing and mockery from friends and enemies alike. The egalitarianism of the symposium is, however, of a special sort and never implies an advocacy of complete social equality. The symposium encloses a homogeneous group, usually members of the same social class, which is open to other members of the same class, but closed to all others. In Castiglione's court, this elite class is defined rather broadly, in part because of the constantly changing social world of Renaissance Italy. It contains noblemen like Ludovico da Canossa, artists like Giancristoforo Romano, churchmen like Bembo, and poets like Aretino. Moreover, the equality its characters share lasts only for the duration of the symposium and could never be extended indefinitely. While Castiglione's characters sit and talk, they treat one another as equals, but during the rest of the time they spent together each day, in Renaissance society it is certain that complex expressions of deference and reinforcements of status would have been not the exception but the rule.

When the characters of a symposium abandon the hierarchies and status of society and sit in a circle expressive of their equality, they do not cease to make evaluative distinctions or to create hierarchies among themselves. These hierarchies, however, are really a tribute to the distance separating the symposium world from the one outside it, since they inevitably parody, invert, contradict, or somehow set aside the normal hierarchies of that world.[27] Plato's and Xenophon's symposia, for example, celebrate the intellectually superior, but socially inferior, Socrates, while in Plutarch's *Banquet of the Seven Sages* a political ruler holds his feast as a tribute to the seven wise men, none of whom comes from the upper classes. Note that Castiglione gives the last and best speech in his work not to a nobleman like Ludovico, but to the writer and intellectual Bembo. What distinguishes the evaluations and hierarchies made by characters in a symposium is that they in no way depend upon external social structures but are generated independently as a result of the discussions held and the games played within its enclosing walls.

The fact that Castiglione's courtiers and ladies revere the duchess would seem to deny the contention that prior social and political hierarchies are ignored in their symposium. Castiglione's work seems an exception to the genre insofar as the symposium world it depicts is also, simultaneously, part of the permanent social world with which it has merged. Within this both permanent and temporary social order, the duchess enjoys a special status and authority which are a direct reflection of her political position in the state over which she and her husband rule. Nevertheless, in keeping with the symposium's desire to maintain its freedom and distance from the social world about it, Castiglione's characters define the reverence they pay the duchess as a tribute freely granted her because of their esteem for her personal, moral superiority. To some extent, this reverence could even be interpreted as a parody of the normal social order, since men, not women, occupied the positions of authority in Renaissance society, and at least some of Castiglione's characters, misogynists like Gasparo and Ottaviano, show a resistance to the social inversion they perceive.[28] Thus, although the duchess's authority results in part from her political position in real life, the courtiers see their reverence for her as freely offered and based on their own values, not on those of the actual political hierarchy. By viewing the situation in this way, they make the inequalities of their real world seem consistent with the egalitarianism and distance from normal hierarchies that characterize the symposium.

Because of its festive character, its egalitarianism, independent values, and communal spirit, the symposium has a literary struc-

ture that distinguishes it from other forms of the dialogue. Where
the philosophical debate is a relentless quest for truth, often involving victory for some of its characters and defeat for others,
and where the educational dialogue offers the extended, usually
uninterrupted, exposition of a subject, the symposium is structured topically into a sequence of speeches and presentations with
considerable allowance for interruptions, questions, and digressions. Often the artist reserves his characters' best speeches for
last, a practice honored by Plato, Xenophon, and Castiglione, in
order to provide a resounding finale for the work. Nevertheless,
even though one speaker may display a talent, eloquence, or wisdom no one else could equal, his speech is not presented as negating those of all the others, but as complementing and perfecting
them. Thus, Socrates' brilliant speech does not cancel out the
appealing wit of Aristophanes' fable or Pausanias's distinction between the earthly and heavenly Aphrodites, and Bembo's vision of
love serves as a complement for the others' more mundane conceptions. Note that Castiglione has Emilia Pia tug at Bembo's robe
and make a sardonic comment to him precisely to correct for the
elevated tone and distinctive manner of his speech; it is the author's way of insuring that the speech will not be interpreted as
going beyond the limits of the symposium in spite of its drama
and brilliance.[29] Although some opinions are clearly better than
others, the rules of the symposium—including Castiglione's—dictate that its participants must tolerate all opinions and respect
every person's right to hold and defend his own.

Knowing that they live in a world of opinion where the absolute
truth of things is difficult to fathom, and knowing likewise that an
individual's bias strongly colors his opinions of reality, Castiglione's characters carry the symposium's tolerance even farther by
refusing to make exaggerated claims concerning the absolute
truth and preferability of their own opinions. Count Ludovico
announces formally before beginning his presentation in Book I
that he cannot describe *the* ideal courtier, but only the one he
appreciates most, and when he later insists that arms, not letters,
should be the courtier's chief profession, he defends his position
not on the grounds that it is right or the best, but on the grounds
of personal preference, since it is his own ideal courtier he is
creating (I, 13, 102 and I, 45, 165). Similarly, in Book III, the
Magnifico defends his requirements for the ideal *donna di palazzo*
as a matter of fashioning her in his own manner (III, 4, 341: "a
modo mio"), essentially as a matter of personal taste (see also III,
8, 347). Moreover, when Castiglione's characters debate, there are

no declared winners or losers; no one ever seriously admits that his opinions are false or that he has been beaten, nor is he expected to do so by the others. Thus, although the Magnifico handily refutes all the arguments Gasparo can bring up against women, the latter never recognizes or acknowledges defeat, and when the former claims victory, he does so in a way that invites further debate and encourages the retorts Gasparo never fails to supply (see, for example, III, 18, 359 and III, 31, 380). Instructively, at one point in the debate of Book III, after Cesare Gonzaga has carried on at some length in praise of women, Ottaviano ironically does urge his fellow misogynists to admit defeat.

> Allora il signor Gasparo, essendosi fermato messer Cesare di parlare, cominciava per rispondere; ma il signor Ottaviano ridendo,—Deh, per amor di Dio,—disse,—datigliela vinta, ch'io conosco che voi farete poco frutto; e parmi vedere che v'acquistarete non solamente tutte queste donne per inimiche, ma ancora la maggior parte degli omini—. Rise il signor Gasparo e disse:—Anzi ben gran causa hanno le donne di ringraziarmi; perché s'io non avessi contradetto al signor Magnifico ed a messer Cesare, non si sariano intese tante laudi che essi hanno loro date—.
>
> (III, 51, 410)

> Messer Cesare had ceased speaking and signor Gasparo was about to reply, when signor Ottaviano said, laughing: "In Heaven's name, grant him the victory, for I know that you have little to gain in this; and, as I see it, you will make not only all these ladies your enemies, but the greater part of the men as well."
>
> Signor Gasparo laughed and said: "Nay, the ladies have very good reason to thank me; because, if I had not contradicted signor Magnifico and messer Cesare, we should not have heard all the praises they have given to women."
>
> (256)

The laughing, mocking tone of the two fellow misogynists here clearly indicates that they do not offer their admission of defeat seriously, and even while he supposedly excuses his own, misogynistic attacks, Gasparo maliciously insinuates that the Magnifico's and Cesare's praise of women was nothing more than flattery, thus spurring them on to renewed debate.

In order to avoid the sort of acrimonious arguments that might arise over the absolute truth of an issue, since individuals normally feel deep commitment to what they judge to be the truth, Castiglione's characters implicitly agree to treat the issues they raise as matters of personal opinion. The rivalry of painting and sculpture, the place of women in society, the superiority of monarchy to republican government—all are issues which could, theoretically at least, be presented in terms of right and wrong, truth and falsehood, but which instead are almost always argued less intensely from a wide variety of shifting positions. Occasionally, deeper feelings and commitments surface—as when the Magnifico criticizes irreverent friars and Federico insists upon pursuing the debate on language—but the two female umpires intervene quickly in all such cases and steer the discussion away from danger. As a result, although Castiglione's symposium lacks the intensity and excitement characteristic of a Platonic debate, it celebrates the ideals of tolerance, diversity, and respect for the right of each person to his own opinion. What is more, because no debate ends decisively in victory for one and defeat for another, and no character pretends that he has cornered the truth, the discussions in Castiglione's book seem capable of almost infinite extension, far beyond the last, purposefully inconclusive exchange between Gasparo and Emilia.

The seeming endlessness of discussion which Castiglione emphasizes in his last pages is related to the most important change he and certain other Renaissance writers made in the symposium form they inherited from antiquity. Ancient symposia were always temporary experiences, a fact underscored by Plato when he has his work begin with Socrates walking to Agathon's house and end the next morning with him leaving it. Even encyclopedic works like Macrobius's *Saturnalia* and Athenaeus's *Deipnosophists,* where the discussions continue for several days, are carefully delimited in time and have definite beginnings and endings. To be sure, in the first pages of *The Laws,* Plato presents the symposium as a model for the well-ordered society at peace, because of its creation of a harmonious community, but he does not confuse a limited model with a complex reality or pretend that it could be a suitable, permanent replacement for society without the extensive modifications he spends the rest of his long work describing.

During the Renaissance, while writers like Alberti and Ficino remain faithful to the character of the symposium as an interlude, a tendency appears in others to present it as though its community could or should be a permanent and separate society. Perhaps because of his Christian revulsion for the viciousness of the fallen world, Erasmus imagines in his *Convivium religiosum* an ideal environment for the Christian humanist, an environment he dreams could be self-sustaining and independent of the outside world, [30] and when Rabelais describes the ideal kingdom of Gargantua and Pantagruel, it is striking that social life there consists almost entirely of festivities of every sort and particularly of banquets and symposia. In his *Cortegiano,* not only does Castiglione present a symposium world that incorporates something of the social hierarchies of the real one into its own structures, but he also strives to create the impression that Urbino's social life is nothing but a continuous festival. Thus, although he stresses the exceptional nature of the pope's visit, which has increased the level of festivity in the court, and although he indicates clearly that his courtiers and ladies hold their *ragionamenti* only in the evening, presumably after the day's work is done, he effectively blurs the distinction between work-time and feast-time, day and night. Note how he pointedly refrains from describing whatever serious military, political, or administrative activities might have been attended to during the day. Instead, he glowingly recounts how the courtiers used to joust, play games and music, and hold feasts all the time in their ideal court (see I, 3, 84). He thus seems to suggest that their activities during their working days were exactly like the activities he presents in the four books of his *Courtier.* Moreover, although he notes that Francesco Maria worked in accompanying the pope out of Urbino, that work meant riding in a triumphal procession, a kind of holiday parade. Only during the fourth evening, when Ottaviano objects to the frivolity of a life spent in continual games, is there some attempt to find meaningful work for courtiers to do as they engage themselves in educating and advising their political leader and contributing to the order and prosperity of the state. Only in the fourth book does a real consciousness emerge that a continual symposium, however satisfying its ideal community may seem, offers an inadequate substitute for a real society.

One way to understand why the symposium is an inadequate substitute for society is to focus on its character as a world of play, which Castiglione's characters emphasize from the start by speaking of their activities as a game.[31] The symposium not only contains games and contests, but is a game itself. Like all games, it has or creates its own special time and space, which are separated psychologically, socially, and symbolically from the time and space of the ordinary world. Within its confines, the symposium game

171

temporarily offers the individual freedom from the burdens of normal routines and replaces the confused rules operative in everyday life with its own more precise and limited set. Finally, to a large extent the symposium game is its own end; it is unproductive when judged in terms of the economic needs of society. It is played for the pleasure it gives of itself, as individuals pursue the self-generated goals it erects independent of, but hardly indifferent to, outside hierarchies and values. Nevertheless, the symposium does serve a tremendously important social end, for it allows individuals to reaffirm their sense of community, which is as essential for society as its hierarchical structures are. Moreover, the symposium not only invites its particpants to release emotions and instincts that normally operate at a fairly low level and in an unregulated manner in everyday life, but its rules actually facilitate a deepening and intensifying of such emotions, albeit only within the limited space and time of the game, in order to permit individuals the profound exhilaration of confronting and playing them out without sacrificing the order or harmony of their society.[32] The symposium is truly a holiday experience which refreshes its players and allows them to return to social routines with renewed vigor and commitment. Logically, if the symposium game is a holiday from society, it cannot be equated with society; its definition depends, in part, on its necessary separation and difference from society. Nevertheless, such an equation is exactly what Castiglione wishes to produce, in spite of the reservations he feels about it and expresses through Ottaviano, and his attempt is responsible to some degree for the hostility many later Renaissance writers felt towards courts and courtliness, however much they may have admired Castiglione's ideals.[33]

Games, like the symposium, can be played only as a result of self-imposed limitations codified in their rules; they operate successfully by simplifying life for the sake of order and an increased intensity of experience. The beauty and grace of Castiglione's symposium are purchased necessarily by turning away from significant areas of human and social reality, by channeling only certain emotions for the sake of release and ignoring others that the game cannot accommodate (e.g., the desire for material possessions), and by playing out life as though most serious economic, social, and political concerns did not exist. The symposium wears blinders, and if its brave, new world were to be substituted for society, it would stand defenseless before the perversions of passions it had not seen in its controlled intensity; it would succumb before the complex problems of economic, social, and political organization it had ignored in its relative simplicity. Thus, although practically everyone in the Renaissance upper classes kept *Il Cortegiano* on the bookshelf and applied it to the letter, doing so made it all the easier for them to ignore its spirit. In his *Malpiglio overo de la corte,* Tasso has his spokesman lead a youth, who had read Castiglione and been impressed by the glitter of contemporary courts, to sense that the glitter is mere tinsel and that beneath it, courts are really hostile to men of talent and learning.[34] The people of Gascoigne's *Master F. J.* and the courtiers in the tragedies of Shakespeare, Middleton, and Webster used Castiglione's vision to create a superficially brilliant, but essentially hollow, image of civilization and refinement. Like the characters in Spenser's House of Pride, they played the game of symposium on the surface while betraying its fundamental values of civility, community, and controlled emotional release in the grimmer underlying game of power and lust. Taken as a model for the whole of society, the limited symposium game of Castiglione's book actually encourages its own perversion. It leads men to dream that life can become a continuous banquet, and when they try to realize their dream, they find that the court has become—to paraphrase Hamlet's mocking reference to the dead Polonius—a banquet not where men eat together, but where they are eaten.

By seeking to identify the symposium holiday with everyday life, Castiglione also threatens to eliminate the psychological and social benefits that sort of experience gives its participants, benefits which resemble those derived from rituals in more primitive cultures.[35] Both symposia and rituals have a tripartite, diachronic structure: separation from the profane world of everyday; an experience of seclusion in what has been described as the liminal state (from *limen,* threshold), a state "betwixt and between" on the fringes or margins of society; and a final return to society and reintegration with it.[36] Moreover, the liminal state is characterized generally in terms that fit the festive world of the symposium perfectly, for it involves egalitarianism, inversions of social hierarchies, and images like night, death, madness, and being in the womb, which contrast with images describing the everyday world.[37] This central episode in many rituals also combines masking with the experience of intoxication or ecstasy, the wearing of masks creating a communal bond among the celebrants and providing an anonymity and freedom which facilitates an exhilarating release from restraint.[38] Similarly, the experience of the symposium involves a metaphorical masking and a release of emotion which for the Greeks was insured by drinking wine and for later cultures is often restricted to verbal play, wit, and games. To be sure, symposia are not primitive rituals: they are held by small groups in private rather than being a significant aspect of the public life of an entire community; they are a leisure-time activity distinguished sharply from work, whereas no such distinction concerning rituals obtains for primitive societies; and although they are sometimes related to important occasions, like weddings or dramatic festivals, they are not connected with seasonal cycles or individuals' status changes in the community and can theoretically be celebrated at arbitrary times completely dependent on individual whim.[39] Nevertheless, symposia can be classified along with other occasions of social festivity in modern, industrialized societies, activities ranging from Masonic rites to sporting events and carnivals, which possess a ritual-like structure involving movement from the everyday world through something like the liminal state and then back again into normal society.[40] Although established arbitrarily and limited to a select group set apart from the rest of society, the festive symposium world, like the liminal state of primitive rituals, provides its participants with an intensified experience of community and an exhilarating release of emotion. And the entire symposium experience, like primitive ritual, gives the individual a sense of being reborn as he emerges from the womb of his secluded world to assume his place in society once again with renewed vitality and commitment.

It is precisely this experience of rebirth that Castiglione minimizes in the first three books of *Il Cortegiano* insofar as he minimizes the distance between his characters' symposium festivity and the real world they live and work in. The rebirth that the symposium experience can bring about demands not only that its participants depart from ordinary reality in some way, but also that they return to it at the end of their festivity, and, in his first three books, Castiglione provides little to suggest that such a return has been made or that the symposium world is really significantly different from the one around it. In his fourth book, however, he modifies the style, tone, and behavioral routines established in the first three, almost as though he consciously wished to resurrect the ritual pattern underlying the symposium and to insure that his entire work would leave its participants with a powerful and satisfied feeling of renewal at its end.

Essentially, Castiglione makes the fourth book a kind of holyday within a holiday. By intensifying the tone of its discussions, making them more serious and weighty, and increasing his characters' earnestness and involvement, he raises the entire book to a

174

level quite above that of the first three and allows it ultimately to soar to the heights of ecstasy on the wings of Bembo's discourse. Though his performance may be more serious than those of speakers of the previous three nights, when Bembo begins his discussion of Neoplatonic love he is nonetheless exposed to criticisms and interruptions just as they had been. As he continues his eloquent ascent up the stairway of love, however, dialogue gradually turns into monologue. Bembo's language changes, becoming increasingly more rhetorical and hence excited as the declarative form of his exposition yields to the optative subjunctive when he urges his companions to become true lovers. It reaches an impassioned climax in direct address, a prayer to the god of love, as Bembo flies upward to the ultimate vision itself, which is beyond words. In the course of his speech, Bembo takes the symposium far beyond the emotional release embodied in wit and games. He becomes intoxicated with the heady wine of his imagination, and for a few moments after the close of his oration, he completely transcends his normal state, speechlessly contemplating the vision of love. He does not, however, keep this wine to himself but, like a shaman or priest, offers it to the other celebrants and takes them up along with him to share in his final moment of vision. He provides his audience, which begs for more when the speech is done, with a bit of ecstasy, of intoxicated release and freedom, more intense than anything previously experienced in their symposium game. He takes their play up to its highest limits, gives everyone the chance for profound emotional release, and thus makes it possible for them to experience a sense of renewal and rebirth when they discover, as they are about to wend their way to bed, that day has dawned.[41] After the community achieved through their masking and especially after the intoxication of Bembo's wine, their long night of seclusion reaches its dawn; like the celebrants in many primitive rituals, they return from their liminal state and are symbolically reborn into the world of day.

Their ritual rebirth is, however, extremely ambiguous, for the courtiers and ladies of Urbino do not really return to a daylight world in which people carry on the practical affairs of life and fulfill necessary military, diplomatic, and political duties. Rather, they return to playing life as a symposium game which Ottaviano's seriousness and Bembo's ecstasy appear to have interrupted only temporarily. Significantly, Castiglione does not simply terminate his book with a return to day after four long nights of discussion, thus implying that Urbino's game has come to its end, but he concludes instead with a final set of witty exchanges between his

175

misogynists and their opponents. The end of Castiglione's work touches its beginning, for this last skirmish between Gasparo and Emilia in the sexual war that has raged throughout every book of *The Courtier* effectively leads the entire work back in a circle to where it began, to the exchange between the pair that opened the discussions on the first evening. This ending can hardly be said to anticipate a re-entry into the real world of daytime activities; it is merely a renewal and continuation of the courtly festivities that have been in progress from the start. Moreover, to emphasize even further the ambiguous character of his courtiers' rebirth, Castiglione does not present them gazing up at a morning sky lighted by a brilliant sun, because that might suggest too forcefully a return to the normal daytime world of practical affairs. Rather, he has them look at the morning star, the star of love, as it gently irradiates a pastoral landscape filled with birdsong, caressed by gentle breezes, and dreamily distant from a workaday world of struggles and hardships. This entrancing twilight world, ruled over by "la dolce governatrice del ciel di Venere" (IV, 73, 544: "the sweet mistress of the heaven of Venus"[359]), seems infused with all the benevolence and love that grace Urbino's harmonious community, almost as though the entire world had been magically transformed into a grand and continuing symposium. Thus, thanks to the intensification of their discussions during the fourth night and to their marvelous arrival at the dawn of a new day, Castiglione's characters can experience an exhilarating feeling of rebirth without ever abandoning their brilliant, festive symposium game.

6/ Ottaviano's Interruption

Castiglione emphasizes the patterned, stylized character of social life at his ideal court by dividing *Il Cortegiano* into four separate evenings of discussion and having each evening open in approximately the same fashion: the group has assembled at the usual time in the usual place; the duchess or Emilia Pia entreats the principal speaker to expound his views; and after the latter has played some variation on the elaborate deference ritual performed by every principal speaker before beginning his exposition, he does in fact accept his assignment, and the discussions finally get under way. For this highly formalized opening Castiglione could have found no precedent in dialogue writers like Plato or Cicero; even Bembo, who has *Gli Asolani* take place on three successive afternoons, presents his characters' discussions as exceptional occurrences, not as parts of a regularly recurring, elaborately patterned, social routine. Moreover, comparison between the final, published text of *Il Cortegiano* and Castiglione's earlier versions of the work reveals him consciously revising his manuscript in order to underscore the ceremonial character of life at Urbino. For instance, not only does the *Seconda redazione* of *Il Cortegiano*, which Castiglione completed sometime before 1520 or 1521, have one less book than his final version and thus one less opportunity to display the routines of his characters' social life, but its first book opens by describing a full day's activities at the court rather than focusing immediately and exclusively, as the final text does, on the elaborate ceremonies that initiate the after-dinner discussions.[1] The *Seconda redazione* also contains fewer direct references to the patterned, game-like nature of life at Urbino, and at one point it actually stresses the great variety of disparate activities in which the courtiers engage themselves: "E benché questa vita non fosse sempre di una medema [*sic*] stampa, pur mai d'altro che di vertuose operazioni non era variata" (I, 3, 8: "And although this life was not always of the same character, it was really never varied by other than virtuous activities"). Castiglione carefully excised this sentence from his final text lest it impair the impression he wished to create of stylization and ritualization at his ideal court.

Consequently, because *Il Cortegiano* establishes so firmly the repeated patterns distinguishing Urbino's social life, when Ottaviano Fregoso interrupts its standard opening procedures at the start of Book IV, his delicate, subtly calculated action acquires great force by frustrating the well-entrenched expectations of courtiers and readers alike. Castiglione describes how, at the beginning of that fourth evening, the lords and ladies of Urbino have come together "all'ora consueta" (IV, 3, 448) in the usual place, and are waiting with anticipation for the arrival of Ottaviano, who has strangely been in retirement all day. No Ottaviano appears, however, and after searching for him in vain, the courtiers and ladies turn to dancing. By the time Ottaviano finally does walk in unexpectedly sometime later, his small alteration of the normal routine must appear a brilliantly calculated, dramatic gesture which proves him a true embodiment of the courtly ideal. For while it does not threaten the others, because it puts Ottaviano in the slightly indecorous position of arriving late, it interrupts the routine just enough to surprise everyone and to gain the fixed attention of the entire company for the speech he is about to give (IV, 3, 449: "stando ognuno con molta attenzione").

Castiglione's revisions of his book reveal that he paid particular attention to this passage describing Ottaviano's late entry and that he altered it in several significant ways. In the first place, although both the *Seconda redazione* and the final text begin by describing how Ottaviano spent the day in retirement, the earlier version suggests facetiously that he was hiding because of the odious nature of his task (i.e., defending his misogynism), while the final text simply stresses his need for solitude in which to think carefully about what he would say and thus implies a greater respect for the seriousness of his ideas and his concern. Secondly, although both passages then describe how all the inhabitants of Urbino arrived in the duchess's chambers at the usual hour and had to search out the missing Ottaviano, both passages continue and conclude in strikingly different fashions:

> . . . bisognò con diligenzia fa[r] cercare il signor Ottaviano; il quale in ultimo venne, e vedendo messer Camillo in mezo delle donne, che ciascuna come suo diffensore lo accarezzava, disse: "Fategli vezzi, ché lo merita, volendo

dire così gran bugie per amor vostro come si apparecchia di far questa sera!"

(Sec. red., III, 3, 186–87)

. . . they had to have signor Ottaviano searched out with diligence; finally he came, and seeing messer Camillo in the midst of the women each of whom caressed him as her defender, he said: "Give him those endearments, since he merits them in wanting to tell such grand lies for your love as he is preparing to do this evening!"

. . . bisognò con diligenzia far cercar il signor Ottaviano, il quale non comparse per bon spacio; di modo che molti cavalieri e damigelle della corte cominciarono a danzare ed attendere ad altri piaceri, con opinion che per quella sera più non s'avesse a ragionar del cortegiano. E già tutti erano occupati chi in una cosa chi in un'altra, quando il signor Ottaviano giunse quasi più non aspettato; e vedendo che messer Cesare Gonzaga e 'l signor Gaspar danzavano, avendo fatto riverenzia verso la signora Duchessa, disse ridendo: —Io aspettava pur d'udir ancor questa sera il signor Gaspar dir qualche mal delle donne; ma vedendolo danzar con una, penso ch'egli abbia fatto la pace con tutte; e piacemi che la lite o, per dir meglio, il ragionamento del cortegiano sia terminato così.

(IV, 3, 448)

. . . a diligent search had to be made for signor Ottaviano, who for a good while did not appear; so that many cavaliers and ladies of the court began to dance, and engage in other pastimes, thinking that for that evening there would be no more talk about the Courtier. And indeed all were occupied, some with one thing and some with another, when signor Ottaviano arrived after he had almost been given up; and, seeing that messer Cesare Gonzaga and signor Gasparo were dancing, he bowed to the Duchess and said, laughing: "I quite expected to hear signor Gasparo speak ill of women again this evening; but now that I see him dancing with one, I think he must have made his peace with all of them; and I am pleased that the dispute (or rather the discussion) about the Courtier has ended so."

(287–88)

179

Note the differences: the later text increases and underscores the length of time Ottaviano is absent; it establishes that the others feel he will not come at all, thus implicitly acknowledging the total interruption of their previous routines which they themselves have reaffirmed in deciding to dance instead of talk; finally, the later text dramatizes Ottaviano's last minute entry and stresses its complete unexpectedness ("quasi più non aspettato"). Clearly, as Castiglione reworked his book for publication, not only did he increasingly stress the repeated patterns of Urbino's social life, but he also placed far greater emphasis on the small but dramatic interruption Ottaviano creates by means of his strategically delayed entrance.

Castiglione emphasizes Ottaviano's interruption precisely because it serves as a symbolic cue introducing the greater seriousness and weightiness of the fourth book in comparison with the first three. Such emphasis would not have suited earlier versions of *Il Cortegiano* nearly so well as it does the final text. In the *Seconda redazione,* as in the final version, Castiglione begins his last book with an elegiac passage based on the opening of the last book in Cicero's *De Oratore,*[2] and in both versions, Ottaviano then expounds his elevated conception of the courtier's social and political functions.[3] The final book of the *Seconda redazione* was, however, essentially still in a transitional state; a rambling debate about women and love, it did not end on the high note of Bembo's Neoplatonic idealism but on the low note of Gasparo's misogynistic denunciation of women.[4] As Castiglione reworked this earlier version of his *Cortegiano,* he not only added Bembo's speech, but, more importantly, he also divided and re-arranged all of his material, separating the less lofty debates about women and love, which became his new Book III, from the speeches of Ottaviano and Bembo, which Castiglione's own characters consider more serious and which constitute the present Book IV. As Castiglione moved beyond his earlier conceptions, leaving behind him those popular treatises on women's place in court society that once may have served as a significant motivation for his work, he conceived the speeches of his new fourth book as the most elevated definition of the meaning and purpose of courtly life that he could imagine, and thus as the most fitting conclusion for his masterpiece.[5]

In order to underscore the more elevated, serious character of this last book and its new conceptions, he must have decided that he also had to rewrite the passage describing Ottaviano's interruption. Perhaps his decision was influenced by what Alberti and

Bembo had done in the final books of their dialogues, where the former introduced a change of locale and the latter added a crowd and an elaborate ceremony in order to signal the slightly more elevated status of the conceptions about to be offered. In any case, in the final version of the passage, Castiglione stresses the way that Ottaviano's interruption has created an inversion of the normal order of events established on previous evenings: before, the dancing had followed, not preceded conversation, while now, on this fourth evening, conversation takes place only after the implicitly less serious business of dancing is done with. Secondly, Castiglione describes how Ottaviano spent the entire day and, by implication, part of the evening as well, meditating upon his assignment, and nowhere does he suggest that his speaker's absence results from embarrassment over charges of misogynism. Finally, by stressing the considerable amount of time the group spends dancing before Ottaviano finally appears, Castiglione not only makes it seem more reasonable that their conversations should last until morning, but he places their discussions clearly in the middle of the night, perhaps a time of deception and unreality but also traditionally a time of greater truths and more profound exploration of mysterious realms.[6] Ottaviano's interruption is hardly a simple gesture, and it should alert the reader, as it does the lords and ladies of Urbino, to expect the unexpected, to anticipate discussions that probe more deeply and more seriously than before. Thus though Ottaviano re-establishes the ritual forms by his first jesting remarks to the company and by his expected refusal to speak until ordered to do so by the duchess, he has used the social forms available to him in order to prepare auditors—and readers—for the discussions that follow.

Ottaviano's interruption preludes the far-reaching changes the speakers of the fourth book wreak upon the ideal courtier. Ottaviano and Bembo adopt a far more serious tone in presenting their ideals, replacing the witty, informal presentations of the first three nights with more technical analyses in which explanations and clarifications, formerly less essential, now become prominent. Each implicitly rejects some essential feature of the earlier ideal, Ottaviano criticizing the courtier's uselessness and lack of social productivity, while Bembo rejects the sensual and earthly, though legitimate, love of Book III in favor of the world-denying ecstasy of his Neoplatonic vision.[7] Each speaker redefines the ideal in terms of his own values and attitudes, transforming someone conceived primarily as an actor and an artist, whose prime purposes were to serve his lady and achieve personal honor and dignity, into a mystic lover seeking self-transformation into pure spirit, and a humanist whose sole justification is the service he performs for his prince as educator and advisor.

Castiglione, however, does more than merely emphasize the superiority of this new ideal to the conceptions of previous books; he stresses its absolute differences from them as well. Just as he utilizes Ottaviano's interruption to signal the new and different ideals of Book IV, he has his characters themselves indicate forcefully that Ottaviano's and Bembo's visions of the ideal courtier are essentially incompatible in some basic respects with the vision of the first three books. Ottaviano's conception is rejected because he has turned the ideal courtier into a humanist *maestro di scuola* (IV, 36, 491), and when he later argues that Plato and Aristotle exemplify his ideal, even his fellow misogynist, Gasparo Pallavicino, feels moved to mock his assertion with an ironic comment:

> Io non aspettava già che 'l nostro cortegiano avesse tanto d'onore; ma poiché Aristotile e Platone son suoi compagni, penso che niun più debba sdegnarsi di questo nome. Non so già però s'io mi creda che Aristotile e Platone mai danzassero o fossero musici in sua vita, o facessero altre opere di cavalleria.
>
> (IV, 48, 510)

> I certainly did not expect our Courtier to be honored so; but since Aristotle and Plato are his companions, I think no one henceforth ought to despise the name. Still, I am not quite sure that I believe that Aristotle and Plato ever danced or made music in their lives, or performed any acts of chivalry.
>
> (333)

Similarly, although Bembo claims he accepts earlier notions of sensual love when framing his own ideal, the self-absorbed, spiritual passion he approves for the courtier is possible only after earthly and bodily concerns like sensual love have been transcended. Consequently, his notion of Neoplatonic love really appears the antithesis of the courtly love celebrated by the group in Book III.[8] Clearly, although Castiglione wants the reader to regard Book IV as an essential part of his work, the changes he effects in basic conceptions and which he so forcefully and self-consciously calls attention to open a vast gulf between the ideas and ideals of the fourth book and those of the first three.

At least two fundamentally different approaches to the problem of explaining why Castiglione chose to create a new conception of the courtier in his last book are possible. The first of these, the biographical approach, looks to the details of Castiglione's life in order to explain the changes in his book: it generally argues that the author originally intended a work in three books which he finished in 1515 or 1516, that he subsequently experienced significant changes in his life—the dissolution of the court at Urbino, his rise to prominence in papal service, the death of his wife, and his assumption of holy orders—and that these experiences led him to add the material that eventually became the supplemental fourth book. The last night of discussions is thus considered a revision of earlier material, an attempt to remold the ideal in the light of a greater political and religious seriousness.[9] Yet these biographical explanations accounting for the relationship between the fourth book and the first three by pointing to the genesis of Castiglione's work simply do not satisfy. Either they turn *Il Cortegiano* into disguised autobiography, following the lead of Vittorio Cian,[10] or they simply content themselves by substituting consideration of external, biographical details for analysis of internal structure. In either case, they look beyond the book itself rather than within it; they do violence to *Il Cortegiano* as a carefully wrought work of art and fragment its unity into a series of biographical moments. Consequently a second and better way of approaching the changes in the fourth book would be to examine the themes and structure of the work itself, seeking primarily within it explicit reasons for Castiglione's alteration of his ideal. Looked at in this way, *Il Cortegiano* would reveal its meaning from within: the new seriousness of the fourth book could be read as a direct response to certain inadequacies in the first three; its double reworking of the ideal courtier could be considered an attempt to solve or at least avoid the two major problems that dogged Castiglione's heels throughout the earlier books—the problems of deception and triviality.

Considering the first of these problems, it is remarkable how often the first three books encounter the issue of deception while failing or refusing to solve the problems it raises. Some issues, like the question of language and the relative merits of painting and sculpture, remain unresolved because they are peripheral to the ideal. Other issues, like the questions of nobility and the relative superiority of arms and letters, require compromises, and the courtiers leave them behind almost as soon as they have achieved a satisfactory compromise formulation. Only in the case of the debate on women, which is generated by the structural imbalance between men and women in Urbino's society and is essentially unresolvable, and in the matter of deception, do the courtiers return to the same issues repeatedly. Deception poses an especially complex and troubling problem for them, because they live in a world where appearance reigns supreme and where their chief task is learning how to recognize, understand, and manipulate it. But they worry most about deception because the courtly actor they fashion is the master of masking, the brilliant creator of his social personality who could, on that account, be considered a subtle deceiver, and consequently something less than morally ideal.

Leading the attack on the courtier's masking as deception, Gasparo Pallavicino expresses his reservations on three separate occasions, moving from oblique criticism to head-on assault. A rambunctious spirit of contradiction, Gasparo first attacks Ludovico da Canossa in Book I on the issue of inherited nobility, forcing him to abandon his original position, which simply assumed nobility was something valuable in itself for the ideal courtier, and to argue for it instead on the pragmatic grounds that it disposes others to receive the courtier favorably and thus facilitates his success. Recognizing "no ancestor but Adam,"[11] the egalitarian Gasparo wants a courtier who will win praise and honor through his real qualities and achievements, not through the gifts granted him by fortune or the credulity of men. In other words, by attacking inherited nobility, Gasparo really attacks obliquely a kind of deception where appearances, rather than real qualities, claim the rewards of praise and honor.[12]

Later, in the second book, Gasparo's attack on the courtier's masking as deception becomes much more explicit when he rejects Federico Gonzaga's concern over the ideal's dress and appearance. Criticizing such a concern as a reprehensible affectation for the trivial, Gasparo declares:

> A me non pare, . . . che si convenga, né ancor che s'usi tra persone di valore giudicar la condicion degli omini agli abiti, e non alle parole ed alle opere, perché molti s'ingannariano; né senza causa dicesi quel proverbio che l'abito non fa 'l monaco.
>
> (II, 28, 233)

> It does not seem fitting to me, or even customary among persons of worth, to judge the character of men by their dress rather than by their words or deeds, for then many

would be deceived; nor is it without reason that the proverb says: "The habit does not make the monk."

(123)

Gasparo's challenge forces Federico to abandon his far too simple assertion that in this world "le cose estrinseche spesso fan testimonio delle intrinseche" (II, 27, 232: "external things often bear witness to inner things"[122]), and to agree that he does not think men should be judged by their dress. But he refuses to yield an inch on the importance of external appearances, for in a world of façades where men are usually forced to judge by what they see long before they can judge by what they know, Federico surely argues sensibly that the courtier should try to manipulate his appearance so that it expresses his best qualities. Of course men should be judged by their words and deeds, but in this world, says Federico,

> ancor l'abito non è piccolo argomento della fantasia di chi lo porta, avvenga che talor possa esser falso; e non solamente questo, ma tutti i modi e costumi, oltre all'opere e parole, sono giudicio delle qualità di colui in cui si veggono.
>
> (II, 28, 234)

> . . . a man's attire is no slight index of the wearer's fancy, although sometimes it can be misleading; and not only that, but ways and manners, as well as deeds and words, are all an indication of the qualities of the man in whom they are seen.
>
> (123)

In this statement Federico hastens over the problem of deception that has troubled his fellow courtier, admitting only parenthetically ("avvenga che talor possa esser falso") that his ideal courtier could really be a master of deceit. Like Ludovico da Canossa in Book I, Federico refuses to think of the ideal in that way, but prefers to see him as a brilliant actor, the artisan of his appearance and personality. Although Ludovico and Federico would prefer to avoid the unpleasant fact of the courtier's deception, Gasparo's challenges make them face it again and again, for if the courtier deceives, what moral authority can he have?

A few pages after the interchange over the courtier's dress, the issue finally comes into the open. Federico has been describing an ideal strategy for the courtier: he should claim excellence only in his profession, even though he may possess it in other areas, so that when people see him perform well in what is not his profession, they will think him even better at what is. "Quest'arte," concludes Federico, "s'ella è compagnata da bon giudicio, non mi dispiace punto" (II, 39, 252: "Such an art, when accompanied by good judgment, does not displease me in the least"[138]). It does, however, displease Signor Gasparo:

> Questa a me non par arte, ma vero inganno; né credo che si convenga, a chi vol esser omo da bene, mai lo ingannare.
>
> (II, 40, 252)

> This seems to me to be not an art, but an actual deceit; and I do not think it seemly for anyone who wishes to be a man of honor ever to deceive.
>
> (138)

In responding to Gasparo's straightforward, moral indictment, Federico performs a series of intellectual somersaults, first claiming that such deception is really an adornment for the courtier, then admitting it is deception, but not to be blamed, then finally arguing for the identity of deception and art.

> Questo . . . è più presto un ornamento, il quale accompagna quella cosa che colui fa, che inganno; e se pur è inganno, non è da biasimare. Non direte voi ancora, che di dui che maneggian l'arme quel che batte il compagno lo inganna! e questo è perché ha più arte che l'altro. E se voi avete una gioia, la qual dislegata mostri esser bella, venendo poi alle mani d'un bon orefice, che col legarla bene la faccia parer molto più bella, non direte voi che quello orefice inganna gli occhi di chi la vede! E pur di quello inganno merita laude, perché col bon giudicio e con l'arte le maestrevoli mani spesso aggiungon grazia ed ornamento allo avorio o vero allo argento, o vero ad una bella pietra circondandola di fin oro. Non diciamo adunque che l'arte o tal inganno, se pur voi lo volete così chiamare, meriti biasimo alcuno.
>
> (II, 40, 252–53)

> This . . . is an ornament attending the thing done, rather than deceit; and even if it be deceit, it is not to be cen-

sured. Will you also say that, in the case of two men who
are fencing, the one who wins deceives the other? He wins
because he has more art than the other. And if you have a
beautiful jewel with no setting, and it passes into the
hands of a good goldsmith who with a skillful setting
makes it appear far more beautiful, will you say that the
goldsmith deceives the eyes of the one who looks at it?
Surely he deserves praise for that deceit, because with
good judgment and art his masterful hand often adds
grace and adornment to ivory or to silver or to a beautiful
stone by setting it in fine gold. Therefore let us not say
that art—or deceit such as this, if you insist on calling it
that—deserves any blame.

(138–39)

In reply to Gasparo's blunt moral attack, Federico slips out of the
line of fire under the cover of a semantic smokescreen where once
again aesthetics replace morals and deception metamorphoses
into art. Although Gasparo allows the issue to rest without further
ado, Federico's slippery redefinition of terms has by no means
solved the problem.

Deception also poses another, not unrelated problem for these
courtiers, the problem of trusting appearances. While the ideal
courtier deceives only to insure the favorable reception of his
good qualities, and while behind the illusion he manipulates there
supposedly lies the larger reality it figures forth, not every courtier is an ideal courtier. Sometimes the jewel in Federico's gold and
silver setting is not a diamond, but cut glass whose false beauty
easily deceives men's eyes, which are never sufficiently sharp-
sighted, especially at first glance. For instance, the Magnifico explicitly condemns men's astuteness in playing false roles as they
successfully flatter women into serving their wicked ends (III, 54,
415), and Ottaviano complains in Book IV that contemporary
princes need good advisors precisely because they are surrounded
by packs of lying sycophants who successfully, continuously veil
the truth from them (IV, 6, 452). Pietro Bembo, especially, reveals
the anguish that results from too trusting an acceptance of appearances:

Però essendo a me intervenuto più d'una volta l'esser in-
gannato da chi più amava e da chi sopra ogni altra persona aveva confidenzia d'esser amato, ho pensato talor da
me a me che sia ben non fidarsi mai di persona del

mondo, né darsi così in preda ad amico, per caro ed
amato che sia, che senza riserva l'omo gli comunichi tutti i
suoi pensieri come farebbe a se stesso; perchè negli animi
nostri sono tante latebre e tanti recessi, che impossibil è
che prudenzia umana possa conoscer quelle simulazioni,
che dentro nascose vi sono.

(II, 29, 236)

Thus, since it has happened to me more than once to be
deceived by the one whom I most loved and by whom I
was confident of being loved above every other person—I
have sometimes thought to myself it would be well for us
never to trust anyone in the world, or give ourselves over
to any friend (however dear and cherished he may be) so
as to tell him all our thoughts without reserve as we would
tell ourselves; for there are so many dark turns in our
minds and so many recesses that it is not possible for
human discernment to know the simulations that are la-
tent there.

(125)

In this passage, Bembo is not speaking of chance acquaintances
whom he has had little time to get to know well, but of those who
pretended to love him. Perhaps Bembo's bad experiences may be
attributed to some hypothetical inability on the part of this bookish mystic to judge men with sufficient discrimination, but if it can
be assumed that on the contrary he is as reasonable as his statement above suggests, then his remarks open a most disturbing
vista indeed within Castiglione's book, the vista of a shadowy
world where all is appearance and men are never, or seldom,
what they seem. A potentially terrifying question must gnaw away
in the hidden recesses of the courtiers' minds: how can truth be
separated from appearances? how do you know your best friend
is not your worst enemy? To this question of truth and appearance, which the indefatigable Gasparo poses to Federico Fregoso
at one point, the latter's reply shows obvious discomfort that the
subject has even come up: "Perdonatemi; . . . io non voglio entrar
qua, ché troppo ci saria che dire, ma il tutto si rimetta alla discrezion vostra" (II, 23, 226: "Excuse me, . . . I do not wish to go into
that, for there would be too much to say; but let the whole question be left to your discretion"[117–18]).

Federico's evasive responses do not succeed in laying the question of deception to rest, and whether it continued to bother

Castiglione or not in the years after he finished his first three books, he nevertheless revives it in Book IV. This time, however, he offers solutions to the two general problems involved. In the first place, while Ottaviano's new courtier is still a deceiver, he justifies this deception by giving it a moral function. The courtier becomes a humanist educator who will not alienate his prince with the corrections and rebukes of a *severo filosofo* (IV, 8, 456) but will use his talents to make himself and his moral lessons pleasing and ingratiating to his master in order to educate and advise him.[13] In other words, he will deceive the prince into a love of learning and morality by making the unpleasant seem pleasurable, leading his unwitting master up the steep hill of virtue, "ingannandolo con inganno salutifero" (IV, 10, 457: "beguiling him with salutary deception"[294]). In such an educator, the artful manipulation of his personality is not merely excusable; the courtier's good acting is absolutely essential for the ultimate good of the state. No wonder, then, that none of Castiglione's courtiers should think to attack the ideal courtier's deception now.

If Ottaviano solves the first problem of deception by having the courtier use it to serve his prince's, not his own interest, Bembo's monologue offers a way of dealing with the general problem of deception posed by a world where truth and appearance seem indistinguishable. Toward the beginning of his speech, Bembo identifies the beautiful with the good, and he is immediately challenged by the mockery of Morello da Ortona, who claims he has known many a wicked beauty (IV, 55, 520: "molte belle donne malissime"). Bembo cannot deny that what Morello says of beautiful women is often true, but he does insist that beauty itself, the Platonic idea of beauty, can never be evil. Beauty can become evil only when it is immersed in the world of matter, incarnated in the flesh of men and women. In other words, the problem of beauty's deceptiveness—really, the problem of all earthly deceptiveness—is unavoidable as long as the world of matter exists and men remain parts of it. In order to enjoy true beauty, which is free from deception and imperfection, Bembo tells the courtier to turn away from the mundane sphere entirely, to contemplate the idea of beauty within himself, and finally to mount the stairway of love to a divine realm which is unchanging, eternal, simple, true. Bembo would have the courtier conquer deception and come to know true beauty, not by changing an unredeemable world, but by transcending it and its illusions completely.

While the ideals of Ottaviano and Bembo may thus be considered implicit responses to the problems deception creates in the first three books, Ottaviano and Bembo present their speeches much more explicitly as responses to what is really the most discussed and debated issue within them, the question of what the courtier's relationship should be to women. This issue holds great importance for both Ottaviano and Bembo because they link it to the courtier's involvement in his society and its courtly games. Both are disturbed that their ideal should engage in what they feel are totally trivial activities that women demand as service and define as the only activities proper to life in society, over which they rule. Thus, while Bembo may begin his speech as a praise of woman's beauty and courtly love, he soon turns to a love of ideal beauty instead, urging the courtier to transcend women entirely at the same time that he transcends the trivialities and transitoriness of courtly life. More explicitly than Bembo, Ottaviano minces no words in denouncing the former ideal courtier as trivial and useless and in linking his defects to his courtly service of his lady. Having already revealed himself as something of a misogynist in Book III, Ottaviano begins his speech—and his attack—on the courtier by distinguishing things which are good in themselves, like temperance, fortitude, and health, from those which are good only with respect to the ends they serve. The ideal courtier is an example of things good only in respect to their ends:

> ché in vero se con l'esser nobile, aggraziato e piacevole ed esperto in tanti esercizi il cortegiano non producesse altro frutto che l'esser tale per se stesso, non estimarei che per conseguir questa perfezion di cortegiania dovesse l'omo ragionevolmente mettervi tanto studio e fatica, quanto è necessario a chi la vole acquistare; anzi direi che molte di quelle condicioni che se gli sono attribuite, come il danzar, festeggiar, cantar e giocare, fossero leggerezze e vanità, ed in un omo di grado più tosto degne di biasimo che di laude; perché queste attillature, imprese, motti ed altre tai cose che appartengono ad intenimenti di donne e d'amori, ancora che forse a molti altri paia il contrario, spesso non fanno altro che effeminar gli animi, corrumper la gioventù e ridurla a vita lascivissima; onde nascono poi questi effetti che 'l nome italiano è ridutto in obbrobrio, né si ritrovano se non pochi che osino non dirò morire, ma pur entrare in uno pericolo.

> (IV, 4, 450)

For indeed if by being of noble birth, graceful, charming, and expert in so many exercises, the Courtier were to bring forth no other fruit than to be what he is, I should not judge it right for a man to devote so much study and labor to acquiring this perfection of Courtiership as anyone must do who wishes to acquire it. Nay, I should say that many of those accomplishments that have been attributed to him (such as dancing, merrymaking, singing, and playing) were frivolities and vanities and, in a man of any rank, deserving of blame rather than of praise; for these elegances of dress, devices, mottoes, and other such things as pertain to women and love (although many will think the contrary), often serve merely to make spirits effeminate, to corrupt youth, and to lead it to a dissolute life; whence it comes about that the Italian name is reduced to opprobrium, and there are but few who dare, I will not say to die, but even to risk any danger.

(288–89)

In this opening assault on the ideal Ottaviano not only attacks its lack of some serious purpose, such as the political service to prince and state he will propose, but he also rejects the beautiful social game, the dancing, singing, and playing, as well as the acts of knightly service to the lady that formerly distinguished the courtier's life. Ottaviano even goes so far as to link the courtly games, and especially the courtier's service to his lady, to moral charges of degeneracy and effeminacy as well as to the contemporary political decay of Italy. Ottaviano's tone clashes with the tone that prevailed for three nights of discussion; it is the serious, humorless tone of a committed statesman and moralist. Moreover, Ottaviano's attack cannot be dismissed out of hand, for while his charge of degeneracy seems emotional rhetoric, his other charges, of triviality and uselessness, go right to the heart of the earlier ideal.

The courtier of the first three books is a creature of leisure fashioned in the image of those real courtiers at Urbino who seem to do nothing but play games and converse entertainingly. To be sure, their discussions, dancing, and other amusements supposedly occupy only their evenings, but Castiglione gives no description of the activities that occupy their days. Consequently it is entirely consistent that such a society, seemingly always at leisure, would fashion a courtier whose ideals and activities duplicate its own. While his creators supply him with the practical duties of serving his lord and practicing the profession of arms, they refrain from much comment on either activity. Instead, they are

obsessed by other concerns, by his successful performance of social roles at court, by his ability to entertain those around him, by
his acquisition of social standing and the approval of his peers and
superiors. From his perspective, no wonder Ottaviano condemns
this courtier as an effeminate, inconsequential social butterfly!

Ottaviano is clearly disturbed by the self-imposed limitations,
the narrow circle of activities, the courtiers and ladies accept and
likewise impose upon their ideal. Essentially, he is disturbed by
their transformation of social life into a game which, like all
games, is played by setting up boundaries and imposing limitations codified in rules. The rules for Urbino's game are, moreover, especially restrictive: they forbid delving too deeply into
difficult problems or exploring profound, personal differences.
While they permit raising questions about the issue of deception,
they make it a breach of decorum to brood on it too long and thus
risk the possible social dislocation, the fears and worries, to which
such brooding might expose the group. Likewise, the rules of
their game dictate that the courtiers turn the debate about
women's place and nature in Book III away from potentially more
troubling, philosophical considerations and transform it into an
inconclusive, less directly disturbing exchange of stories displaying female virtue and vice. Moreover, because the rules of Urbino's symposium game require that everyone participate as an
equal in open, public discussion, they forbid private and intimate
tête-à-têtes, discussions that transcend the intellectual competence
or experiential spheres of those present, and monologues or
speeches that do not permit interruptions or are not offered def-
erentially as forms of entertainment, as Bibbiena's comic performance is in Book II.

It is true that from Ottaviano's political and social perspective,
this limited game-world could be judged "un-serious." Looked at
from other perspectives, Urbino's symposium game, like many
other games, is a most serious affair indeed. Not only does it have
its participants play parts that will guarantee them substantial social and political rewards from their lord and lady, but the game is
serious in an even more profound way as well. It allows its players
to articulate deep feelings of aggression and status rivalries, sexual antagonisms and fantasies, in a controlled and limiting situation; the game's rules minimize the destructive possibilities involved and allow the participants to perform roles of some consequence to themselves and even ultimately to achieve a measure of
conscious recognition and order for some of their deepest
drives.[14] Thus while its rules prevent Castiglione's society from

going beyond a restricted round of activities and conversations, they are also clearly indispensable not only for the orderly maintenance of social life but for the deeply experienced pleasure, the exuberant joy, and the self-realization that Urbino's inhabitants find in social intercourse.[15] In making his criticisms, Ottaviano adopts the role of spoilsport; he wants his fellow courtiers to stop turning civilization into their wonderful game, and he wants to insist on a notion of seriousness that denies the very possibility of play.

As Ottaviano rejects the symposium game played at Urbino, he likewise rejects the women who reign over it and keep it within its proper, limited bounds. Women set the high, refined, joyful tone for courts and courtiers alike, inspiring men's imaginations and animating their passions. Cesare Gonzaga, defending women from the attacks of the courtly misogynists in Book III, reprimands the latter:

> Voi sete in grande errore, . . . perché come corte alcuna, per grande che ella sia, non po aver ornamento o splendore in sé, né allegria senza donne, né cortegiano alcun essere aggraziato, piacevole o ardito, né far mai opera leggiadra di cavalleria, se non mosso dalla pratica e dall'amore e piacer di donne, così ancora il ragionar del cortegiano è sempre imperfettissimo, se le donne, interponendovisi, non danno lor parte di quella grazia, con la quale fanno perfetta ed adornano la cortegiania.
>
> (III, 3, 340)

> You are greatly mistaken, . . . because just as no court, however great, can have adornment or splendor or gaiety in it without ladies, neither can any Courtier be graceful or pleasing or brave, or do any gallant deed of chivalry, unless he is moved by the society and by the love and charm of ladies: even discussion about the Courtier is always imperfect unless ladies take part in it and add their part of that grace by which they make Courtiership perfect and adorned.
>
> (204–5)

Later, the Magnifico will reinforce Cesare's argument by examples, and Cesare will continue his argument that men produce all their noble virtues and manners, all the refinements of civilized life, from their desire to please the ladies (III, 51–52, 410–13).

The relationship between women and the beautiful game of civilization played at Urbino could not be made more explicit. The ring of chairs at Castiglione's symposium is simply the outermost edge of the duchess's skirt.

Both Ottaviano and Bembo respond in the last book to the question of the ideal courtier's relationship to women and to the "trivial" symposium game they rule over by radically changing the nature of both the ideal and his world. They provide the courtier with motivations and goals that either remove him from the influence of women into Ottaviano's exclusively masculine world of politics and social responsibility or allow him to love and serve beautiful women only as the first step in transcending them altogether. In the very language they use, they deny the essentially self-contained, firmly bounded, static social world in which previous versions of the courtier implicitly would operate and which is mirrored in the elegant society of Urbino's court. Rather than see him as a permanent denizen dancing about within the narrow, fixed circle of their court, the playground of their symposium game, Ottaviano and Bembo make him a figure of dynamic movement. As they erect definite goals for him to pursue beyond the symposium game at court, they force him to move decisively through the space of the real world, to undertake a journey or quest that leads him definitively outside the tight circle of their court. Moreover, both Ottaviano and Bembo replace the essentially static, cylical conception of time reflected in Urbino's repetitious, ritualized social life with a dynamic, linear conception organizing time sequentially. They thrust the courtier into history and give him a mighty propulsion forward into an anticipated future.

Ottaviano reveals this new, dynamic conception of the courtier and his world at the very start of Book IV when he declares that while some things are good in themselves, others, like the courtier, are good only in terms of the *goal* to which they *direct* themselves (IV, 4, 449: "per lo fine al quale s'indrizzano"). To be sure, all the courtiers at Urbino speak in characteristic spatial metaphors, but as they talk of entering and leaving a conversation, of staying within or going out of bounds, it is clear that the space they have in mind is the area enclosed within their symbolic circle of chairs and that the only movement they make takes them in to its center and never leads them beyond its periphery. Ottaviano, on the other hand, speaks continually in terms of roads and journeys, imagining the courtier's life not as the achievement of a static self-perfection but as a dynamic progress through space and time. As he says, it is not sufficient for the courtier to produce the flower of self-realization; he must grow beyond that point and produce the substantial fruit of social and political benefits (IV, 5, 450–51). Thus Ottaviano instructs his ideal to become the educator, servant, and advisor of his prince, leading him up to higher goals along the austere path of virtue (IV, 10, 457: "la austera strada della virtù"). Ottaviano then makes the prince an equally dynamic figure, who is provided with the task of ruling well so that his realm can also move forward and reach the ultimate goal of peace and prosperity under his good reign, when all men will be happy and once again the Age of Gold will return to earth (IV, 18, 469: "il che solo basteria per far gli omini felici e ridur un'altra volta al mondo quella età d'oro, che si scrive esser stata quando già Saturno regnava").

Several ironies result from Ottaviano's redefinition of the courtier's role and the world in which he is to operate. In the first place, if man's temporal existence becomes meaningful, justifiable, and serious only because it possesses a goal to be reached in the future, the achievement of that goal, the restoration of the Golden Age, can only mean the obliteration of time itself. Moreover, there is a second irony: why should the courtier struggle through time to a paradise which he already possesses in the timeless round of activities at Urbino? To this question, however, there is an answer, for when Castiglione wrote his dedicatory letter to Don Michel de Silva, and perhaps by the time he began writing Ottaviano's speech, he had become aware that the Golden Age of Urbino had faded away, and by prefacing his work with the letter, he deliberately made his readers aware that such a loss had occurred. Urbino emerges from *Il Cortegiano* not as an enduring paradise, an oasis of perfection spared the ravages of time, but rather as an Arcadia from which death has dispelled the illusion of timelessness. In the context of this nostalgic vision, Ottaviano's new conception of the courtier and his activity, which attempts to make temporal process meaningful, becomes all the more understandable and compelling.[16] Though Urbino's brilliant court has vanished, Ottaviano's courtier can look forward with hope to a better future and can journey forth in quest of a new Golden Age in the larger world to replace the little circle of friends whom Castiglione once knew and loved.

Complementing Ottaviano, Bembo also creates an ideal courtier who will break out of the boundaries established for Urbino's symposium game and reject the cyclical, repetitive movement of courtly existence in favor of directed movement toward some ultimate future goal. Specifically, Bembo rejects the ideal of an earthly lover trapped in the cycle of sexual desire, and he espouses the ideal of a Neoplatonic mystic who follows his course upward and away from the earth, leaving behind its frustrating cycles of life. Like Ottaviano's, Bembo's entire speech is grounded in metaphors that organize movement through space and time and turn the courtier's static dance into a pilgrimage. Bembo speaks of the *divina strada amorosa* (IV, 62, 528) and the *vero camino* on which the courtier will journey, with divine guidance, away from the *cieco labirinto* (IV, 70, 540) of this world up to heaven. Bembo also characterizes human life as having a positive temporal development in its movement from the passion of youth to the ideal contemplation of age. But while his metaphors, like Ottaviano's, would seem to organize experience in terms of horizontal, linear movement through time and space toward a future goal, Bembo's basic metaphoric conception, the *scala d'amore,* involves vertical ascent from the *infimo grado* of sensual pleasure to the "sublime stanzia ove abita la celeste, amabile e vera bellezza" (IV, 69, 539: "lofty mansion where heavenly, lovely, and true beauty dwells" [355]). Ottaviano's and Bembo's conceptions are thus in some respects quite different: Ottaviano's courtier moves horizontally through time and space toward a new Age of Gold, while Bembo's moves vertically upward to heaven; Ottaviano's quest involves people other than the courtier himself, while Bembo's is a solitary experience; Ottaviano's ultimate goal is social and earthly, whereas Bembo's transcends society and this world completely; and finally, where the first strives to give man's actions in time, and time itself, significance, the second at best tolerates the temporal processes of human life, really desiring immediate, direct transcendence that would abolish time altogether. Nevertheless, in spite of their differences, both create ideal courtiers who have a direction and purpose far beyond repeated participation in the symposium game that goes on night after night in the self-contained playground of Urbino's palazzo.

Clearly, a profound gulf yawns between the ideals of the first three nights and the fourth. Replacing the well-rounded man, the perfect amalgam of medieval knight and urbane, humanist-trained gentleman, are Ottaviano's *maestro di scuola* and Bembo's Neoplatonic lover.[17] Neither reformulation of the ideal, however understandable as a response to problems and objectionable features in the original conception, should be thought of as being particularly original on Castiglione's part. Quite the contrary, in order to deal with his problems, he has simply turned to two of the more accessible intellectual traditions in his culture: the educational philosophy of antiquity and contemporary humanism, and the Neoplatonism of Bembo and the Florentine Academy.[18] But in segregating the "wisdom" of those traditions along with his new versions of the courtier in the fourth book, Castiglione revealed that "wisdom" to be as fundamentally incompatible with the attitudes and concepts of the first three books as Bembo's and Ottaviano's courtiers are with the earlier ideal. In other words, in solving the problems attached to certain ideals by turning to others, Castiglione polarized courtly love and Neoplatonic love, revealing their basic incompatibility, and he split apart two educational ideals which had been assumed compatible since antiquity. He developed the Hellenistic ideal of well-roundedness and elevated amateurism in the first three books, then replaced it in the last book with the more Roman and earlier Greek notion of education as training for service to the state.[19] He polarized the ideal of training a man for aesthetic self-realization in the essentially apolitical game called civilization and the ideal of training him for practical, political purposes, such as serving to educate and advise his prince. Finally, if the ideal courtiers of the first three and the last books make poor bedfellows, the worlds they would live in are hardly more compatible; a world content with itself, its ceremonies, and its brilliance is the diametric opposite of one consumed by struggle for goals beyond itself. For the first courtier, conversation is its own end, a civilized, humane art, while for Ottaviano's ideal it can only be the means to some higher end, and for Bembo's it will cease entirely as he rises to higher levels of reality, just as surely as conversation yields to monologue and then to silence during Bembo's exposition. In no uncertain terms, by the changes Castiglione makes in his fourth book, he has separated its courtiers, cultural traditions, and ideal worlds from those of the first three.

Although insofar as the fourth book answers questions raised in the first three it can be said to possess a definite, dialectical relationship to them, its divergent ideals nevertheless create a significant problem for grasping the unity of *Il Cortegiano* as a work of art. Had Castiglione's book been written as a treatise or handbook, there would be no question that its contradictory concepts render it a most disunified work. The major criteria applicable to such a book would be the tests of logical consistency and intellectual coherence, and it would have clearly failed those tests. Castiglione's *Cortegiano,* however, declares itself from the start to be neither a treatise nor a handbook, but a dialogue, a symposium;

and its essential unity derives from the utter consistency with which Castiglione maintains the distinctive form and the distinctive fiction of his work.[20] By opposing ideas and ideals he adds significant, dramatic tensions which enliven, energize, and complicate his work, but at the same time, by consistently respecting its basic character as a symposium, he simultaneously contains the piquant dissonances of his concepts within the broader harmonies of his form and its fiction of elegant, civilized conversation. By virtue of great artistic control, he maintains the fundamental unity of his work, in spite of the constant shifts in emphasis he gave its ideas between the time of its inception, sometime after 1506, and its final publication in 1528.[21]

In the first place, because his work is cast in the form of a symposium, Castiglione rarely presents his ideas *in propria persona*, but rather through the mouths of his characters, thereby detaching those ideas from himself to some extent and attaching them instead to the personalities of the characters who assert them. Note that although at times he allows certain figures to express what clearly are his own prejudices, he never makes one of them his exclusive representative, and, in every instance, he allows the other characters to voice often quite substantial objections to the speaker's views. Moreover, he endows each speaker with his own individual personality and set of distinctive biases, of which the rest of the group is often quite conscious. Instructively, his characters never pretend to create *the* ideal courtier, but rather a composite figure made out of their shared ideals and about which broad areas of disagreement are still possible without detracting from its essentially ideal quality. They all applaud Ludovico da Canossa, who begins discussion of the courtier by stressing his inability to do more than describe "quella sorte di cortegiani ch'io più apprezzo" (I, 13, 102–3: "that manner of Courtier that I most esteem" [28]). The other courtiers can take it or leave it, and Ludovico will not insist that his ideal is better than theirs, "ché non solamente a voi po parer una cosa ed a me un'altra, ma a me stesso poria parer or una cosa ed ora un'altra" (I, 13, 103: "for not only can you think one thing and I another, but I myself may sometimes think one thing and sometimes another" [28]). Since Castiglione's courtiers realize that no one of them possesses the ideal absolutely, they implicitly authorize others to interpret their statements always as at least partially personal utterances revealing character or bias as much as objective assessments of truth. Since Castiglione's work is neither a treatise nor a handbook, but a symposium which presents its ideas always partially as projections of its characters' personalities, the presence of two new versions of the courtier in Book IV by no means interrupts the form of the work or vitiates its basic fiction, but merely provides interest and novelty by the injection of new ideas. Ottaviano's and Bembo's new ideals are as easily embraced by the form of Castiglione's work as Socrates' transcendent vision of love was contained within the form of Plato's *Symposium,* a work Castiglione clearly kept in mind while restructuring his masterpiece to reach its conclusion in Book IV. Consequently, while it would be incorrect to assert that Ottaviano's and Bembo's ideals are to be placed on no higher plane of seriousness than those of everyone else, it would be equally incorrect to see such an increase in seriousness as alien to the symposium form or to think that these new ideals are divorced from the personal qualities of their advocates, from Ottaviano's antifeminism and Bembo's intellectualism and Neoplatonic mysticism. Ultimately, Castiglione's book lives not in its ideas, but in the complex dialectical play of ideas and reality, precept and example, an imagined ideal and real men replete with their petty vices, defects, and limited points of view. Consequently, a conflict of ideas cannot really impair the unity of Castiglione's book, for its substance is the wedding of ideals and personalities, not merely one or the other, and Castiglione celebrates that wedding consistently from beginning to end.

No matter how serious their conceptions, both Ottaviano and Bembo remain participants in the complex social game played at Urbino, the symposium game that is the real substance of *Il Cortegiano.* Consequently, they must deal with the questions, arguments, verbal attacks, and personal gibes that others direct against them just as they directed them against all the principal speakers on previous evenings. Ottaviano especially must defend himself and the premises on which he bases his ideal, answering charges to define terms, explaining seeming contradictions, clarifying doubts. Practically every courtier has a chance to join in the assault, for they obviously do not consider his more serious exposition of the ideal courtier sacrosanct. In fact, some of them ultimately reject his ideal and mock his seriousness; they protest that Ottaviano has described a schoolteacher, not a courtier, and twit him mercilessly when he declares Plato and Aristotle examples of his ideal simply because at times in their lives they were the teachers of princes.

Unlike Ottaviano—or any of the other principal speakers in *Il Cortegiano* except Bibbiena—Bembo enjoys a relative immunity from attack; only his identification of beauty and goodness man-

199

ages to raise a few protests. Perhaps the difficulty in attacking
Bembo's Neoplatonic idealism explains the general lack of hostility towards him, for any attack would have to be an attack on the
basic premise of Bembo's philosophy, on the ontological belief in
a supersensible world of ideas. None of the courtiers is willing to
make such an attack, either because they share Bembo's Neoplatonic assumptions, or, more likely, because they respect sufficiently the rules of the game that prohibit that sort of profound and
profoundly personal argument. Another explanation for Bembo's
relative safety from attack might be that he, like Bibbiena, is considered essentially an entertainer, an artist who puts his talents at
the service of the group in order to amuse and edify it. Frequent
interruptions would impair the enjoyment of such artistic performances, and for this reason the other courtiers and ladies restrain
their otherwise exuberant questions and attacks. Nevertheless,
Castiglione will not permit the illusion that Bembo's unchallenged
exposition should be granted special status. In the first place,
Bembo's oration fits his character and biases perfectly, solitary
ecstasy and solitary monologue going hand in hand with his
avowed disappointments in love, his earnestness, and his philosophical temperament. Moreover, at repeated intervals during the
speech, Castiglione allows Signor Morello da Ortona to voice unhappiness with a Neoplatonic love that would deny him the pleasures of beauty in the flesh. A parody of Bembo's old courtier in
love, Morello is teased by the others for his philandering ways, but
he is a constant qualification to Bembo's idealism, a reminder of
the reality of sexual desire and that from the perspective of desire
Bembo's speech is little more than magnificent sublimation.

Castiglione thus maintains the unity of the last book with the
first three by maintaining the form of the work intact from beginning to end. Ottaviano may turn his courtier into the prince's
maestro di scuola, and Bembo urge escape from this world through
Neoplatonic contemplation, but these men are speakers and courtiers like all the rest, participating through new and personal
means in the social game they have all been playing. Though their
speeches may lead to troubling considerations and may alter the
concept of the courtier drastically from what it was before, Ottaviano and Bembo still live in the world of Urbino, stretching its
limits perhaps, but ultimately accepting its patterns of behavior
and intellectual assumptions, obeying its rules, and serving its
ideals. While they introduce a new note of seriousness into the
game, they participate in it neither more nor less seriously than all
the rest. Thus although the fourth book signals its new serious-

ness when Ottaviano's interruption alters the patterns previously established for beginning the game each evening, those patterns are not destroyed, and Urbino's symposium game, raised to new heights, retains its fundamental character.

Nowhere is the triumph of the game, its ability to absorb Ottaviano's and Bembo's serious new ideals, more assured than in the last pages of Castiglione's book. At this point, Bembo has brought his impassioned monologue to its final vision of God, a wordless moment of ecstatic, mystic contemplation that temporarily dissolves the game in silence. His courtly audience—and generations of his readers—are momentarily enraptured as well, gazing up with him toward celestial realities.[22] Suddenly, Emilia Pia's intervention breaks the spell and prevents the game from disappearing utterly. With consummate art and mischief, this witty skeptic brings Bembo—and everyone else—back down to earth and the reality of Urbino.[23]

> Avendo il Bembo insin qui parlato con tanta veemenzia, che quasi pareva astratto e fuor di sé, stavasi cheto e immobile, tenendo gli occhi verso il cielo, come stupido; quando la signora Emilia, la quale insieme con gli altri era stata sempre attentissima ascoltando il ragionamento, lo prese per la falda della robba e scuotendolo un poco disse: —Guardate, messer Pietro, che con questi pensieri a voi ancora non si separi l'anima dal corpo. —Signora, —rispose messer Pietro, —non saria questo il primo miraculo, che amor abbia in me operato—.
>
> (IV, 71, 541)

> Having spoken thus far with such vehemence that he seemed almost transported and beside himself, Bembo remained silent and still, keeping his eyes turned toward heaven, as if in a daze; when signora Emilia, who with the others had been listening to his discourse most attentively, plucked him by the hem of his robe and, shaking him a little, said: "Take care, messer Pietro, that with these thoughts your soul, too, does not forsake your body."
>
> "Madam," replied messer Pietro, "that would not be the first miracle Love has wrought in me."
>
> (357)

Appropriately, one of the two leading female figures in the group, this brilliant representative of the ideal civilization depicted in *Il Cortegiano,* is given the task of gently, but firmly, reasserting the conversational mode of the symposium game and bringing Bembo's speech back down to earth.[24] From the perspective of the game, which has once more reasserted itself, Bembo's momentary, silent transcendence of its limits is a threat to continued, successful social conversation, and Emilia's intervention effectively avoids the embarrassment of a continuing, awkward silence by mildly ridiculing Bembo's deed and putting him in the defensive position of one who has committed a slight faux pas. She has effectively restored the game of conversation by laughing at that which threatens to end it, and Bembo, who, like all the others, has had a moment to regain his composure, replies with a bit of delicate, self-deprecating humor that tacitly acknowledges his error and endorses Emilia's act of restoration.

Although the crowd then urges Bembo to continue, the divine rapture has passed, and without more ado—surely without any feeling that some new vision has really transformed everyone—Bembo sits back in his chair, becoming just one courtier among many once again. Immediately and significantly, these courtiers who followed Bembo in his ascent return without any feeling of incongruity to their mundane debate about women. Ironically, while many readers have felt that Bembo's speech is a fitting resolution to Castiglione's work[25]—and surely it does allow *Il Cortegiano* to end with memorable, rhetorical display—it has resolved nothing for these courtiers, because nothing is ever resolved in the symposium game they play night after night in their castle. That game permits no single vision, no individual conception of truth, to possess an absolute validity transcending or negating the views of others, and it declares that at Urbino there are no winners, no real losers.

As if to insist that nothing has been resolved at Urbino, Castiglione ends his book neither with Bembo's speech nor Emilia's gesture. He does not even end it with the marvelous but significantly rather ambiguous discovery that the group has talked out the night and that a glorious day has dawned. To be sure, the vision of day, lighted by the morning star, could be interpreted as a symbolic transformation of the world through the power of divine love that Bembo celebrated in his speech.[26] But it could also be interpreted as an equally miraculous transformation of the entire world into an expanded version of Urbino, animated by the kind of fraternal affection and love that characterizes its society. Moreover, the return to day can be read equally well as a release from—and a denial of—the hermetically sealed little room and Bembo's hot-house ecstasy; it marks a return to the more mundane, but more comfortable reality of everyday life at Urbino. Note that Castiglione chooses to emphasize the resurrection of normal, everyday reality by not terminating his book with the marvelous vision of dawning day. Instead, he ends it by making a full-scale return to the witty, entertaining, animated debate between the misogynists and their opponents that Ottaviano's self-proclaimed seriousness and Bembo's ecstasy temporarily eclipsed.[27] This return is, however, only a summary one, limited to a pair of brief exchanges which give *Il Cortegiano* a particularly open-ended quality; Castiglione closes his book not with a fervent resolution, a climax of intense feeling, or a triumph of logic and argument, but with a reaffirmation of the more mundane debate which is the lifeblood of his ideal society and which he dramatically interrupts before it has fully begun to flow again. The next-to-last statement in his work is calculated specifically to leave the members of the group—and the readers—anticipating a renewed skirmish between Gasparo and the Magnifico on the next evening, and the final words contain the unanswered challenge that the clever, sharp-tongued Emilia Pia directs at her arch-enemy Gasparo and that will doubtless provoke him to new heights of anti-feminine wit in the battle to come.

> . . . e quando già erano per uscir dalla camera, voltossi il signor Prefetto alla signora Duchessa e disse:—Signora, per terminar la lite tra 'l signor Gaspar e 'l signor Magnifico, veniremo col giudice questa sera più per tempo che non si fece ieri—. Rispose la signora Emilia: — Con patto che se 'l signor Gaspar vorrà accusar le donne e dar loro, come è suo costume, qualche falsa calunnia, esso ancora dia sicurtà di star a ragione, perch'io lo allego sospetto fuggitivo.

> (IV, 73, 544)

> . . . and as they were about to leave the room, the Prefect turned to the Duchess and said: "To put an end to the dispute between signor Gasparo and the Magnifico, we will come with the judge earlier this evening than yesterday."

> Signora Emilia replied: "On condition that if signor Gasparo wishes to accuse and slander women further, as is his wont, let him give bond to stand trial, for I cite him as a suspect and fugitive."

> (359–60)

The open-ended conclusion of Castiglione's work significantly reinvokes the one debate that has surfaced in every single book, from the opening exchange between Gasparo and Emilia at the start of the first evening, through the fully developed "war" between the misogynists and the ladies' "knights" in Books II and III, down to Emilia's final jab at Gasparo on *Il Cortegiano*'s last page. These ever-recurring gibes and arguments concerning women clearly occupy a central position both in Urbino's society and in Castiglione's *Cortegiano*. They do so partly because, unlike the discussions of humor, Neoplatonism, and even the ideal courtier, they involve a subject about which everyone at the court can express an opinion and argue a set of beliefs; they do not encourage one-man shows, but the lively free-for-all of open debate and vigorous repartée. Moreover, since they spring from the basic, structural imbalance in power between men and women in Urbino's society and from the aggressive tensions which that imbalance necessarily generates, the debates about women are clearly bound to recur frequently and enjoy continuing prominence. They offer Urbino's society a dependable, unchanging, easily tapped source of emotional energy which will quickly revitalize discussion whenever it seems to flag. When joke telling has gone on so long that it stops being funny, or when a Neoplatonic mystic delivers a powerful speech whose finality seems to preclude further discussion, a timely quip from the perky Gasparo or one of his fellow misogynists always suffices to resuscitate conversation and involve the entire group in it once again. Thus, the open ending of Castiglione's work is not at all the result of artistic indecision or failure, but a final, significant reminder of the source of Urbino's vitality, which is also the guarantee of its viability as a society. It is one last demonstration that Castiglione conceived his *Cortegiano* not primarily as a handbook or a treatise, but as a memorial celebrating a brilliant court and its ability to play human life as a witty, decorous, animated game. Artfully, this conclusion leaves the reader with a strong final impression not of Castiglione's courtly doctrines, but of Urbino's courtly society. It gives him one last vision of that *amorevole compagnia* who performed the always marvelous feat of transforming ordinary human life into an elegant, vital, and enduring work of art.

Abbreviations for Journals
Cited in Notes and Bibliography

CL	*Comparative Literature*
ELH	*English Literary History*
ELR	*English Literary Renaissance*
GSLI	*Giornale storico della letteratura italiana*
JEGP	*Journal of English and Germanic Philology*
JHI	*Journal of the History of Ideas*
MLN	*Modern Language Notes*
MLR	*Modern Language Review*
PMLA	*Publication of the Modern Language Association of America*
PQ	*Philological Quarterly*
SEL	*Studies in English Literature*
SP	*Studies in Philology*
SRen	*Studies in the Renaissance*

 Notes

Introduction

1. Sir Thomas Hoby, *The Book of the Courtier from the Italian of Count Baldassare Castiglione,* with introduction by Walter Raleigh (London, 1900), pp. 368–77 (hereafter cited as "Hoby").

2. See John L. Lievsay, *Stefano Guazzo and the English Renaissance* (Chapel Hill: University of North Carolina Press, 1961), pp. 40–41.

3. For the influence of *The Courtier* as a handbook of manners, see Vittorio Cian, *Un illustre nunzio pontificio del Rinascimento: Baldassar Castiglione, Studi e testi,* 156 (Vatican City: Biblioteca Apostolica Vaticana, 1951), p. 229; and Erich Loos, *Baldassare Castigliones "Libro del Cortegiano": Studien zur Tugendauffassung des Cinquecento, Analecta Romanica,* 2 (Frankfurt am Main: Vittorio Klostermann, 1955), p. 23. For some studies of its reception and use outside Italy, see: Daniel Javitch, *"The Philosopher of the Court:* A French Satire Misunderstood," *CL* 23 (1971): 119–20; W. J. Schnerr, "Two Courtiers: Castiglione and Rodrigues Lôbo," *CL* 13 (1961): 138–53; David J. Welsh, "Il Cortigiano polacco," *Italica* 40(1963): 22–27; William L. Wiley, *The Gentleman of Renaissance France* (Cambridge: Harvard University Press, 1954), passim.

4. On courtesy books, see Thomas F. Crane, *Italian Social Customs of the Sixteenth Century and Their Influence on the Literatures of Europe* (New Haven: Yale University Press, 1920), pp. 323–86; William M. Rossetti, *Italian Courtesy Books, Early English Text Society,* Extra Series, no. 8 (London, 1869), pp. 8–75; James W. Holme, "Italian Courtesy Books of the Sixteenth Century," *MLR* 5(1910): 145–60; and John E. Mason, *Gentlefolk in the Making* (Philadelphia: University of Pennsylvania Press, 1933), pp. 4–20.

5. Rossetti, *Italian Courtesy Books,* pp. 14–32.

6. On this difference, see the intelligent remarks of Hilary Adams, " 'Il Cortegiano' and 'Il Galateo,' " *MLR* 42 (1947): 457–66; and Piero Floriani, "Esperienza e cultura nella genesi del *Cortegiano,*" *GSLI* 146(1969): 508–10.

7. For some perceptive comments on the subject of masking in Renaissance literature, I am indebted to Walter R. Davis, "Masking in Arden," *SEL* 5(1965): 151–63; and Margaret E. Dana, "Heroic and Pastoral: Sidney's *Arcadia* as Masquerade," *CL* 25(1973): 308–20.

8. Denis Diderot, *Le Neveu de Rameau* (Paris: Gallimard, 1966), pp. 133–34.

9. In my discussion of festivity I am indebted to a number of works: Mikhail Bakhtin, *Rabelais and His World,* trans. Helene Iswolsky (Cambridge, Mass.: M. I. T. Press, 1968); Victor Turner, *The Ritual Process* (Chicago: Aldine Publishing Co., 1969); Roger Abrahams, "Ritual, for Fun and Profit, or, The Ends and Outs of Celebration," unpublished paper prepared for the Burg-Wartenstein Sym-

posium, no. 59 (1973); and Barbara Babcock-Abrahams, "The Carnivalization of the Novel," *MLN* 89 (1974): 911–37.

10. For a discussion of the notion of mixed genres in Renaissance literature, see Rosalie L. Colie, *The Resources of Kind: Genre-Theory in the Renaissance,* ed. Barbara K. Lewalski (Berkeley: University of California Press, 1973).

11. "Noi in questi libri non seguiremo un certo ordine o regula di precetti distinti, che 'l più delle volte nell'insegnare qualsivoglia cosa usar si sòle; ma alla foggia di molti antichi, rinovando una grata memoria, recitaremo alcuni ragionamenti, i quali già passarono tra omini singularissimi a tale proposito ... " (I, 1, 80–81).

12. See John Shearman's *Mannerism* (Harmondsworth, England: Penguin Books, 1967), passim; Arnold Hauser, *The Social History of Art* (New York: Vintage Books, 1960), II, 84–143; and Anthony Blunt, *Artistic Theory in Italy, 1450–1600* (Oxford: Clarendon Press, 1940), pp. 86–102.

Chapter 1

1. Much of what is said of the ideal courtier applies, mutatis mutandis, to the ideal *donna di palazzo* of Book III. However, insofar as her role is considerably less active than his, there is less inclination to present her as an actress. It should also be noted that in Book IV, the principal speakers abandon the basic metaphors of previous discussions and conceive the courtier alternatively as a schoolmaster-advisor for his prince and as a Neoplatonic mystic. This change in basic conceptions will be discussed at length in Chapter 6.

2. Like the courtier, his prince is also considered a masker and role player. He is thus described as wearing the mask of the prince ("tener la persona di principe") and as taking it off on occasion ("spogliandosi ... la persona di principe" [II, 11, 207]).

3. Joseph Mazzeo has analyzed the aesthetic element in Castiglione's *Courtier* and has stressed the way in which he envisions the self as a work of art. Mazzeo does not suggest, however, that the particular art the courtier masters is the art of acting, nor does he explore the extensive relationship between Castiglione's terms and those used by contemporaries to analyze works of art. See his *Renaissance and Revolution* (New York: Random House, 1965), pp. 131–60.

4. This discussion is based on his *Centuries of Childhood,* trans. Robert Baldick (New York: Vintage Books, 1962), pp. 390–98.

5. Trans. George Lamb (New York: Shad and Ward, 1956). I am indebted to this book for my discussion of ancient Greek, Hellenistic, and Roman education. See especially pp. 138–45 and 327–34.

6. William H. Woodward, *Studies in Education During the Age of the Renaissance, 1400–1600* (Cambridge, 1906), pp. 4–10.

7. Eugenio Garin, *L'Umanesimo italiano* (Bari: Laterza, 1965), pp. 22–27, and his *L'educazione in Europa, 1400–1600* (Bari, 1957), pp. 170–77; and Hiram Haydn, *The Counter-Renaissance* (New York: Harcourt, Brace, and World, 1950), pp. xii–xiii. One reason for the strong emphasis on the student's preparation for involvement in civil affairs was doubtless that most humanists served rulers as secretaries or tutors and dedicated their tracts on education to political figures.

8. Desiderius Erasmus, *Declamatio de pueris statim ac liberaliter instituendis,* ed. Jean-Claude Margolin (Geneva: Droz, 1966), p. 389: "homines, mihi crede, non nascuntur, sed finguntur."

9. Desiderius Erasmus, *Institutio Matrimonii Christiani,* in *Opera Omnia,* ed. J.

Clericus (Lugduni Batavorum, 1703–6), vol. 5, 722C. All the humanists fondly repeated Cicero's definition of the *artes liberales* as those which were worthy of a free man (see *De Oratore*, bk. I, chap. 16), although their notion of freedom was more a metaphysical or existential conception than a political one. This freedom was defined most strikingly by Pico della Mirandola in the opening passage of his oration *De Hominis dignitate*. On the humanists' conception of the formation of a malleable child into a human ideal, see Thomas M. Greene, "The Flexibility of the Self in Renaissance Literature," in *The Disciplines of Criticism*, ed. Peter Demetz, Thomas M. Greene, and Lowry Nelson, Jr. (New Haven: Yale University Press, 1968), pp. 249–56; and Garin, *L'educazione in Europa*, pp. 92–93.

10. R. R. Bolgar, *The Classical Heritage* (New York: Harper Torchbook, 1964), pp. 258–59, 332–40.

11. Cf. Joseph Mazzeo, *Renaissance and Revolution*, pp. 246–50.

12. See my article, "Erasmian Education and the *Convivium religiosum*," *SP* 69 (1972): 131–49. At one point in *The Scholemaster*, Roger Ascham declares that reading books like *The Courtier* at home can teach more in one year than one can learn from travelling abroad in Italy for three; see *The Whole Works of Roger Ascham*, ed. J. A. Giles (London, 1865), vol. 3, p. 141.

13. For the difference between Castiglione and other writers on courtesy, see, among others, Ercole Bottari, "Baldassare da Castiglione e il suo libro del 'Cortegiano,'" *Annali della Scuola Normale Superiore di Pisa* 3(1877): 208–16; Daniel Javitch, "The Philosopher of the Court: A French Satire Misunderstood," *CL* 23 (1971): 105–6; Benedetto Croce, "Libri sulle corti," in *Poeti e scrittori del pieno e tardo Rinascimento* (Bari: Laterza, 1945), vol. 2, pp. 198–206; and Dain Trafton, "Tasso's Dialogue on the Court, " *ELR* Supplements, no. 2 (1973): 3–13.

14. Cf. Daniel Javitch, "Poetry and Court Conduct: Puttenham's *Arte of English Poesie* in the Light of Castiglione's *Cortegiano*," *MLN* 87 (1972): 870.

15. John Shearman, *Mannerism* (Harmondsworth, England: Penguin Books, 1967), pp. 21–22.

16. Mazzeo, *Renaissance and Revolution*, p. 145.

17. Anthony Blunt, *Artistic Theory in Italy, 1450–1600* (Oxford: Clarendon Press, 1940), pp. 93–96.

18. *Grazioso* is the primary adjective Vasari uses to define the style of Raphael's works: see Vicenzo Golzio, *Raffaello nei documenti, nelle testimonianze dei contemporanei e nella letteratura del suo secolo* (Vatican City, 1931), pp. 196–235, especially pp. 206, 225, 227, and 235.

19. Note that the courtier is specifically told that when he is offered gifts and favors, he should resist accepting them and avoid at all costs appearing to beg for them (II, 19, 220–21).

20. Cf. Erich Loos, *Baldassare Castigliones "Libro del Cortegiano": Studien zur Tugendauffassung des Cinquecento, Analecta Romanica*, 2 (Frankfurt am Main: Vittorio Klostermann, 1955), pp. 154–55.

21. *A Rhetoric of Motives* (Berkeley: University of California Press, 1969), pp. 231–32.

22. For a description of this "meliorist" position adopted by Renaissance Catholic humanists who followed late medieval thinkers like Thomas Aquinas, see Hiram Haydn, *The Counter-Renaissance*, pp. 53–59.

23. Vittorio Cian, *Un illustre nunzio pontificio del Rinascimento: Baldassar Castiglione, Studi e testi*, 156 (Vatican City: Biblioteca Apostolica Vaticana, 1951), pp. 18–24.

24. See the discussion of the term in James V. Mirollo, *The Poet of the Marvelous: Giambattista Marino* (New York: Columbia University Press, 1963), pp. 117–18.

25. Ibid., pp. 118, 166.
26. Shearman, *Mannerism*, pp. 106–12, and passim.
27. For the Mannerist delight in the beauty of the monstrous, see Shearman, *Mannerism*, pp. 156–58.
28. For Cicero, see the *Paradoxa Stoicorum*, par. 4, and for Quintilian, see *Institutio oratoria*, bk. IV, chap. 1, par. 40. For Puttenham and the Renaissance conception of the response appropriate to paradox, see Rosalie L. Colie, *Paradoxia Epidemica* (Princeton, N. J.: Princeton University Press, 1966), pp. 3–4, 8. My discussion of paradox and marvel is largely dependent on her suggestive analysis.
29. Colie, *Paradoxia Epidemica*, p. 22.

Chapter 2

1. Orville Prescott, *Princes of the Renaissance* (New York: Random House, 1969), pp. 273–75; and Julia Cartwright, *The Perfect Courtier* (New York: Dutton, 1927), vol. 1, pp. 224–26.
2. Prescott, *Princes*, pp. 357–62.
3. Vittorio Cian, "Dizionarietto biografico," appended to his edition of *Il Cortegiano* (Florence: Sansoni, 1929), 3rd ed., pp. 503, 510.
4. Cartwright, *Perfect Courtier*, vol. 1, pp. 203, 197.
5. See chapter 3, note 8.
6. Among those who see *The Courtier* as a mirror of its society are: Thomas F. Crane, *Italian Social Customs of the Sixteenth Century* (New Haven: Yale University Press, 1920); Henri Hauvette, *Littérature italienne* (Paris: Colin, 1906); and Jacob Burckhardt, *The Civilization of the Renaissance in Italy* (many different editions). For a discussion of this tradition of interpretation, see Erich Loos, *Baldassare Castigliones "Libro del Cortegiano,"* Analecta Romanica, 2 (Frankfurt am Main: Vittorio Klostermann, 1955), pp. 21–22, 24.
7. Most Italian critics condemn Castiglione for his distance from reality. See, for example, G. Prezzolini's introduction to Baldassar Castiglione and Giovanni della Casa, *Opere* (Milan: Rizzoli, 1937), p. 14; and Mario Rossi, *Baldassar Castiglione* (Bari: Laterza, 1946), p. 26. For a discussion of this critical tradition, see Loos, *Baldassare Castiglione*, pp. 23–24.
8. Donald J. Wilcox, *The Development of Florentine Humanist Historiography in the Fifteenth Century* (Cambridge: Harvard University Press. 1969), p. 40: "It is a commonplace in humanist historical thought that an historian should be guided by moral considerations in writing history."
9. Felix Gilbert, *Machiavelli and Guicciardini* (Princeton: Princeton University Press, 1965), p. 217.
10. Berthold L. Ullman, "Leonardo Bruni and Humanist Historiography," in *Studies in the Italian Renaissance* (Rome: Edizioni di storia e letteratura, 1955), p. 331.
11. Peter Burke, *The Renaissance Sense of the Past* (London: Edward Arnold, 1969), p. 106.
12. Gilbert, *Machiavelli and Guicciardini*, p. 209.
13. Giannetto Bongiovanni documents fully Castiglione's interest in the arts; see his *Baldassar Castiglione* (Milan: Alpes, 1929), pp. 48–56.
14. For a brilliant discussion of the relationship between High Renaissance art and culture, see Arnold Hauser, *The Social History of Art* (New York: Vintage Books, 1951), vol. 2, pp. 86–91.

15. Vittorio Cian, *Un illustre nunzio pontificio del Rinascimento: Baldassar Castiglione, Studi e testi,* 156 (Vatican City: Biblioteca Apostolica Vaticana, 1951), p. 185.
16. Rensselaer W. Lee, *Ut Pictura Poesis: The Humanistic Theory of Painting* (New York: Norton, 1967), p. 3; and Robert J. Clements, "The Identity of Literary and Artistic Theory in the Renaissance," in *The Peregrine Muse,* University of North Carolina Studies in Languages and Literatures, no. 82 (Chapel Hill: University of North Carolina Press, 1969), pp. 14–18.
17. Lee, *Ut Pictura Poesis,* p. 7.
18. See Leone Battista Alberti, *Della Pittura Libri Tre,* in *Kleinere kunsttheoretische Schriften,* ed. Hubert Janitschek (Vienna, 1877), p. 149; and John Pope-Hennessy, *Raphael* (London: Phaidon Press, n. d.), p. 34.
19. Lee, *Ut Pictura Poesis,* p. vii; and Clements, "Identity," pp. 18–20. For a discussion of the humanists' reliance on ancient rhetorical theory, see John R. Spencer, "Ut Rhetorica Pictura," *Journal of the Warburg and Courtauld Institutes* 20 (1957): 26–44.
20. Lee, *Ut Pictura Poesis,* p. 3, n. 6.
21. Erwin Panofsky, *Idea,* trans. Joseph Peake (Columbia: University of South Carolina Press, 1968), p. 49.
22. Lee, *Ut Pictura Poesis,* pp. 7–11.
23. *Ibid.,* pp. 9–11; Panofsky, *Idea,* p. 48; and Anthony Blunt, *Artistic Theory in Italy, 1450–1600* (Oxford: Clarendon Press, 1940), pp. 17–18.
24. Blunt, *Artistic Theory,* p. 62.
25. Panofsky, *Idea,* pp. 56–59; Lee, *Ut Pictura Poesis,* pp. 14–15.
26. Alberti, *Della Pittura,* pp. 109, 151.
27. Vicenzo Golzio, ed., *Raffaello nei documenti, nelle testimonianze dei contemporanei e nella letteratura del suo secolo* (Vatican City, 1936), p. 31.
28. Panofsky, *Idea,* p. 65.
29. Lee, *Ut Pictura Poesis,* pp. 17–18.
30. See the introduction to Leone Battista Alberti, *On Painting,* trans. John R. Spencer (New Haven: Yale University Press, 1956), pp. 23–24.
31. Alberti, *Della Pittura,* pp. 117–19: "Quello che prima dà volupta nella storia, viene dalla copia et varietà delle cose . . . " (p. 117). Note that Leonardo in his early *Adoration,* Michelangelo in his *Battle of the Centaurs,* and Raphael in his *Marriage of the Virgin* all follow Alberti's dictum precisely.
32. *Ibid.,* pp. 127–29.
33. Ibid., p. 105. For Leonardo's similar opinion, see Blunt, *Artistic Theory,* p. 34. For Renaissance painters generally, see Lee, *Ut Pictura Poesis,* p. 7.
34. Hauser, *Social History of Art,* vol. 2, pp. 95–96; and Edward Williamson, "The Concept of Grace in the Work of Raphael and Castiglione," *Italica* 24 (1947): 316–24.
35. This discussion of developments in the late quattrocento and the High Renaissance is largely derived from the splendid pages of S. J. Freedberg, *Painting of the High Renaissance in Rome and Florence* (New York: Harper and Row, 1972), vol. 1, pp. 11–17.
36. See Pope-Hennessy, *Raphael,* pp. 175–80.
37. Especially after the 1480s, artists increasingly portrayed figures in religious paintings enveloped in "draperies of a timeless and fashionless type"; see Linda Murray, *The High Renaissance* (New York: Praeger, 1967), p. 19.
38. *Painting of the High Renaissance,* vol. 1, p. 130.
39. Ibid., p. 335.
40. Linda Murray attributes the invention of this genre to Quentin Matsys, in *The Late Renaissance and Mannerism* (New York: Praeger, 1967), p. 117.

41. See, for instance, the figures in Masaccio's frescoes or Donatello's prophets.

42. See his Eremitani frescoes at Padua.

43. Freedberg, *Painting of the High Renaissance,* vol. 1, p. 23.

44. Compacting the figures in a painting into a dense, sculptural mass was a general procedure of High Renaissance artists and is especially apparent in Michelangelo's *Doni Tondo* and in Leonardo's several versions of the *Virgin with St. Anne.*

45. Hauser, *Social History of Art,* vol. 2, p. 96.

46. *Painting of the High Renaissance,* vol. 1, p. 278.

47. Alberti, *Della Pittura,* pp. 121, 127–29. See also Lee, *Ut Pictura Poesis,* pp. 23–25; Blunt, *Artistic Theory,* p. 35; and especially, Spencer, "Ut Rhetorica Pictura," p. 26.

48. Freedberg, *Painting of the High Renaissance,* vol. 1, pp. 334–35.

49. Ibid., pp. 5–6.

50. For examples of his antagonism to others' idealistic pronouncements, see I, 34, 140; II, 8, 200; and IV, 63, 529.

51. Erich Loos praises Castiglione's ability to duplicate the styles of speech possessed by different characters but only notes briefly the most general characteristics of Unico Aretino's, Bibbiena's, and Bembo's styles; see his *Baldassare Castiglione,* p. 165.

52. The *Seconda redazione* shows that originally Ottaviano spoke many of Gasparo's lines, including most of Gasparo's attacks on women, as well as his own, and that Camillo Palleotto, a character who disappears from the final version, gives many of the speeches later assigned to Cesare Gonzaga and the Magnifico. Isolated speeches are also occasionally transferred from one character to another. For instance, where the prefect speaks for himself in the *Seconda redazione* (II, 43, 131), Bembo comes to speak for him in the final text (II, 43, 257), and where Ottaviano suggests that Federico speak more about the courtier (*Sec. red.,* III, 3, 187), later the Magnifico is given that line (III, 2, 337).

53. See the introduction to Pietro Bembo, *Prose e Rime,* ed. Carlo Dionisotti (Turin: Unione Tipografico-Editrice Torinese, 1960), p. 21.

54. Cian, *Un illustre nunzio,* p. 240.

55. The Latin *Urbinum* is not given an etymology in Lewis and Short's *Latin Dictionary,* but it is doubtless derived from *urbs* plus the local or regional ending *inum.* Thus, even in Roman antiquity the generic quality of the name and its connection with *urbs* would have been apparent. Moreover, although the *-ino* ending of the modern name is not a true diminutive, the folk etymology of Urbino as the "little urbs" would certainly have suggested itself readily to Renaissance, as to modern, Italians.

56. Castiglione praises the little state for its triumphs over much larger enemies (I, 2, 82). It clearly also fits the description of Ottaviano's ideal state, whose excellence depends upon the moral character, not the number of its citizens (see IV, 34–35, 490–91).

Chapter 3

1. See Walter R. Davis, *Idea and Act in Elizabethan Fiction* (Princeton, N.J.: Princeton University Press, 1969), pp. 45–49.

2. See John R. Cooper, *The Art of "The Compleat Angler"* (Durham, N. C.: Duke University Press, 1968).

3. This discussion of Castiglione's style is largely dependent on the brilliant

analysis of Maurizio Dardano, "L'arte del periodo nel *Cortegiano*," *Rassegna della letteratura italiana* 67 (1963): 441–62.

4. When explaining how his affection for Alfonso Ariosto moved him to write his book, Castiglione acknowledges the close connection in his mind between love and an intense desire to please others by linking the two concepts together in a single phrase: "affezione e desiderio intenso di compiacere" (I, 1, 79).

5. Vittorio Cian sees Castiglione as a model courtier in turning Vittoria Colonna's refusal to return his manuscript into a courtly compliment; see *Un illustre nunzio pontificio del Rinascimento: Baldassar Castiglione, Studi e testi,* 156 (Vatican City: Biblioteca Apostolica Vaticana, 1951), p. 133.

6. In earlier versions of *Il Cortegiano,* he goes on at length singing the virtues of figures like Francesco Maria della Rovere, Eleonora Gonzaga, and Federico Gonzaga II of Mantua, but in his final text he has pared down every single one of those passages. Compare the original versions in the *Sec. red.,* III, 3, 184–86 and III, 42, 229–30 with the relevant passages in the final text: IV, 2, 447–48 and IV, 42, 501.

7. Some examples: he recounts none of Duke Francesco Maria's particular accomplishments as he lauds the prince's wit and virtue (I, 55, 183; IV, 2, 447); he has his characters use the most general formulas to praise the artistic excellence of both Raphael and Michelangelo (I, 50–51, 174–76); he allows the Magnifico to celebrate the wisdom and virtue displayed by quite a host of famous contemporary women without providing more than a small handful of concrete details to document his claims (III, 36, 387–90).

8. On a few occasions, praising a person in general, conventional terms becomes a matter of diplomatic necessity. Most notably, Castiglione refuses to specify the *inimici* and *disgrazie* which Ottaviano had to endure in his personal triumph of *virtù* over *fortuna* (see *Letter,* 1, 70). Since Ottaviano had been captured by imperial troops when they sacked Genoa in 1522 and had died from mistreatment as the Marchese di Pescara's prisoner in 1524, Castiglione could not risk endangering his master's, the pope's, diplomacy by an open denunciation of his allies, nor would he insult Vittoria Colonna by condemning her husband, the marchese. Nevertheless, Castiglione's oblique allusions to Ottaviano's misfortune do not prevent the well-informed reader from supplying the relevant details, and even if his praise lacks the drama and vividness which their inclusion could provide, it remans a sincere tribute to his friend's courage and endurance. For a more detailed discussion of aviano's capture and death, see Julia Cartwright, *The Perfect Courtier: Baldassare Castiglione* (New York: Dutton, 1927), vol. 2, pp. 155–56.

9. In Castiglione's time this image had wide currency and was used, as it is here, without any intent to suggest negative implications, i.e., that the men inside the horse were not heroes, but slaughterers who destroyed the civilization of Troy. See Giuseppi Bettalli, "Considerazioni su un luogo del Cortegiano," *Belfagor* 11 (1956): 454–57.

10. Although Giuseppe Toffanin notes that nostalgia is what moves Castiglione to write, he does not develop this insight; see his *Il "Cortegiano" nella trattatistica del Rinascimento* (Naples: Libreria scientifica editrice, n. d.), pp. 37–39.

11. Lawrence Lerner, *The Uses of Nostalgia* (London: Chatto and Windus, 1972), pp. 41–47.

12. Lerner, *Uses of Nostalgia,* pp. 41–47; Renato Poggioli, "The Oaten Flute," *Harvard Library Bulletin* 11 (1957): 147–48; Mia I. Gerhardt, *La Pastorale* (Assen: Van Gorcum, 1950), p. 74; Erwin Panofsky, "*Et in Arcadia Ego:* Poussin and the Elegiac Tradition," in *Meaning in the Visual Arts* (Garden City, N. Y.: Doubleday,

1955), pp. 296–304; and Bruno Snell, *The Discovery of the Mind,* trans. T. G. Rosenmeyer (Oxford: Oxford University Press, 1953), p. 291.

13. All references to this text as well as to the translations of the passages cited are taken from the Loeb Library edition, trans. H. Rackham (London, 1942). References are to book, chapter, and page.

14. " . . . furono alcuni, i quali, tratti dalla dolcezza di questa compagnia, partendo il Papa e la corte, restarono per molti giorni ad Urbino; nel qual tempo non solamente si continuava nell'usato stile delle feste e piaceri ordinari, ma ognuno si sforzava d'accrescere qualche cosa, e massimamente nei giochi, ai quali quasi ogni sera s'attendeva" (I, 6, 89).

15. "Castiglione's Urban Pastoral," *Greyfriar* 8 (1965): 5–13.

16. Walter W. Greg, *Pastoral Poetry and Pastoral Drama* (New York: Russell and Russell, 1959), p. 14; Frank Kermode, ed., *English Pastoral Poetry* (London: Harrap, 1952), pp. 14–15; Harold E. Toliver, *Pastoral Forms and Attitudes* (Berkeley: University of Calfornia Press, 1971), pp. 1–3; and Thomas G. Rosenmeyer, *The Green Cabinet: Theocritus and the European Pastoral Lyric* (Berkeley: University of California Press, 1969), pp. 19–23.

17. Greg, *Pastoral Poetry and Pastoral Drama,* pp. 169–72.

18 Snell, *Discovery of the Mind,* pp. 281–309 and especially pp. 281–83.

19. Although I have been unable to locate a direct statement indicating that Castiglione had read the *Arcadia,* it is extremely unlikely that he would not have known such a popular Renaissance work. Many pieces of indirect evidence suggest strongly that he must have been quite familiar with it. His *Tirsi* is filled with phrases and lines which Bruno Maier feels echo those of Sannazaro (see the notes to *Tirsi,* which is contained in his edition of *Il Cortegiano,* pp. 549–71). Note that Castiglione specifically refers to Sannazaro's poetry at one point in *Il Cortegiano* as though it were a cultural staple (II, 35, 245). Finally, Vittorio Cian remarks that while Castiglione did not spend much time in Naples, he did actively correspond with Sannazaro; see his *Un illustre nunzio,* p. 172.

20. Rosenmeyer, *The Green Cabinet,* pp. 119–20.

21. Erwin Panofsky, "The First Page of Giorgio Vasari's 'Libro': A Study in the Gothic Style in the Judgment of the Italian Renaissance," in *Meaning in the Visual Arts,* pp. 169–225.

22. In his original prologue to Book II, Castiglione began with an extended praise of nature's variety and diversity, and hence, of its irregularity (see *Sec. red.,* II, 1, 77–79). By excising this passage from his final text, he not only removed aesthetically irrelevant material from the prologue, but also sharpened the contrast running throughout his books between the regularity of nature and the irregularity and whimsicality of fortune.

23. In other passages fortune is blamed for elevating the unworthy to positions of social pre-eminence while opposing the rise of merit (see I, 15, 106), and Castiglione himself sees it as the force that has oppressed him with continual labors and kept him from completing the manuscript of his *Cortegiano* (see *Letter,* 1, 68).

24. See the *prologo* to Leon Battista Alberti's *I libri della famiglia* for a direct statement of his views on the relationship between *virtù* and *fortuna.* Also see the famous twenty-fifth chapter of Machiavelli's *Il Principe,* which is concerned with the power of fortune and its limits.

25. Similarly, Castiglione implies the existence of a fundamental opposition between fortune and nature when he describes how fortune envied Duke Guidobaldo and afflicted him with gout, thus ruining "un dei più belli e disposti corpi del mondo . . . *nella sua verde età*" (I, 3, 83; my italics).

26. For a concise account of Castiglione's sincere Christianity, see Vittorio Cian, "Religiosità di Baldassar Castiglione," *Convivium* 22 (1950): 772–80. Note, however, that Cian's insistence on Castiglione's religiosity in his life is hardly proof that *Il Cortegiano* is a particularly pious book.

27. Erich Loos feels that Castiglione's book is "pagan" because of its insistence on the way fortune rules this world and its lack of direct, Christian ideology; see his *Baldassare Castigliones "Libro del Cortegiano," Analecta Romanica*, 2 (Frankfurt am Main: Vittorio Klostermann, 1955), pp. 154–55. Castiglione's book is not "pagan," however, in the sense of being anti-Christian, as much as it is secular in emphasis and concern and simply fails to stress elements of Christian dogma, which would not necessarily contradict its expressly formulated doctrines. As Giuseppe Ferrero has noted, it is not opposed to religion, but at the same time not a page in it, except perhaps the end of Book IV, is in any way permeated with a sense of the divine; see his review article, "Studi sul Castiglione," *Rivista di sintesi letteraria* 2 (1935): 476.

28. In his brief elegy for Raphael, *De Morte Raphaelis Pictoris*, Castiglione dwells on the loss of his friend and concludes, without any hint of Christian consolation, that we and all our things are owed to death ("Deberi et Morti nostraque nosque mones"). In *Alcon*, his earlier pastoral elegy on the death of Falcone, Castiglione more fully re-creates the ethos and sentiments of pagan antiquity in response to death. To be sure, he does note that Alcon-Falcone now walks in the Elysian Fields, but there is no final rejoicing about Alcon's resurrection or any hope for rebirth as there would be in a more specifically Christian elegy like *Lycidas*. Rather, Iolas-Castiglione broods extensively on the loss created by his young friend's untimely death, recalls happy moments from their childhood, and finally, after recounting a dream he had in which Alcon came to see him at Rome, laments bitterly that death has prevented this dream from becoming a reality. At the end, Iolas vows to do what Castiglione would do later in his *Cortegiano:* he writes an epitaph for Alcon's tomb—although his poem is also a memorial—in which he emphasizes the universal bereavement that Alcon's death has caused for everyone. Significantly, the last word of the epitaph is "bitter":

Alconem postquam rapuerant impia fata,
Collacrimant duri montes et consitus atra est
Nocte dies: sunt candida nigra, et dulcia amara.

Citations from Castiglione's poems are taken from the edition of letters and poems by Pierantonio Serassi (Padua: G. Comino, 1769–71), vol. 2.

29. Cf. Cicero, *De Oratore*, II, ii, 202, and Castiglione, *Letter*, 1, 71.

Chapter 4

1. Allor messer Federico si levò in piè e disse:—Ascoltatemi, prego, queste poche parole—" (I, 39, 153).

2. Bibbiena repeatedly defines the operation of witty remarks and jokes by saying they bite or stab *(mordere, pungere)* their victims. See II, 66, 289 and II, 80, 305 for examples.

3. Using the language of knightly combat, Bibbiena says it would be a difficult *impresa* worthy of a *grandissimo guerriero* to defend women against Gasparo (II, 96, 328), and Emilia continues his playful use of metaphor a moment later: "noi metteremo in campo un cavalier più fresco, che combatterà con voi, acciò che l'error vostro non sia così lungamente impunito" (II, 97, 329). The women con-

tinually describe the Magnifico and Cesare Gonzaga as their defenders (e.g., III, 17, 358) and Gasparo and Ottaviano as their enemies (e.g., III, 23, 369; III, 76, 441). On at least two separate occasions, the debate on women is consciously referred to in legal metaphors (IV, 42, 500; IV, 73, 544).

4. Thomas F. Crane, *Italian Social Customs of the Sixteenth Century and Their Influence on the Literatures of Europe* (New Haven: Yale University Press, 1920), pp. 1–98.

5. At one point, Roberto da Bari argues against the austerity of the Magnifico's ideal *donna di palazzo*, insisting that she should not be prevented from granting her favors to a worthy knight simply because of conventional moral standards. He is, however, prevented from continuing his argument by the sudden, arbitrary proclamation of the duchess: "Messer Roberto pur contradicea, ma la signora Duchessa gli diede il torto, confirmando la ragion del signor Magnifico; poi suggiunse: — Noi non abbiam causa di dolersi del signor Magnifico, perché in vero estimo che la donna di palazzo da lui formata possa star al paragon del cortegiano. . . . " (III, 60, 423).

6. At times the men praise the duchess so openly that she has to use her authority to silence such embarrassing displays; see III, 4, 340–41 and III, 49, 407. Note that Castiglione himself literally revered her. Not only did he speak of his admiration for her in the introductory paragraphs to *Il Cortegiano* (*Letter*, 1, 71–72), but his biography reveals that he hid away a picture of her behind a mirror along with some sonnets he wrote about her but showed to no one. See Julia Cartwright, *The Perfect Courtier: Baldassare Castiglione* (New York: Dutton, 1927), vol. 1, p. 93.

7. Note that in his speech Gasparo takes literally the metaphorical conceits of Petrarchan and courtly love poetry, turning them back against the ladies rather than following the practice of the courtly lover who internalized them and brooded over his own inadequacy.

8. See Arnold Hauser, *Social History of Art* (New York: Vintage Books, 1951), vol. 2, pp. 86–91.

9. Like Machiavelli, Castiglione sees in men an infinite, insatiable drive for power which is responsible for wars and killing (IV, 27, 481). Ottaviano, however, who makes this analysis, also believes that the courtier can educate his prince to rule well and ultimately restore the Age of Gold (IV, 13–18, 462–69).

10. Ottaviano replies to Gasparo's skepticism that virtue can be taught by declaring that it would be strange if man could tame beasts, but not himself. Ottaviano also views the courtier-schoolmaster as a farmer who plants the seeds of virtue in the soil of his young prince's mind. (For both passages, see IV, 12–13, 460–63.) The conceptions derive ultimately from ancient writers on education like Plutarch and Quintilian and reflect the optimistic assessment of human potential made by many Italian humanists and educators during the fifteenth and sixteenth centuries. For a discussion of humanist views and typical metaphors, see my "Erasmian Education and the *Convivium religiosum*," *SP* 69 (1972): 131–49.

11. Joseph A. Mazzeo, *Renaissance and Revolution* (New York: Random House, 1965), pp. 94–97, 104–7.

12. " . . . l'amore è tenuto da uno vinculo di obbligo, il quale, per essere li uomini tristi, da ogni occasione di propria utilità è rotto . . . " (from chap. 17 of *Il Principe*, in Niccolò Machiavelli, *Il Principe e Discorsi*, ed. Sergio Bertelli [Milan: Feltrinelli, 1960], p. 70).

13. Note his image: the regard which all the courtiers and ladies at Urbino felt for the duchess was "una catena che tutti in amor tenesse uniti . . . " (I, 4, 85–86).

14. The famous chapter 15, on p. 65 of the edition cited in note 12.

15. Erving Goffman, *Encounters* (Indianapolis: Bobbs-Merrill, 1961), pp. 7–9; and *Interaction Ritual* (Garden City, N.Y.: Doubleday, 1967), pp. 54–58.

16. He uses variants of this phrase at the start of every book, even including the first. In addition to the example cited in the text, see I, 6, 89; II, 5, 196; IV, 3, 449.

17. My analysis of deference rituals has profited considerably from Erving Goffman's essay, "The Nature of Deference and Demeanor," in *Interaction Rituaal,* pp. 47–96.

18. Federico Fregoso, for instance, begins the second evening by declaring that his performance will fall below that of Count Ludovico (II, 7, 198), and he continually asks to be excused from speaking (II, 17, 215–16; II, 42, 255). Ludovico, Bibbiena, and Ottaviano similarly seek the duchess's permission to pass the burden of speaking on to another (see I, 54, 182; II, 84, 310; IV, 26, 479).

19. II, 98–100, 331–33; IV, 3, 448–49; IV, 50, 513. Note that the two-stage pattern of refusal and acceptance is varied with great freedom in all these instances but that it remains nevertheless recognizable in all of them.

20. Bibbiena implies the existence of a *forma ordinata* for their discussions when he justifies his own speaking about humor on the grounds that he does not wish to give others the right not to speak by refusing to do so himself (II, 45, 260). Likewise, the Magnifico accepts the task of forming the ideal *donna di palazzo* only "con quei patti che hanno avuti quest'altri signori . . . " (II, 100, 332).

21. "A Theory of Play and Fantasy," in *Steps to an Ecology of the Mind* (San Francisco: Chandler Publishing Company, 1972), pp. 177–93, and especially, pp. 186–88. On p. 188, he explains that a frame is "metacommunicative": it is not a direct communication, but a message giving instructions as to how to interpret the messages with which it is associated.

22. See his *Wit and Its Relation to the Unconscious.* I have found the following insights especially valuable: the presence of exhibitionism and aggression in witticisms and jokes, the importance of play in the forms that wit assumes, the role of the audience or third person in providing the joke teller with reassurance that his disguising of aggression has been successful, and the concept that laughter is a release of energy that would otherwise have to be used for repression.

23. My analysis here owes something to Clifford Geertz's suggestive discussion of the way that games activate tremendous emotional responses in their participants; see his "Deep Play: Notes on the Balinese Cockfight," *Daedalus* 101 (1972): 1–37.

24. I owe this particular comparison between aggression in oratory and *The Courtier* to Daniel Javitch.

25. I have found Erving Goffman's essay, "On Face-Work," in *Interaction Ritual,* pp. 5–46, extremely helpful in analyzing the social crises of Castiglione's society and the way his characters handle them.

Chapter 5

1. The best general statement concerning the Renaissance belief in eloquence and its love for the dialogue is Hanna H. Gray's "Renaissance Humanism: The Pursuit of Eloquence," *JHI* 24 (1963): 497–514. See also Georg Luck, "Vir Facetus: A Renaissance Ideal," *SP* 55 (1958): 107–21.

2. See Thomas M. Greene, "Roger Ascham: The Perfect End of Shooting," *ELH* 36 (1969): 614–18; and his "Flexibility of the Self in Renaissance Literature,"

in *The Disciplines of Criticism,* ed. Peter Demetz, Thomas M. Greene, and Lowry Nelson, Jr. (New Haven: Yale University Press, 1968), pp. 249–56.

3. Johan Huizinga, *Erasmus and the Age of Reformation,* trans. F. Hopman (New York: Harper & Row, 1957), p. 104.

4. Leonardo Bruni Aretino, *Ad Petrum Paulum Histrum Dialogus,* in *Prosatori latini del Quattrocento,* ed. Eugenio Garin (Milan: Ricciardi, 1952), pp. 48–52.

5. Leon Battista Alberti, *I libri della famiglia,* ed. Ruggiero Romano and Alberto Tenenti (Turin: Einaudi, 1969), pp. 99–103.

6. The character Thomas More attacks the idealist Hythloday for his "academic philosophy" *(philosophia scholastica);* see Thomas More, *Utopia,* vol. 4 of *The Complete Works of Saint Thomas More,* ed. Edward Surtz, S. J., and J. H. Hexter (New Haven: Yale University Press, 1965), p. 98. Erasmus has Folly denounce the Stoics repeatedly throughout the *Encomium moriae,* and Castiglione has Ottaviano attack the *severo filosofo* who would lack the courtly tact necessary to bring a prince to love virtue (IV, 8, 456).

7. See Dain A. Trafton's introduction to his edition and translation of Torquato Tasso, *Il Malpiglio: A Dialogue on the Court, ELR* Supplements, 2 (1973): 1–13. For my comments on Tasso's and Castiglione's use of dialogue to express their opinions indirectly, I am indebted to Professor Trafton's introduction and to a lecture he gave at the annual meeting of the Modern Language Association in December 1973, entitled "Philosophic Courtiership: Castiglione and the Tradition."

8. Torquato Tasso, *Discorso dell'arte del dialogo,* in *Prose,* ed. Ettore Mazzali (Milan: Ricciardi, 1959), pp. 333–35, and 339–40. Tasso divides dialogues into three classes depending on whether they present persons conversing, use a narrator to narrate conversations he has heard, or use him to introduce others who do the talking. These three classes of dialogue can each be subdivided into comic, tragic, and mixed modes, making a total of nine possibilities. Needless to say, Tasso's categories deal with minimal characteristics of form and are not particularly useful for the distinctions I make in this chapter.

9. *Letter,* 3, 76.

10. For arguments as to Cicero's influence on Castiglione, see Erich Loos, *Baldassare Castigliones "Libro del Cortegiano," Analecta Romanica,* 2 (Frankfurt am Main: Vittorio Klostermann, 1955), pp. 202–7; L. Valmaggi, "Per le fonti del Cortegiano," *GSLI* 14 (1899): 72–93; and Piero Floriani, "La genesi del 'Cortegiano': Prospettive per una ricerca," *Belfagor* 24 (1969): 373–85.

11. Cicero has the young men Sulpicius and Cotta ask Antonius and Crassus to teach them about oratory in the school *(palaestra)* of their villa; see *De Oratore,* bk. I, chap. 21 Although there are arguments among Cicero's characters, they are few, minor, and quickly settled. Even the major debate between Antonius and Crassus in Book I concerning the orator's need for learning turns out to have been instigated by Antonius to steal Crassus's students and is not indicative, according to Antonius himself, of any substantial difference between the two speakers. See bk. II, chap. 9.

12. Rita Falke suggests that the intrusion of reality at the end of *Il Cortegiano* is related to Alcibiades' entrance at the end of Plato's *Symposium,* but she does not pursue her insight to a general consideration of the formal similarity between the two works. See her *"Furor platonicus* als Kompositionselement im *Cortegiano," Romanistisches Jahrbuch* 10 (1959): 112–18. Erich Loos also notices similarities between Castiglione's work and Plato's but does not pursue his observations either. See his *Baldassare Castiglione,* p. 165. And Piero Floriani claims originality for Castiglione's

dialogue in that it does not depict some great man instructing a group of pupils, but a situation in which each speaker is momentarily primus inter pares. Nevertheless, he fails to see substantial differences between Castiglione's and Cicero's dialogues, and insists that the *De Oratore* offered Castiglione an exclusive model for the form of his work; see his "Esperienza e cultura nella genesi del Cortegiano," *GSLI* 146 (1969): 510–14.

13. See Josef Martin, *Symposion: Die Geschichte einer literarischen Form* (Paderborn, 1931), pp. 2–3; and the articles "Symposion" and "Symposion-Literatur," in *Paulys Realencyclopädie der classischen Altertumswissenschaft*, ed. Georg Wissowa, Wilhelm Kroll, and Karl Mittelhaus (Stuttgart, 1931).

14. See the articles "Symposion" and "Commissatio" in *Paulys Realencyclopädie*.

15. Martin, *Symposion*, pp. 2, 32–36.

16. See Dante Alighieri, *Il Convivio*, ed. G. Busnelli and G. Vandelli (Florence: le Monnier, 1953), 2nd ed., vol. 1, pp. 6–8. A note on p. 8 gives the following quotation from Saint Ambrose, *De Officiis*, bk. 1, chap. 22: "Scriptura divina convivium sapientiae est: singuli libri singula sunt fercula."

17. Erwin Panofsky, *Renaissance and Renascences in Western Art* (Stockholm: Almqvist and Wiksell, 1960), pp. 84–106.

18. Leonardo Bruni Aretino, *Dialogus*, in *Prosatori latini del Quattrocento*, p. 98. This notion of double symposium satisfying both the body with food and the spirit with talk goes back to Plutarch; see the article "Symposion-Literatur," in *Paulys Realencyclopädie*.

19. P. 321.

20. See Rita Falke, *"Furor platonicus,"* p. 118.

21. The subjects for discussion proposed by Castiglione's courtiers at the start of the first book are merely variants of the *questioni d'amore* that were a favored form of social amusement for courtly society from the Provençal courts of the twelfth century to the French salons of the seventeenth. See Thomas F. Crane, *Italian Social Customs of the Sixteenth Century and Their Influence on the Literatures of Europe* (New Haven: Yale University Press, 1920).

22. Josef Martin defines the symposium form in terms of its recurrent character types, of which these are but three; see his *Symposion*, pp. 32–115.

23. Ibid., pp. 117–18.

24. IV, 40, 497–8: " . . . le virtù . . . , per esser mediocrità, sono vicine alli dui estremi, che sono vicii; onde chi non sa facilmente incorre in essi; perché così come è difficile nel circulo trovare il punto del centro, che è il mezzo, così è difficile trovare il punto della virtù posta nel mezzo delli dui estremi. . . . "

25. Homer is generally credited with the earliest representations in literature of a symposium, and Greek writers like Hermogenes usually traced the idea back to him. See Martin, *Symposion*, pp. 64–65, 131–32.

26. Martin claims that the mocking or teasing of the host, which is absent from Plato but present in Xenophon and most other symposia, is one of the defining *topoi* of the genre; *Symposion*, pp. 37–51.

27. Symposia involve what anthropologists would call a "symbolic inversion," that is, "any act of expressive behavior which inverts, contradicts, abrogates, or in some fashion presents an alternative to commonly held cultural codes, values and norms be they linguistic, literary or artistic, religious, or social and political"; see Barbara Babcock, "Introduction," *The Reversible World*, ed. Barbara Babcock (Ithaca, N.Y.: Cornell University Press, forthcoming).

28. Vittorio Cian comments that Urbino was distinguished from other Renaissance courts by the important role women played in it; see his *Un illustre nunzio*

pontificio del Rinascimento: Baldassar Castiglione, Studi e testi, 156 (Vatican City: Biblioteca Apostolica Vaticana, 1951), p. 30. Yet that role was clearly confined to certain spheres of social life and never put the wives of Federico, Guidobaldo, or Francesco Maria actually in the position of making basic political, diplomatic, or military policy decisions.

29. For a more extended consideration of how Bembo's vision is related to previously expounded conceptions of love, see Chapter 6.

30. See my article, "Erasmian Education and the *Convivium religiosum*," *SP* 69 (1972): 131–49.

31. See Johan Huizinga, *Homo Ludens* (Boston: Beacon Press, 1950), passim; and Roger Caillois, *Man, Play, and Games,* trans. Meyer Barash (New York, 1961), pp. 2–10.

32. I am greatly indebted to Clifford Geertz for his concept of "deep play," a notion that certain games involve intense emotional experience because they activate the tensions deep within a culture and both express and safely channel the expression of those tensions. See his "Deep Play: Notes on the Balinese Cockfight," *Daedalus* 101 (1972): 1–37.

33. For other reasons behind this hostility, see, for example, Daniel Javitch, "The Philosopher of the Court: A French Satire Misunderstood," *CL* 23 (1971): 97–124.

34. See Dain A. Trafton's analysis of Tasso's dialogue in the introduction to his edition of *Il Malpiglio: A Dialogue on the Court, ELR* Supplements, 2 (1973): 1–13.

35. For a stimulating analysis of the relationship between ritual and festive celebrations like carnival and the symposium, I am indebted to an unpublished paper by Roger D. Abrahams prepared for the Burg-Wartenstein Symposium no. 59, entitled, "Ritual, for Fun and Profit, or, The Ends and Outs of Celebration." For my concept of ritual I have relied on Victor W. Turner, *The Ritual Process* (Chicago: Aldine Publishing Co., 1969).

36. Turner, *Ritual Process,* pp. 14, 94. Turner's analysis depends on the classic study of Van Gennep, *Les Rites de passage,* published in 1909.

37. Ibid., pp. 95–97, 167–68.

38. See Roger Caillois, *Man, Play, and Games,* pp. 87–97. Caillois analyzes primitive rituals as combining two of his four categories of games, mimicry, and vertigo.

39. I owe these distinctions to Max Gluckman "Les rites de passage," in *Essays on the Ritual of Social Relations,* ed. Max Gluckman (Manchester: Manchester University Press, 1962), pp. 1–52. Gluckman would doubtless classify a symposium not as a ritual, but as a ceremony; see p. 22.

40. I am endebted to several unpublished essays by Victor Turner and to a series of lectures on the subject of "pilgrimage" which he delivered to the University of Texas in the spring of 1974. Professor Turner has coined the term "liminoid" to distinguish the central, secluded phase of modern, ritual-like experiences from the "liminal" state of primitive rituals.

41. Note that a similar discovery of day has been eliminated from the end of Book II. Cf. *Sec. red.,* p. 181 n.

Chapter 6

1. For the date of the second version of *Il Cortegiano,* see Ghino Ghinassi, "Fasi dell'elaborazione del 'Cortegiano,'" *Studi di filologia italiana* 25 (1967): 177–84. In the *Seconda redazione,* Castiglione explains how Duke Guidobaldo spends his time after lunch taking care of official business and describes the varied activities of the

courtiers (I, 2–3, 5–8). Only then does he describe how they ate dinner together and afterwards retired to the duchess's chambers. In the final version of this passage, Castiglione reduces his description of the afternoon activities to a most summary statement in order to move directly to the evening ceremonies: "Erano adunque tutte l'ore del giorno divise in onorevoli e piacevoli esercizi così del corpo come dell'animo; ma perché il signor Duca continuamente, per la infirmitá, dopo cena assai per tempo se n'andava a dormire, ognuno per ordinario dove era la signora duchessa Elisabetta Gonzaga a quell'ora si riduceva . . . " (I, 4, 85).

2. Cf. *Sec. red.*, III, 1, 183 and IV, 1, 445–46 with *De Oratore*, III, i–iii.

3. Cf. *Sec. red.*, III, 5–42 with IV, 4–42. The two passages are by no means identical in every regard.

4. Although the germs of Bembo's oration are present in the *Seconda redazione* (III, 112–16), they are completely overwhelmed by the debate between the misogynists and their opponents that dominates this earlier version of Castiglione's final book from the point where Ottaviano finishes his exposition of the courtier's social and political functions to the very end of the work.

5. Ghinassi, op. cit., 173–75; and Lawrence V. Ryan, "Book Four of Castiglione's *Courtier*: Climax or Afterthought?" *SRen* 19 (1972): 159.

6. Note that Castiglione omits an earlier reference to the coming of dawn at the end of Book II, a reference which would have implied that Bibbiena's speech also went on through the depths of the night and which would thus have deprived Bembo's performance of some of its uniqueness. See *Sec. red.*, p. 181 n.

7. A number of critics have stressed the break between the first three books and the fourth in terms of changes of both content and tone. See, for example, Erich Loos, *Baldassare Castigliones "Libro del Cortegiano,"* Analecta Romanica, 2 (Frankfurt am Main: Vittorio Klostermann, 1955), pp. 120–30; Giuseppe Toffanin, *Il "Cortegiano" nella trattatistica del Rinascimento* (Naples: Libreria scientifica editrice, n. d.), p. 160; and Ghinassi, op. cit., 175.

8. I fundamentally disagree with those critics who feel that there is no contradiction between the courtly love of Book III and the Neoplatonic love of Book IV. See, for instance, Joseph A. Mazzeo, *Renaissance and Revolution* (New York: Random House, 1965), p. 143; and Kenneth Burke, *A Rhetoric of Motives* (Berkeley: University of California Press, 1962), pp. 221–33.

9. Erich Loos sees the fourth book as Castiglione's response to his disillusionment after the dissolution of the court at Urbino in 1516; see op. cit., pp. 202–7. Piero Floriani, relying on the definitive manuscript investigations of Ghino Ghinassi, has argued for composition in three states which reflect Castiglione's concerns with personal problems. The first three books, completed in early 1516, show Castiglione concerned with the courtier's success, something he still had not obtained himself. Ottaviano's speech, completed in 1520 or 1521, sees Castiglione, then a political figure in Rome, meditating on his responsibilities. Finally, Bembo's Neoplatonic vision was probably composed between 1521 and 1524, after Castiglione's wife had died and he had taken holy orders. See Piero Floriani, "La Genesi del 'Cortegiano': Prospettive per una ricerca," *Belfagor* 24 (1969): 373–85.

10. *Un illustre nunzio pontificio del Rinascimento, Baldassar Castiglione, Studi e testi,* 156 (Vatican City: Biblioteca Apostolica Vaticana, 1951), pp. 227–57 and passim.

11. Ralph Roeder, *The Man of the Renaissance* (Cleveland, 1933), p. 347.

12. Compare Gasparo's defense of Lombard noblemen for freely engaging themselves in contests of strength with peasants; see II, 10, 204.

13. Both More and Erasmus similarly reject the "Stoic philosopher" who would present truth unvarnished, and both insist that the educator and statesman has to

be a tactful manipulator of men and even a deceiver if necessary. See Thomas More, *Utopia*, ed. Edward Surtz, S. J. and J. H. Hexter, vol. 4 of *The Complete Works of Saint Thomas More* (New Haven: Yale University Press, 1965), pp. 96–100; and Desiderius Erasmus, *Institutio Principis Christiani*, in *Opera Omnia*, ed. J. Clericus (Leiden, 1703), vol. 4, 594A; and his *Encomium Moriae*, op. cit., vol. 4, 401–504, passim.

14. Johan Huizinga long ago noted that play could be a profoundly serious affair; see his *Homo Ludens* (Boston: Beacon Press, 1950), pp. 5–7. My discussion is more directly dependent, however, on Clifford Geertz's brilliant article, "Deep Play: Notes on the Balinese Cockfight," *Daedalus* 101 (1972): 1–37.

15. There is a well-established and clearly mistaken critical tradition that has consistently attacked the world of *Il Cortegiano* as artificial and trivial. For examples, see Mario Rossi, *Baldassar Castiglione: La sua personalità, la sua prosa* (Bari, 1946), passim; and Giuseppe Prezzolini's introduction to Baldassar Castiglione and Giovanni della Casa, *Opere* (Milan-Rome, 1937), pp. 9–40.

16. Joseph A. Mazzeo (*Renaissance and Revolution*, p. 134) calls Urbino an Arcadia, not a Golden Age, although he does not relate this useful distinction to consideration of the Golden Age envisioned in Book IV or explore its implications.

17. For discussions of the courtier as a combination of the medieval knight and an example of the "amateur," the Hellenistic ideal of well-roundedness which the humanists had revived in their educational and other treatises, see Erich Loos, *Baldassare Castiglione*, pp. 38–42; Joseph A. Mazzeo, *Renaissance and Revolution*, p. 133; and Albert D. Menut, "Castiglione and the Nicomachean Ethics," *PMLA* 58 (1943): 309–21.

18. While there can be no doubt that Castiglione knew Plato and contemporary Neoplatonists or that he knew ancient writers on education like Cicero, Plutarch, and Quintilian, Vittorio Cian can only conjecture that he read the works of fifteenth- and early sixteenth-century humanist educators; see *Un illustre nunzio*, p. 250.

19. Joseph A. Mazzeo, *Renaissance and Revolution*, pp. 22–32; and H. I. Marrou, *A History of Education in Antiquity* (New York, 1956), pp. 309–42.

20. My argument is indebted to the seminal article of Lawrence Lipking, "The Dialectic of *Il Cortegiano*," *PMLA* 81 (1966): 355–62.

21. For two views quite different from my own which argue for the unity of Castiglione's work on the basis of a consistent, harmoniously developed, and clearly articulated intellectual development, see Dain A. Trafton, "Structure and Meaning in *The Courtier*," *ELR* 2 (1972): 283–97; and Lawrence V. Ryan, "Book Four of Castiglione's *Courtier*: Climax or Afterthought?" *SRen* 19 (1972): 156–79. Professor Trafton argues that the first two books move away from an ideal of reasonable, moral service for the courtier and instead turn him into a mere poseur, striving to please others without serious, moral concern. He sees Castiglione's work reaching a nadir in the trivialization of courtiership implied by the joke-fest of Book II, but he then argues that Books III and IV display an ever-increasing seriousness about moral matters and an ever more elevated view of the courtier's role. Professor Ryan, on the other hand, argues that Castiglione revised his original text so that his first three books would contain numerous hints pointing to the themes of Book IV and would be consistent with the last book's concepts and technical, philosophical vocabulary. On this basis, and on the basis of an ever more elevated view of love which moves from sexual trifling to mystical love of God, he labels Book IV the "climax" of Castiglione's work to which all the other books lead directly. Many minor objections might be raised to both views: Professor Trafton,

for instance, misjudges Castiglione's—and Renaissance courtly society's—views about the relative importance of jokes and funny stories, and Professor Ryan is exposed to a methodological objection, namely, that a few remodelled phrases and paragraphs in the first books by no means constitute a demonstration that the ideas contained in those books are consistent with those in the last one. However, the major criticism I direct at both writers is simply that they ignore the clear signals Castiglione himself provides for interpreting the relationship between the last book and the first three. They ignore Ottaviano's crucial alteration of previously established social patterns and criticisms of earlier ideals, as well as many characters' scepticism that Ottaviano's and Bembo's new versions of the courtier are consistent with previous ones. They also tend to deemphasize the return to the game of sexual warfare with which Castiglione ends his work. To be sure, there are definite connections between the conceptions of the first three books and those of the last, but they hardly provide a substantial basis for arguing that Castiglione has composed a unified work. The existence of intellectual interrelationships cannot obliterate the clear oppositions and tensions Castiglione signals his reader to bear in mind as he compares the doctrines of Book IV with those of Books I, II, and III. A stronger argument for the work's unity is based on the reader's fundamental perception of it as a dialogue and on the utter consistency from start to finish with which Castiglione has maintained the fiction of his particular literary form—even in Book IV with its radically different conceptions.

22. See, for instance, Mario Rossi, *Baldassar Castiglione*, pp. 81–85; and J. T. Stewart, "Renaissance Psychology and the Ladder of Love in Castiglione and Spenser," *JEGP* 56 (1957): 225–30.

23. Lawrence Lipking ("Dialectic," p. 362) sees the exchange between Emilia and Bembo as double expression of two ideals, "the rapture of the intellect and the skepticism of worldly wisdom."

24. Rita Falke, in her *"Furor platonicus* als Kompositionselement im *Cortegiano,"* *Romanistisches Jahrbuch* 10 (1959): 114, describes how Emilia used Bembo's last words and their sense "um ihn in die 'Wirklichkeit' zurückzurufen; durch das von ihr hinzugesetzte 'Guardate—ancora non' bringt sie seine und aller Anwesenden Klugheit und Achtsamkeit wieder ins Spiel: jetzt können sie sich alle wieder 'vernünftig' darüber unterhalten, ob die Frauen dieser Liebe, von der Bembo gesprochen hat, denn überhaupt fähig sind. . . . "

25. See the works cited in notes 21 and 22 above.

26. Lawrence Ryan sees the book ending with an unambiguous vision of a dawning world transformed in the image of Bembo's love; see "Book IV," 176–77. Professor Ryan's article, however, leaves one with the mistaken impression that Castiglione ends his last book with the exalted vision of day. That is not correct, for that vision yields to a brief exchange between the prefect and Emilia Pia recalling one final time the warfare between the sexes that has raged throughout *Il Cortegiano*. That last exchange provides the final, decisive impression that Castiglione wishes his reader to take away from his book, a vision of Urbino continuing to play its symposium game.

27. In my analysis, this return to conversation and debate is an aesthetic triumph for the unity of Castiglione's work, and I clearly disagree with critics like Mario Rossi (in his *Baldassar Castiglione,* p. 76) who reprimand Castiglione for being unable to maintain the ecstatic level of Bembo's flight.

Bibliography

1. The Works of Baldassar Castiglione

Il Cortegiano. Edited by Vittorio Cian. 3rd ed. Florence: Sansoni, 1929.

Il Libro del Cortegiano con una scelta delle Opere minori. Edited by Bruno Maier. 2nd ed. Turin: Unione Tipografico-Editrice Torinese, 1964.

La seconda redazione del "Cortegiano." Edited by Ghino Ghinassi. Florence: Sansoni, 1968.

Lettere. Edited by Pierantonio Serassi. 2 vols. Padua: G. Comino, 1769–71. (Latin and Italian poetry in vol. 2.)

2. Secondary Works Concerning Castiglione

Adams, Hilary. " 'Il Cortegiano' and 'Il Galateo.' " *MLR* 42 (1947): 457–66.

Battaglia, Salvatore. "Difesa del 'Cortegiano.' " *Romana* 1 (1937): 160–75.

Bettalli, Giuseppe. "Considerazioni su un luogo del Cortegiano." *Belfagor* 11 (1956): 454–57.

Bianco di Sansecondo, Ernesto. *Baldassare Castiglione nella vita e negli scritti.* Verona: L'Albero, 1941.

Bonadeo, Alfredo. "The Function and Purpose of the Courtier in *The Book of the Courtier* by Castiglione." *PQ* 50 (1971): 36–46.

Bongiovanni, Giannetto. *Baldassare Castiglione.* Milan: Alpes, 1929.

Bottari, Ercole. "Baldassare da Castiglione e il suo libro del 'Cortegiano.' " *Annali della Scuola Normale Superiore di Pisa* 3 (1877): 139–221.

Cartwright, Julia. *Baldassare Castiglione: The Perfect Courtier: His Life and Letters, 1478–1529.* 2 vols. London: Murray, 1908.

Cian, Vittorio. *Un illustre nunzio pontificio del Rinascimento: Baldassar Castiglione. Studi e testi,* 156. Vatican City: Biblioteca apostolica vaticana, 1951.

——————. *La lingua di Baldassare Castiglione.* Florence: Sansoni, 1942.

——————. "Religiosità del Castiglione." *Convivium* 22 (1950): 772–80.

Clough, Cecil H. "Gasparo Sanseverino and Castiglione's *Il Cortegiano.*" *PQ* 43 (1964): 276–80.

Colie, Rosalie. "Castiglione's Urban Pastoral." *Greyfriar* 8 (1965): 5–13.

Corsano, Antonio. "L'ideale estetico morale del Castiglione." *Studi sul Rinascimento,* pp. 58–71. Bari: Adriatica, 1949.

Dardano, Maurizio. "L'arte del periodo nel 'Cortegiano.' " *Rassegna della letteratura italiana* 67 (1963): 441–62.

Faccioli, E. "Il conte Baldassar Castiglione." *Mantova: Le lettere.* Edited by Lanfranco Caretti, vol. 2, pp. 292–303. Mantua: Istituto Carlo d'Arco per la storia di Mantova, 1962.

Falke, Rita. "*Furor platonicus* als Kompositionselement im *Cortegiano.*" *Romanistisches Jahrbuch* 10 (1959): 112–18.

Ferrero, G. G. "Studi sul Castiglione." *Rivista di sintesi letteraria* 2 (1935): 473–80.

Floriani, Piero. "Esperienza e cultura nella genesi del *Cortegiano.*" *GSLI* 146 (1969): 497–529.

—————. "La genesi del 'Cortegiano': Prospettive per una ricerca." *Belfagor* 24 (1969): 373–85.

Ghinassi, Ghino. "Fasi dell'elaborazione del 'Cortegiano.' " *Studi di filologia italiana* 25 (1967): 155–96.

—————. "L'ultimo revisore del 'Cortegiano.' " *Studi di filologia italiana* 21 (1963): 217–64.

Harrison, Thomas. "The Latin Pastorals of Milton and Castiglione." *PMLA* 50 (1935): 480–93.

Javitch, Daniel. "Poetry and Court Conduct: Puttenham's *Arte of English Poesie* in the Light of Castiglione's *Cortegiano.*" *MLN* 87 (1972): 865–82.

Lipking, Lawrence. "The Dialectic of *Il Cortegiano.*" *PMLA* 81 (1966): 355–62.

Loos, Erich. *Baldassare Castigliones "Libro del Cortegiano": Studien zur Tugendauffassung des Cinquecento. Analecta Romanica,* vol. 2. Frankfurt am Main: Vittorio Klostermann, 1955.

Maier, Bruno. "Baldassar Castiglione." *Letteratura italiana: I minori,* vol. 2, pp. 891–925. Milan: Marzorati, 1961.

—————. "Sul testo del 'Cortegiano.' " *GSLI* 130 (1953): 226–48.

—————. Review of Erich Loos, *Baldassare Castigliones "Libro del Cortegiano." GSLI* 133 (1956): 436–44.

Mazzacurati, Giancarlo. "Baldassar Castiglione e la teoria cortegiana: Ideologia di classe e dottrina critica." *MLN* 83 (1968): 16–66.

Mazzeo, Joseph A. *Renaissance and Revolution: Backgrounds to Seventeenth Century English Literature,* chap. 3, "Castiglione's *Courtier:* The Self as a Work of Art," pp. 131–60. New York: Random House, 1965.

Menut, Albert D. "Castiglione and the Nicomachean Ethics." *PMLA* 58 (1943): 309–21.

Momigliano, A. *Storia della letteratura italiana,* pp. 177–80. 3rd ed. Messina: Principato, 1938.

Rebhorn, Wayne A. "Ottaviano's Interruption: Book IV and the Problem of Unity in *Il Libro del Cortegiano.*" *MLN* 87 (1972): 37–59.

Rossi, Mario. *Baldassar Castiglione: La sua personalità, la sua prosa.* Bari: Laterza, 1946.

Russo, Luigi. "Baldassar Castiglione." *Belfagor* 13 (1958): 505–22.

Ryan, Lawrence V. "Book IV of Castiglione's *Courtier:* Climax or Afterthought?" *SRen* 19 (1972): 156–79.

Salamon, Linda B. "*The Courtier* and *The Scholemaster.*" *CL* 25 (1973): 17–36.

Sapegno, N. *Compendio di storia della letteratura italiana,* vol. 2, pp. 127–34. Florence: La nuova Italia, 1941.

Schenk, Wilhelm. "The *Cortegiano* and the Civilization of the Renaissance." *Scrutiny* 16 (1949): 93–103.

Schnerr, W. J. "Two Courtiers: Castiglione and Rodrigues Lôbo." *CL* 13 (1961): 138–53.

Speroni, Charles. "The Obstinate Wife." *Italica* 28 (1951): 181–84.

Stewart, J. T. "Renaissance Psychology and the Ladder of Love in Castiglione and Spenser." *JEGP* 56 (1957): 225–30.

Toffanin, Giuseppe. *Il "Cortegiano" nella trattatistica del Rinascimento.* Naples: Libreria scientifica editrice, 1961.

—————. "Baldassare Castiglione." *La critica e il tempo.* Turin: Paravia, 1930.

Trafton, Dain A. "Structure and Meaning in *The Courtier.*" *ELR* 2 (1972): 283–97.

Valmaggi, L. "Per le fonti del Cortegiano." *GSLI* 14 (1899): 72–93.

Vicinelli, Augusto. *Baldesar Castiglione: Il cortigiano, il letterato, e il politico.* Turin: Paravia, 1931.

Welsh, David J. "Il Cortigiano polacco." *Italica* 40 (1963): 22–27.

Williamson, Edward. "The Concept of Grace in the Works of Raphael and Castiglione." *Italica* 24 (1947): 316–24.

Young, Ruth E. "Introduction to Castiglione and His *Courtier.*" *Smith College Studies in Modern Languages* 21 (1939–1940): 240–57.

Ziino, Michele. "Castiglione e Montaigne." *Convivium* 10 (1938): 56–60.

3. Other Primary Works

Alberti, Leon Battista. *Kleinere kunsttheoretische Schriften.* Edited by Hubert Janitschek. Vienna, 1877.

—————. *I libri della famiglia.* Edited by Ruggiero Romano and Alberto Tenenti. Turin: Einaudi, 1969.

—————. *On Painting*. Translated by John R. Spencer. New Haven: Yale University Press, 1956.

—————. *Opere volgari*. Edited by Cecil Grayson. 2 vols. Bari: Laterza, 1960.

Alighieri, Dante. *Il Convivio*. Edited by G. Busnelli and G. Vandelli. Florence: le Monnier, 1953.

Ascham, Roger. *The Whole Works*. Edited by J. A. Giles. Vol. 3: *The Scholemaster*. London, 1865.

Athenaeus. *The Deipnosophists*. Translated by Charles B. Gulich. 6 vols. London: Loeb Library, 1927.

Bembo, Pietro. *Prose e Rime*. Edited by Carlo Dionisotti. Turin: Unione Tipografico-Editrice Torinese, 1960.

Cicero. *De Oratore, De Fato, Paradoxia Stoicorum, Partitiones Oratoriae*. Translated by E. W. Sutton and H. Rackham. 2 vols. London: Loeb Library, 1959.

Della Casa, Giovanni and Castiglione, Baldassar. *Opere*. Edited by G. Prezzolini. Milan: Rizzoli, 1937.

Diderot, Denis. *Le Neveu de Rameau*. Paris: Gallimard, 1966

Erasmus, Desiderius. *Declamatio de pueris statim ac liberaliter instituendis*. Edited by Jean-Claude Margolin. Geneva: Droz, 1966.

—————. *Opera Omnia*. Edited by J. Clericus. 10 Vols. Leiden, 1703–6.

Ficino, Marsilio. *Commentary on Plato's "Symposium."* Text and translation by Sears R. Jayne. University of Missouri Studies, vol. 19. Columbia: University of Missouri Press, 1949.

Golzio, Vicenzo, ed. *Raffaello nei documenti, nelle testimonianze dei contemporanei e nella letteratura del suo secolo*. Vatican City, 1936.

Hoby, Sir Thomas. *The Book of the Courtier from the Italian of Count Baldassare Castiglione*. Introduction by Walter Raleigh. London, 1900.

Lucian. *Works*. Translated by A. M. Harmon. 8 vols. London: Loeb Library, 1913.

Machiavelli, Niccolò. *Il Principe e Discorsi*. Edited by Sergio Bertelli. Milan: Feltrinelli, 1960.

More, Thomas. *Utopia*. Vol. 4 of *The Complete Works of Saint Thomas More*. Edited by Edward Surtz, S. J. and J. H. Hexter. New Haven: Yale University Press, 1965.

Pico della Mirandola, Giovanni. *De Hominis dignitate, Heptaplus. De Ente et uno*. Edited by Eugenio Garin. Florence: Vallecchi, 1942.

Plato. *The Dialogues*. Translated by Benjamin Jowett. 2 vols. New York: Random House, 1937.

Plutarch. *Moralia*. Translated by Frank C. Babbitt. 14 vols. London: Loeb Library, 1928.

Prosatori latini del Quattrocento. Edited by Eugenio Garin. Milan: Ricciardi, 1952.

Quintilian. *Institutio oratoria.* Translated by H. E. Butler. 4 vols. London: Loeb Library, 1963.

Sannazaro, Jacopo. *Arcadia.* Edited by Enrico Carrara. Turin: Unione Tipografico-Editrice Torinese, 1944.

Tasso, Torquato. *Il Malpiglio: A Dialogue on the Court.* Translated and edited by Dain A. Trafton. *ELR* Supplements, 2 (1973).

—————. *Prose.* Edited by Ettore Mazzali. Milan: Ricciardi, 1959.

Xenophon. *Cyropaedia.* Translated by Walter Miller. 2 vols. London: Loeb Library, 1925.

—————. *Hellenica, Anabasis, Apology, and Symposium.* Translated by C. L. Brownson and O. J. Todd. 2 vols. London: Loeb Library, 1922.

4. Other Secondary Works

Abrahams, Roger. "Ritual, for Fun and Profit, or, The Ends and Outs of Celebration." Unpublished paper prepared for the Burg-Wartenstein Symposium, no. 59 (1973).

Ariès, Philippe. *Centuries of Childhood.* Translated by Robert Baldick. New York: Vintage Books, 1962.

Babcock (Babcock-Abrahams), Barbara. "The Carnivalization of the Novel." *MLN* 89 (1974): 911–37.

—————. ed. *The Reversible World.* Ithaca, N. Y.: Cornell University Press, forthcoming.

Bakhtin, Mikhail. *Rabelais and His World.* Translated by Helene Iswolsky. Cambridge, Mass.: M.I.T. Press, 1968.

Bateson, Gregory. *Steps to an Ecology of the Mind.* San Francisco: Chandler Publishing Co., 1972.

Blunt, Anthony. *Artistic Theory in Italy, 1450–1600.* Oxford: Clarendon Press, 1940.

Bolgar, R. R. *The Classical Heritage.* New York: Harper and Row, 1964.

Burckhardt, Jacob. *The Civilization of the Renaissance in Italy.* Introduction by Hajo Holborn. New York: Random House, 1954.

Burke, Kenneth. *A Rhetoric of Motives.* Berkeley: University of California Press, 1969.

Burke, Peter. *The Renaissance Sense of the Past.* London: Edward Arnold, 1969.

Caillois, Roger. *Man, Play, and Games.* Translated by Meyer Barash. New York, 1961.

Clements, Robert J. *The Peregrine Muse.* University of North Carolina Studies in Languages and Literatures, no. 82. Chapel Hill: University of North Carolina Press, 1969.

Colie, Rosalie. *Paradoxia Epidemica.* Princeton: Princeton University Press, 1966.

——————. *The Resources of Kind: Genre-Theory in the Renaissance.* Edited by Barbara K. Lewalski. Berkeley: University of California Press, 1973.

Cooper, John R. *The Art of "The Compleat Angler."* Durham, N.C.: Duke University Press, 1968.

Crane, Thomas F. *Italian Social Customs of the Sixteenth Century and Their Influence on the Literatures of Europe.* New Haven: Yale University Press, 1920.

Croce, Benedetto. *Poeti e scrittori del pieno e tardo Rinascimento.* 2 vols. Bari: Laterza, 1945.

Crossland, Jessie. "Italian Courtesy Books." *MLR* 5 (1910): 502–4.

Cullen, Patrick. *Spenser, Marvell, and Renaissance Pastoral.* Cambridge: Harvard University Press, 1970.

Dana, Margaret. "Heroic and Pastoral: Sidney's *Arcadia* as Masquerade." *CL* 25 (1973): 308–20.

Davis, Walter R. *Idea and Act in Elizabethan Fiction.* Princeton: Princeton University Press, 1969.

——————. "Masking in Arden." *SEL* 5 (1965): 151–63.

Ehrmann, Jacques, ed. *Games, Play, Literature.* Boston: Beacon Press, 1968.

Empson, William. *Some Versions of Pastoral.* Norfolk, Conn.: New Directions, 1960.

Freedberg, S. J. *Painting of the High Renaissance in Rome and Florence.* 2 vols. New York: Harper and Row, 1972.

Freud, Sigmund. *Basic Writings.* Edited by A. A. Brill. New York: Random House, 1938.

Garin, Eugenio. *L'educazione in Europe, 1400–1600.* Bari, 1957.

——————. *L'Umanesimo italiano.* Bari: Laterza, 1965.

Geertz, Clifford. "Deep Play: Notes on the Balinese Cockfight." *Daedalus* 101 (1972): 1–37.

Gerhardt, Mia I. *La Pastorale: Essai d'analyse littéraire.* Assen: Van Gorcum, 1950.

Gilbert, Felix. *Machiavelli and Guicciardini.* Princeton: Princeton University Press, 1965.

Gluckman, Max. *Essays on the Ritual of Social Relations.* Manchester: Manchester University Press, 1962.

Goffman, Erving. *Encounters.* Indianapolis: Bobbs-Merrill, 1961.

——————. *Interaction Ritual.* Garden City, N. Y.: Doubleday, 1967.

Gray, Hanna H. "Renaissance Humanism: The Pursuit of Eloquence." *JHI* 24 (1963): 497–514.

Greene, Thomas M. "The Flexibility of the Self in Renaissance Literature." *The Disciplines of Criticism.* Edited by Peter Demetz, Thomas

M. Greene, and Lowry Nelson, Jr., pp. 249–76. New Haven: Yale University Press, 1968.

——————. "Roger Ascham: The Perfect End of Shooting." *ELH* 36 (1969): 609–25.

Greg, Walter. *Pastoral Poetry and Pastoral Drama.* New York: Russell and Russell, 1959.

Grotjahn, Martin. *Beyond Laughter.* New York: McGraw Hill, 1957.

Hauser, Arnold. *Mannerism.* Translated by Eric Mosbacher. 2 vols. New York: Knopf, 1965.

——————. *The Social History of Art.* 4 vols. New York: Vintage Books, 1951.

Hauvette, Henri. *Littérature italienne.* Paris: Colin, 1906.

Haydn, Hiram. *The Counter-Renaissance.* New York: Harcourt, Brace, and World, 1950.

Hirzel, Rudolph. *Der Dialog: Ein literarhistorischer Versuch.* 2 vols. Leipzig: S. Hirzel, 1895.

Holme, James W. "Italian Courtesy Books of the Sixteenth Century." *MLR* 5 (1910): 145–60.

Huizinga, Johan. *Erasmus and the Age of Reformation.* Translated by F. Hopman. New York: Harper and Row, 1957.

——————. *Homo Ludens: A Study of the Play-Element in Culture.* Boston: Beacon Press, 1950.

Javitch, Daniel. *"The Philosopher of the Court:* A French Satire Misunderstood." *CL* 23 (1971): 97–124.

Kelso, Ruth. *Doctrine for the Lady of the Renaissance.* Urbana: University of Illinois Press, 1956.

——————. *The Doctrine of the English Gentleman in the Sixteenth Century.* University of Illinois Studies in Language and Literature, vol. 14. Urbana: University of Illinois Press, 1929.

Kermode, Frank, ed. *English Pastoral Poetry.* London: Harrap, 1952.

Lee, Rensselaer. *Ut Pictura Poesis: The Humanist Theory of Painting.* New York: Norton, 1967.

Lerner, Lawrence. *The Uses of Nostalgia.* London: Chatto and Windus, 1972.

Lievsay, John Leon. *Stefano Guazzo and the English Renaissance.* Chapel Hill: University of North Carolina Press, 1961.

Luck, Georg. "Vir Facetus: A Renaissance Ideal." *SP* 55 (1958): 107–21.

Marcel, Raymond. *Marsile Ficin.* Paris: Les belles lettres, 1958.

Marrou, Henri I. *A History of Education in Antiquity.* Translated by George Lamb. New York: Shad and Ward, 1956.

Martin, Josef. *Symposion: Die Geschichte einer literarischen Form.* Paderborn, 1931.

Mason, John E. *Gentlefolk in the Making*. Philadelphia: University of Pennsylvania Press, 1933.

Merrill, Elizabeth. *The Dialogue in English Literature*. New York: Henry Holt and Co., 1911.

Mirollo, James V. *The Poet of the Marvelous: Giambattista Marino*. New York: Columbia University Press, 1963.

Murray, Linda. *The High Renaissance*. New York: Praeger, 1967.

——————. *The Late Renaissance and Mannerism*. New York: Praeger, 1965.

Panofsky, Erwin. *Idea: A Concept in Art Theory*. Translated by Joseph Peake. Columbia: University of South Carolina Press, 1968.

——————. *Meaning in the Visual Arts*. Garden City, N. Y.: Doubleday, 1955.

——————. *Renaissance and Renascences in Western Art*. 2 vols. Stockholm: Almqvist and Wiksell, 1960.

Paulys Realencyclopädie der classischen Altertumswissenschaft. Edited by Georg Wissowa, Wilhelm Kroll, and Karl Mittelhaus. Stuttgart, 1931.

Poggioli, Renato. "The Oaten Flute." *Harvard Library Bulletin* 11 (1957): 147–84.

Pope-Hennessy, John. *The Portrait in the Renaissance*. New York: Bollingen Foundation, 1966.

——————. *Raphael*. London: Phaidon, n. d.

Prescott, Orville. *Princes of the Renaissance*. New York: Random House, 1969.

Rebhorn, Wayne A. "Erasmian Education and the *Convivium religiosum*." *SP* 69 (1972): 131–149.

Robb, Nesca Adeline. *Neoplatonism of the Italian Renaissance*. London: Allen and Unwin, 1935.

Roeder, Ralph. *The Man of the Renaissance*. New York: Viking Press, 1933.

Rosenmeyer, Thomas G. *The Green Cabinet: Theocritus and the European Pastoral Lyric*. Berkeley: University of California Press, 1969.

Rossetti, William M. *Italian Courtesy Books*. Early English Text Society, Extra Series, no. 8. London, 1869.

Segre, Cesare. "Edonismo linguistico nel Cinquecento." *GSLI* 130 (1953): 145–77.

Shearman, John. *Mannerism*. Harmondsworth, Eng.: Penguin Books, 1967.

Snell, Bruno. *The Discovery of the Mind*. Translated by T. G. Rosenmeyer. Oxford, 1953.

Spencer, John R. "Ut Rhetorica Pictura." *Journal of the Warburg and Courtauld Institute* 20 (1957): 26–44.

Strauss, Leo. *The Political Philosophy of Hobbes*. Translated by Elsa M. Sinclair. Oxford: Clarendon Press, 1936.

Tayler, Edward W. *Nature and Art in Renaissance Literature.* New York: Columbia University Press, 1964.

Toliver, Harold E. *Pastoral Forms and Attitudes.* Berkeley: University of California Press, 1971.

Turner, Victor. *The Ritual Process.* Chicago: Aldine Publishing Co., 1969.

Ullman, Berthold L. *Studies in the Italian Renaissance.* Rome: Edizioni di storia e letteratura, 1955.

Vallone, Aldo. *Cortesia e nobiltà nel Rinascimento.* Asti: Arethusa, 1955.

Wilcox, Donald J. *The Development of Florentine Humanist Historiography in the Fifteenth Century.* Cambridge: Harvard University Press, 1969.

Wiley, William L. *The Gentleman of Renaissance France.* Cambridge: Harvard University Press, 1954.

Woodward, William H. *Studies in Education During the Age of the Renaissance, 1400–1600.* Cambridge, 1906.

ᴖ Index

(With the exception of the works of Castiglione, the titles of all works discussed in this book are listed after the author's or the artist's name in the Index.)

54, 55–58, 103, 107, 111–12; in *De Oratore*, 101–103, 112–13; Renaissance conventions of, 57–58
Hobbes, Thomas, 132
Hoby, Thomas, 11–12
Holbein, Hans: *Erasmus*, 75
Horace, 61, 91, 160
Humanist education, 27–28, 27n.7, 28n.9, 132n.10, 197; and *The Book of the Courtier*, 28–29

Idealism, 13–14, 16, 18, 55–56. *See also* Court, ideal; Courtier, ideal; *Donna di palazzo*
Isabella of Castille, 53
Istoria, 61, 63

Jonson, Ben, 104
Julius II (pope), 53–54, 59
Juvenal, 91

Latini, Brunetto: *Il Tesoretto*, 12
Laurana, Luciano, 59
Leo X (pope), 21, 59
Leonardo da Vinci, 59, 61, 63, 63n.31, 68, 69–70, 74, 76n.44, 80; *Adoration of the Magi* (1481), 68, 74, 80; *Cena*, 76; *Mona Lisa*, 74, 76
Libro del Cortegiano, Il. See Book of the Courtier
Livy, 57
Lucian, 153, 158, 160
Ludovico il Moro (duke of Milan), 59

Machiavelli, Niccolò, 16, 110, 120, 121, 131, 148; *Il Principe*, 15, 95, 132–33
Macrobius: *Saturnalia*, 160, 170
Mannerism, 33, 49
Mantegna, Andrea, 75
Maraviglia, 47–51
Marrou, H. I., 26
Masking: in Castiglione and Verdi, 149–50; and characterization, 60–61; defined, 14, 16; and festivity, 16–17; literal, 39–40; in ritual, 173–74; in symposium, 165–73. *See also Book of the Courtier*, deception in; Courtier, ideal; Persona
Michelangelo Buonarroti, 20, 21, 48, 59, 62, 63, 63n.31, 64, 65, 68, 74, 75, 76n.44, 86, 94
Middleton, Thomas, 173
Milton, John, 91; *Lycidas*, 113, 114n.28
Misogynism, 81–82, 85–86, 126–31, 193–94. *See also* Women, debate on
More, St. Thomas, 119; *Utopia*, 145–46, 149, 152, 153

Neoplatonism, 175, 182, 189, 195–97, 199–200
Nonchalance. *See Sprezzatura*
Nostalgia, 96–98, 99–103, 108

Odysseus, 165
Ovid, 91

Panofsky, Erwin, 160
Pastoral, 99, 103–4; *The Book of the Courtier* as, 104–8, 111
Performance. *See* Masking
Persona (mask): in Renaissance literary theory, 91–92. *See also Book of the Courtier*, Castiglione's persona in; Masking
Petrarch, Francesco, 91, 107, 151
Petronius, 160, 166
Pico della Mirandola, Giovanni, 28n.9, 152
Piombo, Sebastiano del, 69
Plato, 57, 151, 157, 158, 161, 162, 163, 168, 170, 177, 182, 199; *The Laws*, 170; *Parmenides*, 153; *Phaedrus*, 153, 154; *The Republic*, 153, 154, 155, 164; *Symposium*, 153, 160–62, 167. *See also* Symposium
Plutarch, 26, 45, 132n.10, 161, 162, 163; *Banquet of the Seven Sages*, 160, 167; *On the Education of Children*, 27
Poliziano, Angelo, 104
Pollaiuolo, Antonio, 64, 75
Pontano, Gioviano, 27
Prince, ideal, 25n.2
Proust, Marcel, 114
Puttenham, George, 49

Questioni d'amore, 126, 161n.21
Quintilian, 26, 27, 45, 49, 132n.10

Rabelais, François, 119, 152, 171; *Gargantua*, 146
Raphael Sanzio, 20, 41, 48, 49, 59, 60, 62, 63, 63n.31, 64, 65, 68, 69–70, 72, 78–80, 84, 86, 88, 94, 114n.28, 130; *Andrea Navagero and Agostino Beazzano*, 74–75; *Castiglione*, frontispiece, 73–78, 80, 83; *Leo X with the Cardinals Giulio de' Medici and Luigi Rossi*, 72; *Madonna of the Chair*, 69–70, 74; *Mass of Bolsena*, 75; *School of Athens*, 79, 80
Role-playing. *See* Masking
Rovere, Francesco della, 21
Ryan, Lawrence V., 198n.21

Sadoleto, Jacopo, 27
Sallust, 57
Salutati, Coluccio, 151–52

237

Wayne A. Rebhorn was born in Philadelphia, Pennsylvania, in 1943. A graduate of the University of Pennsylvania, he received his Ph.D. from Yale University. He is an associate professor of English at the University of Texas at Austin.

The book was edited by Saundra Blais. The book was designed by Gary Gore. The typeface is Linotype VIP Baskerville, a transitional cutting which has survived several hundred years without substantial "improvement."

The text is printed on International Bookmark text paper and the book is bound in Joanna Mills' Arrestox A linen cloth over binder's boards. Manufactured in the United States of America.